Collins

I0876492

Cambridge IGCSE™

Literature in English

STUDENT'S BOOK

Also for Cambridge IGCSE (9-1) and Cambridge O Level

Noel Cassidy, Mike Gould, Chris Green,
Kurt A. Johnson, Alexandra Melville
Series Editor: Anna Gregory

William Collins' dream of knowledge for all began with the publication of his first book in 1819.

A self-educated mill worker, he not only enriched millions of lives, but also founded a flourishing publishing house. Today, staying true to this spirit, Collins books are packed with inspiration, innovation and practical expertise. They place you at the centre of a world of possibility and give you exactly what you need to explore it.

Published by Collins
An imprint of HarperCollins*Publishers*
The News Building, 1 London Bridge Street, London, SE1 9GF, UK

HarperCollins*Publishers*
Macken House, 39/40 Mayor Street Upper, Dublin 1, D01 C9W8, Ireland

Browse the complete Collins catalogue at
collins.co.uk

10 9 8 7 6 5 4 3 2 1

British Library Cataloguing-in-Publication data
A catalogue record for this publication is available from the British Library.

ISBN 978-0-00-878119-4

Authors: Noel Cassidy, Mike Gould, Chris Green, Kurt A. Johnson, Alexandra Melville
Series editor: Anna Gregory
Publisher: Catherine Martin
Product manager: Jennifer Hall
Product developer: Daniela Mora Chavarría
Development editor: Judith Walters
Project manager: Just Content Ltd
Copyeditor: Catherine Dakin (1st ed)
Proofreader: Claire Throp (1st ed), Tanya Solomons (2nd ed)
Cover design: Kevin Robbins and James Hunter
Typesetter: Six Red Marbles
Production controller: Alhady Ali
Printed In India by Multivista Global Pvt. Ltd.

collins.co.uk/sustainability

Endorsement indicates that a resource has passed Cambridge International Education's rigorous quality-assurance process and is suitable to support the delivery of their syllabus. However, endorsed resources are not the only suitable materials available to support teaching and learning, and are not essential to achieve the qualification. For the full list of endorsed resources to support this syllabus, visit www.cambridgeinternational.org/endorsed-resources
Any example answers to questions taken from past question papers, practice questions, accompanying marks and mark schemes included in this resource have been written by the authors and are for guidance only. They do not replicate examination papers. In examinations the way marks are awarded may be different. Any references to assessment and/or assessment preparation are the publisher's interpretation of the syllabus requirements. Examiners will not use endorsed resources as a source of material for any assessment set by Cambridge International Education.
While the publishers have made every attempt to ensure that advice on the qualification and its assessment is accurate, the official syllabus, specimen assessment materials and any associated assessment guidance materials produced by the awarding body are the only authoritative source of information and should always be referred to for definitive guidance.
Our approach is to provide teachers with access to a wide range of high-quality resources that suit different styles and types of teaching and learning.
For more information about the endorsement process, please visit www.cambridgeinternational.org/endorsed-resources
Cambridge International Education material in this publication is reproduced under licence and remains the intellectual property of Cambridge University Press & Assessment.
Third-party websites and resources referred to in this publication are not endorsed.

Acknowledgements:
With thanks to Abhinandan Bhattacharya at Finland International School for their review comments.

The publishers gratefully acknowledge the permission granted to reproduce the copyright material in this book. Every effort has been made to trace copyright holders and to obtain their permission for the use of copyright material. The publishers will gladly receive any information enabling them to rectify any error or omission at the first opportunity.

FSC www.fsc.org
MIX
Paper | Supporting responsible forestry
FSC® C199630

Contents

Introduction

Collins *Cambridge IGCSE™ Literature in English Student's Book*: introduction

The Collins *Cambridge IGCSE™ Literature in English Student's Book* offers a skills-building approach to the Cambridge IGCSE™, IGCSE (9–1) and O Level Literature in English syllabuses. It is designed to help you develop the skills you need to be successful in the study of literature, to explore your set texts in depth and tackle examinations and coursework with confidence.

In every chapter, you will read an exciting range of texts from different eras and cultures, chosen to expand your experience and enjoyment of literature in English.

How the book is structured

Chapters 1 and 2

Chapters 1 and 2 introduce the concepts, terminology and skills that underpin the Cambridge syllabuses. You will learn about writers' methods, and how to explore them in writing. These chapters could be used as part of your transition from lower secondary, to recap and reinforce your existing knowledge.

Chapter 1 introduces you to the key concepts of literary study, from characterisation to form and structure. It is designed to help you begin to talk about the effects of writers' choices and to give you a vocabulary with which to do so.

Chapter 2 introduces you to the key skills you need to develop as a student of English Literature. These range from demonstrating your understanding of literary texts, to analysing language in depth, to responding in personal and original ways.

The focus here is on your own analytical writing: how you can write convincingly about the effects of writers' choices and begin to construct your own interpretations of texts.

Chapters 3, 4 and 5

Chapters 3, 4 and 5 provide a starting point from which to explore each of the major forms you will study in your course. The key concepts from Chapter 1 will be revisited in the context of poetry, prose or drama to help you appreciate what is unique about each form and the different methods poets, novelists and dramatists have at their disposal.

Your analysis and writing skills will be developed throughout. At the end of each chapter, you will be given the opportunity to apply your skills to a range of practice tasks, writing an essay, and, in Chapters 3 and 4, a response to unseen poems or prose passages.

These chapters can be used as a way into each of your set play(s), novel and poems or they can be dipped into throughout the course, in particular to hone your ability to respond to unfamiliar or unseen texts.

Chapter 6 for Cambridge IGCSE™ students taking the coursework route

If your school is following the coursework route, Chapter 6 shows you how to apply your skills and understanding to best effect in your two coursework tasks. You will prepare and write your own two essays: one comparing two poems, and one comparing two longer whole texts.

How each lesson is structured

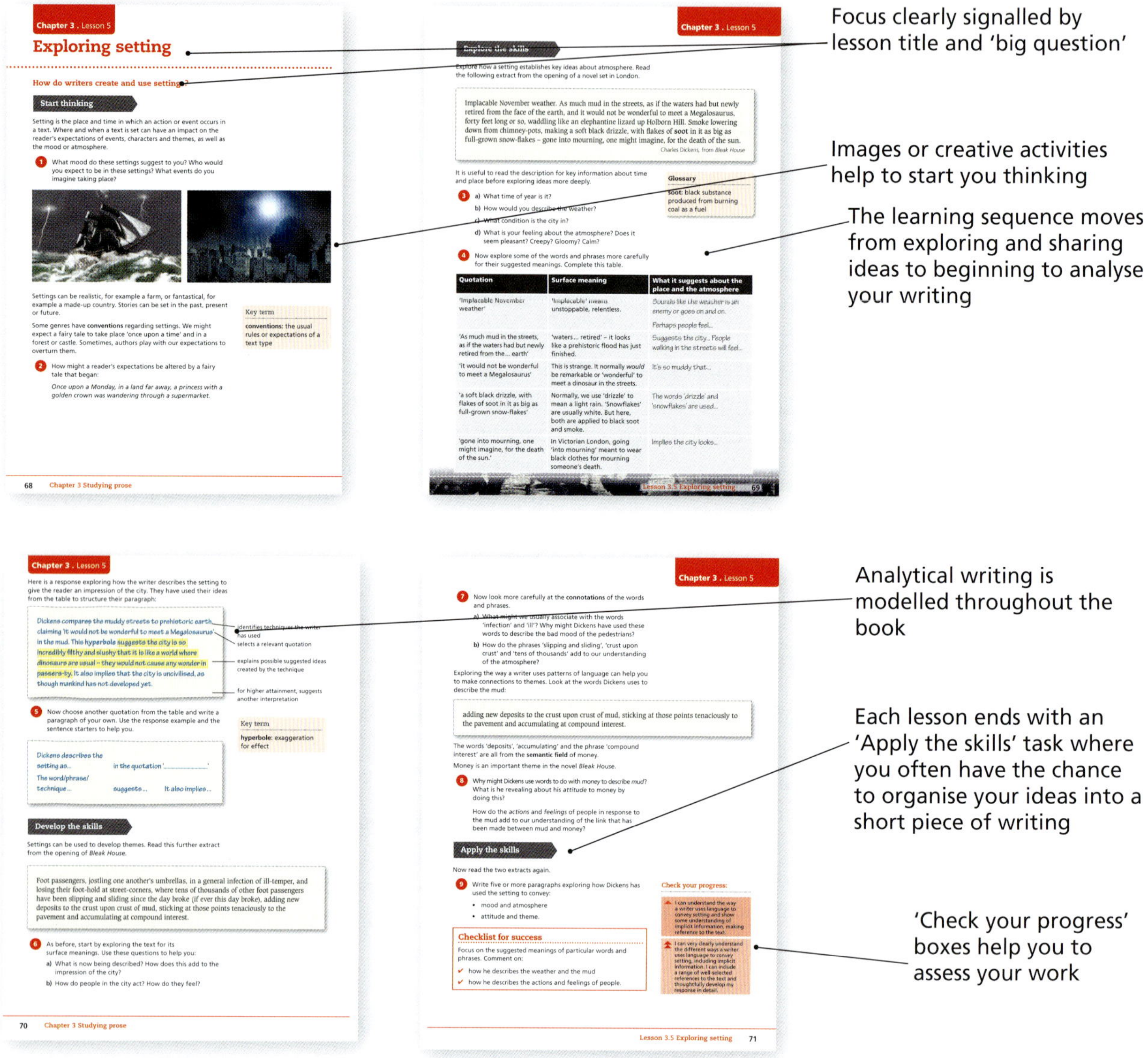

Checking your progress

Tasks are included throughout the book that could be used as assessment opportunities to help you gauge progress. The longer practice tasks are supported by sample responses at different levels to help you understand how you can improve your work. These sample tasks, responses and all commentary on the responses have been written by our author team, not by Cambridge International Education.

We hope our skills-building approach helps you not only to navigate through your Cambridge Literature in English course, but also to discover a world of fascinating literary texts.

Noel Cassidy

1 Understanding writers' methods

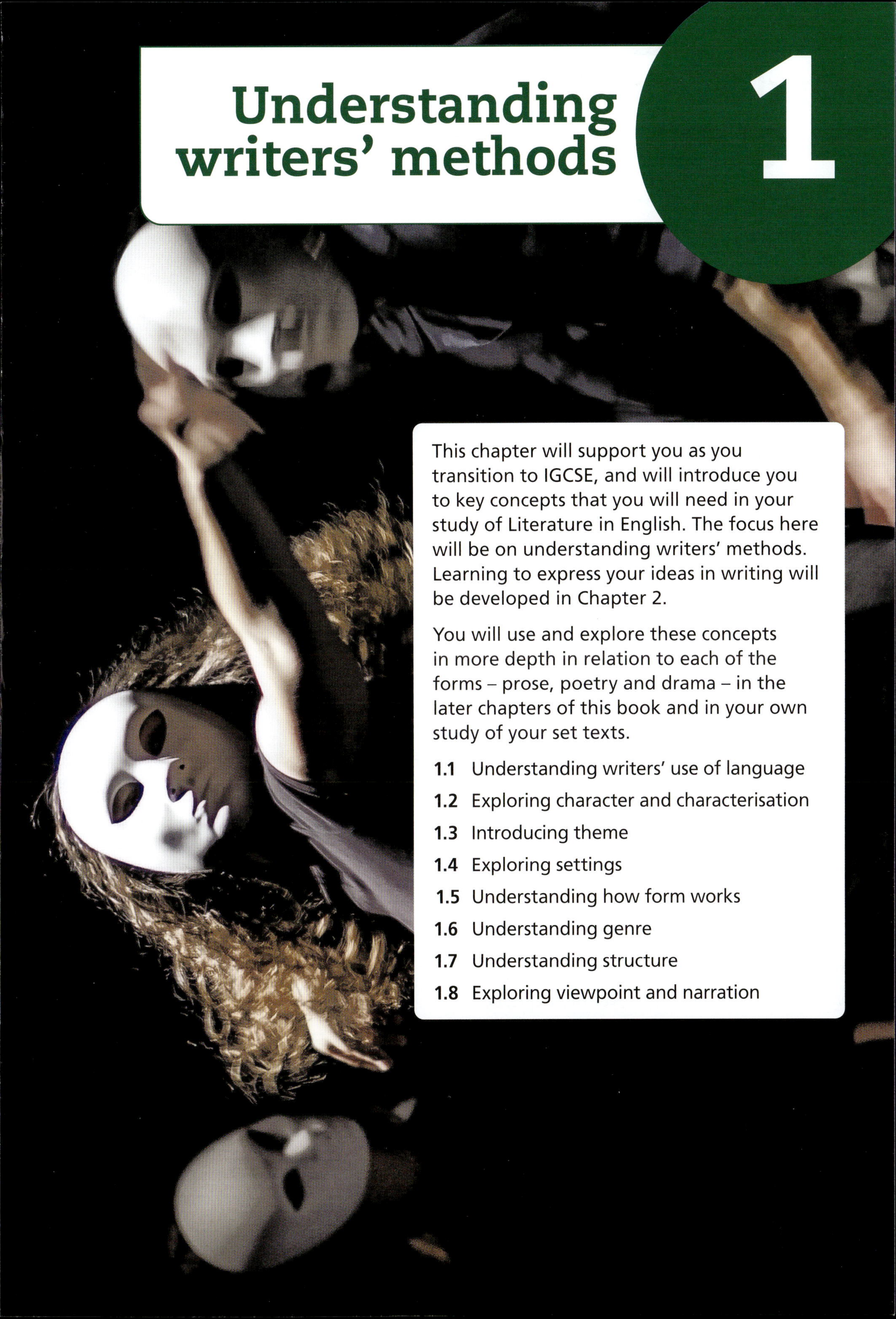

This chapter will support you as you transition to IGCSE, and will introduce you to key concepts that you will need in your study of Literature in English. The focus here will be on understanding writers' methods. Learning to express your ideas in writing will be developed in Chapter 2.

You will use and explore these concepts in more depth in relation to each of the forms – prose, poetry and drama – in the later chapters of this book and in your own study of your set texts.

Understanding writers' use of language

How do writers use language to create different effects?

Start thinking

Even simple word choices can create very different meanings.
For example, imagine you are describing a tree. You could write:

tall, emerald tree

But just think of how many other descriptions you could create by simply replacing the two **adjectives**.

1 Write five further descriptions using this structure:

.... [*adjective*] ....[*adjective*] tree

Think of adjectives to do with shape, colour, movement – or anything else. Make them as different as possible!

Key term

adjectives: words that describe a noun

Explore the skills

As you look closely at language, you should ask:

- What particular language choices has the writer made?
- How do these choices make me – and perhaps other readers – feel, or what do they make me think?
- What is the writer trying to express or make me imagine?

Read one poet's description about a place:

> By a dim road, o'ergrown with dry thin grass,
>
> Mary Coleridge, from 'Cut it down'

Working with a partner, answer these questions:

2 What two things has the writer chosen to describe?

3 What adjectives has she used in each case?

4 What feelings do these descriptions immediately evoke? Think of their **connotations**. Use the nouns from this word bank.

wildness	richness	joy	loneliness	secrecy
well-being	isolation	bleakness	neglect	

Key term

connotations: ideas or associations brought to mind beyond the literal or surface meaning

Now read the rest of the opening to the poem.

By a dim road, o'ergrown with dry thin grass,
    A little straggling, wild, wind-beaten tree,
Stood, like a sentry, where no feet might pass,
    And storm-swept by the sea.

5 **a)** What do you imagine and feel when you read the verse? You could copy the lines onto a sheet of paper and write as many reactions as you can to individual words or phrases.

Look at the spider diagram below:

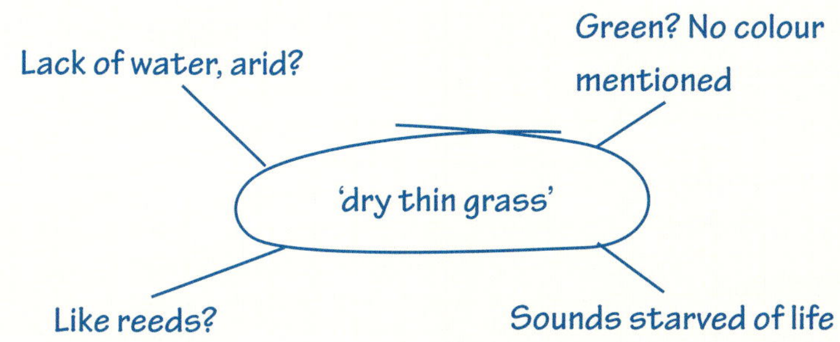

b) Complete the diagram for the rest of the poem, focusing on the adjectives in particular.

Key term

imagery: vivid pictures created by words and phrases

Imagery

Writers also use **imagery** to create effects. But what is imagery?

Device	Example	Effect
simile: comparison made between two different objects, people, and so on, using the word 'like' or 'as'	'a wind-beaten tree… like a sentry'	The comparison suggests the tree is watching over or guarding something – unwelcoming!
metaphor: a stronger form of comparison that states that something really *is* something else	Mary Coleridge could have written, 'a wind-beaten tree, *a sentry*, where no feet might pass…'	This stronger comparison stresses the impression that the tree is protecting or blocking out all humanity.
extended metaphor: takes a central comparison and revisits it in different ways through a text or extract	Mary Coleridge could have added: 'It stands guard along the road, warning us to keep away While armies of clouds gather in battle lines above…'	

6 How is the metaphor developed or extended in the third example? Which words link to the idea of conflict – and what impression is given of nature as a whole?

Sense effects

Writers often choose words that appeal to the senses.

7 **a)** Which of the five senses (sight, sound, touch, taste and smell) are evoked by the opening verse of this poem?

The wind one morning sprang up from sleep,
Saying, "Now for a frolic! now for a leap!
Now for a mad-cap, galloping chase!
I'll make a commotion in every place!"
So it swept with a bustle right through a great town,
Creaking the signs, and scattering down
Shutters; and whisking, with merciless squalls,
Old women's bonnets and gingerbread stalls.
There never was heard a much lustier shout,
As the apples and oranges trundled about;
And the urchins, that stood with their thievish eyes
Forever on watch, ran off each with a prize.

William Howitt, from 'The Wind in a Frolic'

b) The highlighted parts in the poem create sound effects. Match the techniques to the highlighted sections.

Technique	Definition	Example
assonance	the repetition of vowel sounds in a sequence of words with different consonant beginnings	'*rustling, bustling* sound of her large wedding dress'
onomatopoeia	the sound of the word matches its meaning	'The car hit the wall with a *bang*, followed by the loud *hiss* as the tyre burst and air rushed out.'
repetition	repeated words or phrases for impact or rhythmic effect	'*Out, out*, brief candle!' (Shakespeare)
alliteration	repeated consonant sounds at the start of a sequence of words	'His *soul swooned slowly*...' (James Joyce)

8 What overall effect about the wind is created by these uses of sound? Think about: pace and rhythm, mood and atmosphere.

Develop the skills

Sentence structure and variety

Writers also choose the shape, type and length of sentences carefully to create effects.

The following extract is from a novel about Claire, a piano teacher in Hong Kong in the 1940s.

9 What different sentence lengths and styles do you notice here? Look for:

- short or simple **statements**
- **exclamations** or **minor sentences**
- longer sentences developing thoughts or ideas.

It started as an accident. The small **Herend** rabbit had fallen into Claire's handbag. It had been on the piano and she had been gathering up the sheet music at the end of the lesson when she knocked it off. It fell off the doily (a doily! On the **Steinway**!) and into her large leather bag. What had happened after that was perplexing, even to her. Locket had been staring down at the keyboard, and hadn't noticed. And then, Claire had just... left. It wasn't until she was downstairs and waiting for the bus that she grasped what she had done. And then it had been too late. She went home and buried the expensive porcelain figurine under her sweaters.

Janice Y. K. Lee, from *The Piano Teacher*

Key terms

statements: sentences in which a main idea or event is declared

exclamations: phrases or sentences that indicate surprise, shock or anger

minor sentences: phrases that stand for a whole sentence but omit an element, such as the subject

Glossary

Herend: a type of luxury, hand-painted porcelain

Steinway: a very expensive type of piano

10 Why do you think the writer has used a range of sentence types and styles? Read the text aloud, listening for the changes in pace and tone, and then consider:

- how the writer arouses our curiosity
- how the writer emphasises points for emotional power or surprise
- how the writer explains things the character does.

Apply the skills

11 What overall impression do you get of Claire and her thoughts from this paragraph, based on the points you have considered above?

Check your progress:

- I can recognise the language choices writers make.
- I can explain the effects of these choices.

Exploring character and characterisation

What are 'characters' and how do writers create them?

Start thinking

Most successful stories involve a central character – a person who you would say the story is about.

1 **a)** As a game, in one minute, work in pairs to write down as many names of main characters as you can think of – and the story or tale each character comes from. For example:

Mowgli – *The Jungle Book*

Dracula – *Dracula* (!)

b) Spend a minute or two thinking about or discussing what it is about these characters that makes them so memorable. How do they influence the plot?

Explore the skills

The process of creating characters is called characterisation. The methods writers use to make their inventions come to life include:

- describing their appearance and clothing
- showing how they speak and what they say
- showing how they move (gestures and actions) and behave
- showing how others speak or react towards them.

2 Look at this image of a well-known character from a Charles Dickens novel. How do you imagine he would move and speak, based on his appearance?

Setting is also part of characterisation: the place a character lives or spends time in can give an insight into what they are like.

3 For example, imagine each of these was a stage design for a play. What sort of character might be found in:

- a modern grey-walled apartment, functional with no artwork or books, plain sofa and hard metal chairs
- a dusty sitting room with battered old leather sofa, shelves of old books, and an oak desk looking out onto a sunny orchard
- a narrow alleyway with grimy water running down the middle and shadows cast by a flickering iron lamp high up on a window-ledge?

Use your imagination! You could add a sentence introducing your character to each description. You could start: *Enter a ....*

Characters are sometimes categorised. This can help writers and readers to understand their function – what they are *for* in a story. For example:

the protagonist	The main character whose actions we follow – and is the main 'driver' in the plot; he or she is aiming to do something, get somewhere, learn something.
the antagonist	Often an equally important character, but in the story is the one who causes problems or is an obstacle to the protagonist.
minor character	A character who may influence the story but is not the main focus.
'flat' character	Minor characters may be – though not always – straightforward and 'flat' in that the reader never really gets to see their thought processes or **empathises** with them in the same way as a main character.
'rounded' or multi-dimensional characters	'Rounded' characters are characters we learn a lot about and whose feelings and motives are explained. Multi-dimensional characters are those who have a range of aspects to them – perhaps surprising ones (for example, an apparent villain who we learn is a carer for his old mother).

You can usually tell who the protagonist of a story is from the **narration**. If the story is told in the first person ('I') then it is likely that this person is the protagonist – the reader is following their experiences.

Key terms

empathises: able to put yourself in the shoes of someone else and understand their situation

narration: the telling, or manner of telling, of a story

Read this extract about a young Cypriot girl called Ada on the last day of term in school who can't remember what her teacher asked her earlier in the lesson.

'We were talking about family heirlooms,' said Mrs Walcott with a tired smile. 'Zaafar mentioned his grandmother's hope chest. Then Jason said, why is it always women who cling to these souvenirs and knick-knacks from the past? And I wanted to know if you agreed with that statement.'

Ada swallowed drily. Her pulse thudded in her temples. Silence, thick and glutinous, trickled into the space around her. She imagined it spreading out like dark ink on to crocheted white doilies – like the ones she had once found in the drawer of her mother's dressing table. Neatly cut into obsessively small pieces, destroyed, they had been placed between layers of tissue paper, as if her mother could neither keep them as they were, nor bring herself to throw them away.

'Any thoughts?' said Mrs Walcott, her voice tender but insistent.

Elif Shafak, from *The Island of Missing Trees*

4 Which five characters are mentioned in the extract?

a) Who might be the protagonist? Why do you think this?

b) Is there an obvious adversary? Are there any 'flat' characters here?

5 Consider the characterisation of each of the three people mentioned in the extract. Copy and complete this table, filling in any information that is given in the text.

Glossary

heirlooms: items you inherit from someone who has died

crocheted doilies: knitted, ornamental mats

Character	Appearance	Speech, thoughts or actions	How others react	Overall impression?
Ada	n/a	Can't speak Her mouth is ... Imagines ...	Her teacher ...	Girl who ... Anxious when ...
Mrs Walcott				
Ada's mother				

Develop the skills

A key aspect of characterisation is change: the 'journey' a character goes on. This could be a literal or emotional one – or both. In Ada's case, after this extract her aunt from Cyprus helps her overcome some deep personal problems.

Much later in the novel, Ada returns to school for the first day of the new term.

> In a few minutes, Mrs Walcott walked in.
>
> 'Hello, everyone. How wonderful to see you all! Hope you had a great break. I'm assuming you have all interviewed an elderly relative and learned a lot about their lives. Please get out your assignments and I will come round and collect them.'
>
> Without waiting to hear their responses, Mrs Walcott moved straight into the lesson. Ada looked back at Emma-Rose and saw her roll her eyes. She couldn't help smiling at the juvenile gesture [...]. She skimmed her interview notes and essay, and felt a surge of pride at the thought of Mrs Walcott reading about her aunt's life.

6 How has Ada changed from the earlier extract? How has the writer conveyed this through Ada's thoughts and actions?

> **Key terms**
>
> ***Bildungsroman***: German term meaning 'education or growth novel'
>
> **adversary:** enemy or rival

A character's 'journey' can take many forms.

A character:

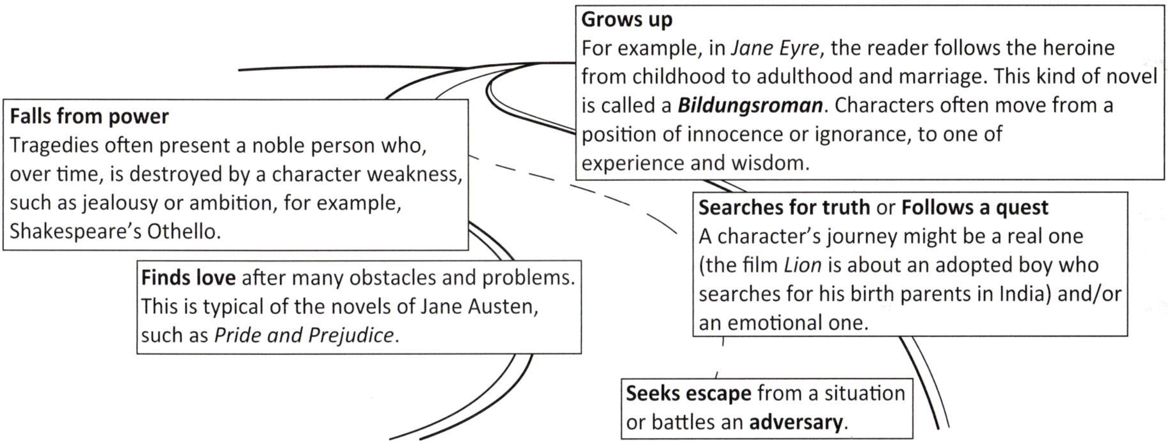

Of course, many stories combine these elements too.

Apply the skills

7 Thinking of your set texts, or any stories you know, are there any examples where a character goes on a journey – either an emotional one or a real one (or both)?

a) What are they like at the beginning?

b) How does what they experience change them?

c) What are they like at the end of the story?

> **Check your progress:**
>
> ▲ I can understand the different sorts of characters that can be found in texts.
>
> ▲▲ I can explain the techniques writers use to develop characters.

Introducing theme

What are themes and how can I identify them in texts?

Start thinking

In very simple terms, there are three ways to approach a text:

- The first is to explore *what* story it tells: what happens when, where and to whom.
- The second is to consider *how* it is told – for example, the writer's structural or language choices.
- The third is: *why* it is told. Does the writer, or the text, have something more to say or show readers than a set of interesting events or vivid descriptions? What larger issues or experiences does the text make readers think about?

This third approach relates to the **themes** of the text – the *ideas* that arise or are explored by the writer through the *what* and the *how*. These are often expressed in **abstract** nouns or phrases such as 'Ambition', 'Conflict' or 'Growing up'.

Key terms

themes: key ideas running through a text

abstract: the opposite of concrete; something that cannot be seen, like an emotion

1 Here are the blurbs from two well-known stories/films. Can you identify the words or phrases from the blurbs that suggest what the themes are?

Two young lovers from rival families in Verona fall in love. Can they escape the violent conflict between their families, or the hand of Fate? Or will their hopes and dreams end in tragedy?

An actress and a jazz pianist in Los Angeles are unsure whether to follow their dreams and ambitions, or stay together for love. Whatever path they choose, someone will get hurt…

Explore the skills

2 Think of any recent film or story that you have seen or read.

a) Briefly jot down the events: the *what*, *who*, *where* and *when*.

b) Then, look at some of these 'theme words'. Which, if any, fit the film/story you're thinking of? Can you think of others?

loneliness regret love loss family change
memory childhood poverty fate

Often, it is useful to describe themes in more specific ways.

For example:

How ambition *can destroy a reputation*

Conflict *between old and young*

Growing up *in the 1960s*

But how do you identify the core idea or theme?

Read the following verse from a poem about a successful farmer called Yusman Ali.

His life fell and broke like a brown jug on a stone
In middle age his four sons drowned in one boat up a pleasant river,
The wife's heart cracked and Yusman Ali was alone, alone, alone.
Madness howled in his head. His green fields died.
He burns the wild wood in his barren yard alone...

Ian Macdonald, from 'Yusman Ali, Charcoal Seller'

3 What are the bare facts of the story? Do they tell you anything? (For example, are they happy, sad, funny or weird?)

4 How does the language make you feel? Does it create a particular mood? Copy and complete the table below.

Word or phrase	Meaning	Mood or emotion suggested
'His life *fell and broke* like *a brown jug on a stone*' And 'Wife's heart *cracked...*'	His life as he knew it ended. His wife died or was heartbroken. Both were like ornaments that were broken and couldn't be mended.	Tragic – it is so sudden Sad – he loses everything
'alone, alone, alone...' and 'in his *barren* yard *alone*'		
'Madness *howled...*'		
'Green fields *died...*'		

From this sort of analysis, you can start to deduce the theme(s). Read two explanations of this part of the poem:

Jed:

> The poem is incredibly sad; you can't help but feel sorry for Ali who is left totally 'alone' after the tragic accident. He even loses his business – it seems like everything is against him. Even his 'green fields' die.

Nadja:

> The poem explores loss and the effect it has on people. The simile of the broken jug and the linked metaphor of the 'cracked' heart show how deep the suffering is. Another key idea is isolation – how a sudden tragic event can leave you totally alone in the world.

5 Which of these two sample responses focuses more on the *themes* of the poem? Write down any 'theme words' used by Jed or Nadja that suggest this.

Develop the skills

Another key skill you will need to develop is being able to trace themes across a text. This might be through the different verses of a poem – or in different chapters of a book, or acts of a play. The way a writer treats or explores a theme may change, or the theme may be broken up into different sub-themes. For example:

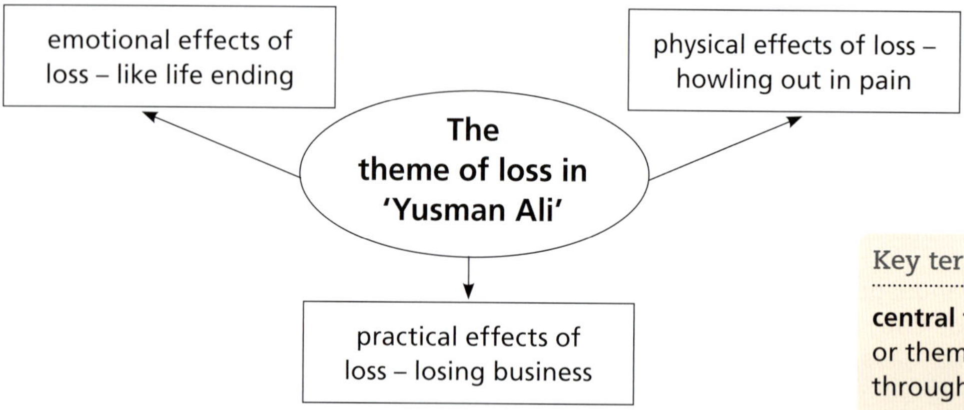

The main theme is loss, but each line from the poem deals with a different aspect of it.

Equally, writers often explore more than one theme in a text. Some of these will be **central themes**, others **secondary** or less important themes or ones that are especially relevant to a particular part of the text.

Key terms

central theme: key idea or theme that occurs throughout a text

secondary theme: a less important theme or idea that is either explored in less depth, or is only relevant to certain parts of the text

Read this summary of Laila Lalami's short story, 'The Homecoming'.

Aziz has been away working in Spain for five years sending money back to his wife in Morocco. Finally, he returns for two weeks but his time away has changed him, and Morocco has changed too. He finds it difficult to fit back into life, is bored and struggles to connect with his wife, even though he still finds her 'beautiful'. When she realises he is not coming home for good, she decides to join him in Madrid, but he tells her he hasn't earned enough for her papers and leaves.

6 Based on this summary, what do you think the themes of the story are? Consider:

- the main or central themes
- the secondary themes.

For example, would 'how Morocco has changed' be a central or secondary theme?

Apply the skills

Now read this short extract from the end of 'The Homecoming' and answer the questions that follow. Aziz is about to leave Morocco to return to Madrid.

'When are you sending me the papers?' she asked, at last.

'I don't know,' he replied.

Zohra started crying. Aziz tapped her shoulder in an awkward attempt at consolation. He couldn't imagine her with him in Madrid. She was used to the neighbours' kid pushing the door open and coming in. She was used to the outdoor market, where she could haggle over everything. She was used to having her relatives drop by without notice. He couldn't think of her alone in an apartment, with no one to talk to, while he was at work. And he, too, had his own habits now. He closed his suitcase and lifted it off the bed. It felt lighter than when he had arrived.

Laila Lalami, from 'The Homecoming'

7 How is the theme of separation explored in this extract? Think about:

a) how Zohra responds to Aziz

b) what Aziz thinks about Zohra coming to Madrid

c) what he says about himself.

8 Are any other secondary themes touched upon in this extract? If so, which?

9 Why does the writer choose to end with the image of the suitcase? Think about what Aziz says about its weight at the start and end of his stay.

Check your progress:

- ▲ I understand what themes are and can identify them in some texts.
- ▲▲ I understand and can explain some of the different ways themes are explored by writers.

Exploring settings

How does understanding a writer's use of setting help me understand the text as a whole?

Start thinking

1. Imagine you were telling a 'rags to riches' story about a poor young man or woman. Discuss with a partner what different settings you would choose to show the change in their life?

Explore the skills

Writers often convey important ideas or plot development through settings, but the term can mean different things.

For example, it can refer to:

- a specific physical place – a hallway, a building or a lake
- a more general place, such as a city or country
- an event or occasion, such as a football match or a wedding.

Glossary

azaleas: shrub with colourful spring flowers

2. Which kind of setting is being described in each of these examples?

a) It is a northern country; they have cold weather, they have cold hearts.

Cold; tempest; wild beasts in the forest. It is a hard life.

Angela Carter, from 'The Werewolf'

b) Bolted and locked since the war by long-dead hands,
Next to the shadowy church, the closed school stands.

Raymond Wilson, from 'The Closed School'

c) She clutched her fan, and, gazing at the gleaming, golden floor, the **azaleas**, the lanterns, the stage at one end with its red carpet and gilt chairs and the band in a corner, she thought breathlessly, "How heavenly; how simply heavenly!"

Katherine Mansfield, from 'Her First Ball'

3 How would you describe the mood created by each of the descriptions above? Focus on particular words or phrases and what they reveal as you explain your answer.

Select a sentence or phrase and annotate it with your ideas.

For example:

> … they have cold weather, they have cold hearts.
>
> Cold; tempest; wild beasts in the forest. It is a hard life.

'cold' here means bad weather – which links to the storm

'cold' in this case means unfriendly, or emotionless

How do the other descriptions add to the unwelcoming mood?

4 Which of the descriptions of setting provides an insight into a character's feelings? What particular features of the setting tell us this?

Develop the skills

Now read this longer extract from 'The Homecoming' by Laila Lalami. Aziz has returned, after some years, to his home town. He is on a bus.

> Aziz sat by a window and looked at the streets passing by. New buildings had sprung up everywhere, squat apartments with tiny windows that had been outlined with Mediterranean tiles, in a futile attempt to make them more appealing. Internet cafes were now interspersed with tailor shops and hairdressers. He was startled away from the window when a bus coming in the other direction passed by, only inches away.
>
> Laila Lalami, from 'The Homecoming'

5 What do the highlighted sections tell us about the city, as Aziz experiences it? Make notes on:

- how the city has changed
- what the traffic is like.

6 What do these descriptions suggest about Aziz himself?

Apply the skills

7 Write a paragraph about 'The Homecoming', explaining how the setting reveals Aziz's state of mind.

Check your progress:

- I can recognise the way settings are used by writers for different effects.
- I can explain how particular words and phrases related to setting create meaning and impact.

Understanding how form works

How can I recognise aspects of form in texts?

Start thinking

Look at the short text below:

'Twas on the shores that round our coast
  From Deal to Ramsgate span.
That I found alone on a piece of stone
  An elderly naval man.
His hair was weedy, his beard was long,
  And weedy and long was he,
And I heard this **wight** on the shore recite,
  In a singular minor key: [...]

W. S. Gilbert, from 'The Yarn of the Nancy Bell'

1. What *sort* of text is this? *(a poem? a novel? a play?)*
2. What clues tell you this?

Glossary

wight: creature

Explore the skills

Each **form** has its own conventions or patterns and, by paying attention to these, you can explore the effects created.

Key term

form: a set of agreed conventions or rules, which give an identifiable shape to a piece of literary writing

3. Read the following descriptions of different **forms**. Which one describes:
   - novels
   - poetry
   - drama (plays)?

a. Has a series of events, uses descriptive detail, characters, and takes the reader on a journey towards a conclusion. Usually split into chapters.
b. Presents a story, using mostly dialogue and movement to show events and characters to the reader/audience. Often divided into scenes or acts.
c. Condenses ideas, using the ideas behind the words, sounds of the words (sometimes in rhyme or through rhythms), and ways they are organised to tell a story or describe a feeling or an idea.

Develop the skills

Certain forms suit particular stories or ideas. Oscar Wilde's plays depend on social interaction and witty use of speech – perfect for drama. In groups of three, with one of you reading the stage directions, read the opening to *A Woman of No Importance*.

Lawn in front of the terrace at Hunstanton.

[Sir John and Lady Caroline Pontefract, Miss Worsley, on chairs under large yew tree.]

LADY CAROLINE. I believe this is the first English country house you have stayed at, Miss Worsley?

HESTER. Yes, Lady Caroline.

LADY CAROLINE. You have no country houses, I am told, in America?

HESTER. We have not many.

LADY CAROLINE. Have you any **country**? What we should call country?

HESTER. [*Smiling.*] We have the largest country in the world, Lady Caroline. They used to tell us at school that some of our states are as big as France and England put together.

LADY CAROLINE. Ah! you must find it very draughty, I should fancy.

Oscar Wilde, from *A Woman of No Importance*

4 What do you notice about the form? Look closely at:

- the layout: where the names are, how speech is shown
- the language: how movement or style of speaking is shown; the tense used for actions.

Glossary

country: probably means 'countryside'

5 How well suited is the form to its story, in your opinion? Would it work as well as a poem?

Now read the following extract.

"There never is anyone in the mill, surely!" exclaimed Mary, as the sea of upward-turned faces moved with one accord to the eastern end, looking into Dunham Street, the narrow back lane already mentioned.

The western end of the mill, whither the raging flames were driven by the wind, was crowned and turreted with triumphant fire. It sent forth its infernal tongues from every window hole, licking the black walls with amorous fierceness; it was swayed or fell before the mighty gale, only to rise higher and yet higher, to ravage and roar yet more wildly.

Elizabeth Gaskell, from *Mary Barton*

6 Which literary form (play, poem or story) does this passage belong to? What conventions does it use?

7 What would you need to do to turn it into a piece of drama? What challenges would you face?

Check your progress:

- I can recognise how the form of plays, poems and stories differ.
- I can recognise different forms of writing and understand how these can influence their impact or meaning.

Apply the skills

8 Rewrite part or all of the passage above as a poem using what you know of poetic form. Once you have finished, consider what has been gained or lost.

Chapter 1 . Lesson 6

Understanding genre

Why is it important to know about different styles and types of text?

Start thinking

1 Look at these four covers of plays or novels. Can you tell what genre of text each one is? Which would appeal to you the most?

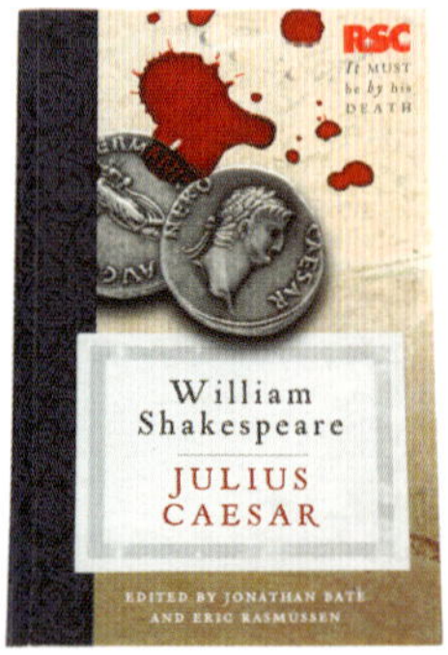

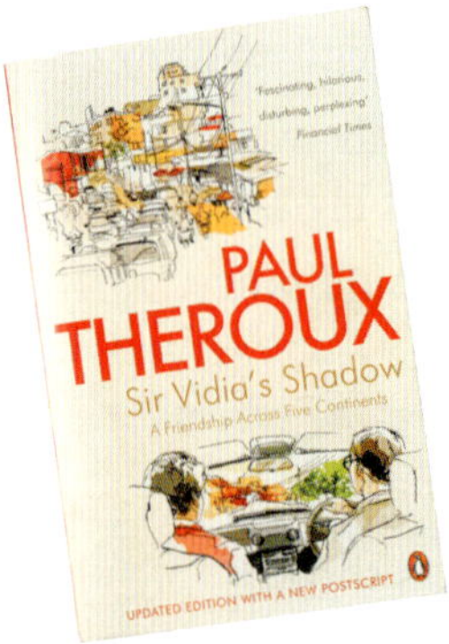

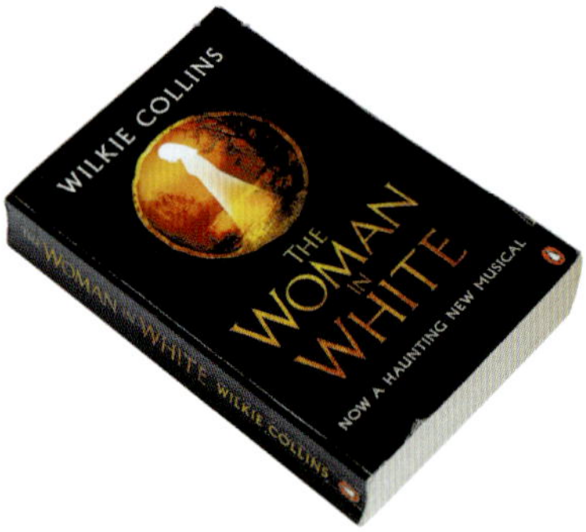

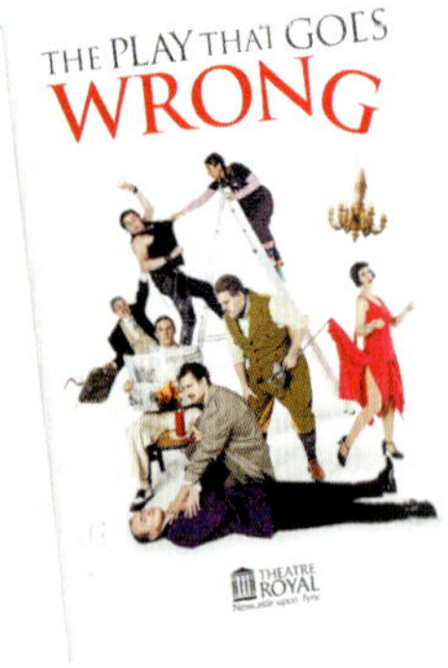

Explore the skills

The term 'genre' means 'group' or 'type'. Each of the texts above belongs to a particular genre. This means that the text shares features with other similar texts.

For example:

> **Key terms**
>
> **flaw:** a character weakness, such as pride
>
> **pastoral:** of the countryside

Genre	Comedy	Tragedy
plot	A misunderstanding, disguises, someone trying to fool another person, people falling in or out of love. Often ends in marriage or reconciled rivals.	A noble or important person who suffers a fall from grace due to some sort of character **flaw**. Has powerful emotions and may include violent or dramatic events. Usually ends in death or suicide for the hero or main character/s.
setting or background	Often, but not always, homely settings such as family houses, streets, **pastoral** scenes.	Wartime or tribal/political conflict; battlefields, castles or government buildings.
characters	Young lovers, but sometimes older people as figures of fun.	Royalty or important/respected people.

2 In what way does the following play description fit one of the two genres above?

> A young prince believes his father, the King, was murdered by his Uncle. He contemplates revenge but makes the mistake of thinking too much about the situation, thus causing a chain of events which leads to the death of others and, ultimately, himself.

The other two genres represented by the covers opposite are 'Gothic' and non-fiction 'travel writing'.

3 **a)** What would you expect the main **conventions** of travel writing to be?

b) Have you heard of **Gothic literature**? Can you think of any typical Gothic tales?

Develop the skills

Language can also give a clue to a text's genre. Silly **puns** and other forms of word-play are common in comedies, while heightened language (exaggerated or powerful descriptions of setting or behaviour) is a key feature of tragedy or Gothic stories.

For example:

> He looked wildly round him, expecting that some dreadful apparition would meet his eyes, the sight of which would drive him mad. A cold shivering seized his body, and he sank upon one knee.
>
> Matthew Lewis, from *The Monk*

4 Replace the highlighted words and phrases with the following. How do they change the effect? Do they make it less Gothic?

uncertainly	nasty	disturb him a bit	got hold of	went down

Apply the skills

Texts do not always belong to just one genre. Often they will combine elements of different genres.

5 Consider any of the plays, poems or novels you are studying. Write a paragraph explaining:

- what genre or genres you believe they are influenced by
- any reasons why this might be the case.

Key terms

conventions: typical features of a text

Gothic literature: a popular form of storytelling that came to prominence in the 18th century. It is a very broad genre but often includes supernatural or dream-like happenings; a villain who seeks to destroy or corrupt an innocent, younger person; gloomy, remote settings such as castles or ruins in mountainous areas or forests

pun: usually playing on two meanings of the same word or two words with the same sound to create humour. For example: 'I know the best *plaice* to buy fish'

Check your progress:

- I can identify some basic conventions of well-known genres.
- I can explain how texts can be a mix of different genres.

Understanding structure

What is structure and why is it important?

Start thinking

1 Imagine you are writing an **autobiography** of your life so far.

- Where would you begin? (With your birth? Or would you choose a different focus, such as your family's background?)
- How would you divide it up? (Would you have chapters for every year you have lived – or separate it in a different way?)
- What would you include? (Everything? Or particular key moments?)

These kinds of decisions would help to shape the structure of your story. This is a vital element of any text, and affects the way the reader responds.

Across a whole text, structure can refer to the following:

- the plot: the order or sequence in which events or information is revealed to the reader (for example, whether it is **chronological** or involves **flashbacks**, what tense/s are used)
- how a text is divided up (for example, through verses or paragraphs and what is included or left out of them)
- repeating patterns (for example, some old stories involve a traveller meeting three different people or facing three challenges during a **quest**)
- how a text begins and ends (for example, whether the ending returns to the start).

2 Think of a well-known folk or fairy tale from your own culture or that you heard as a child. Make brief notes on its structure. (What order is it told in? Are there any repeated patterns or links?)

Key term

autobiography: someone's life story told from their own point of view

Key terms

chronological: told in the order in which things actually happened

flashback: the story cuts backwards in time to an event that happened earlier

quest: a journey in search of something or someone

Explore the skills

One way of describing structure in stories is through a five-stage pyramid, which shows how the plot or action develops.

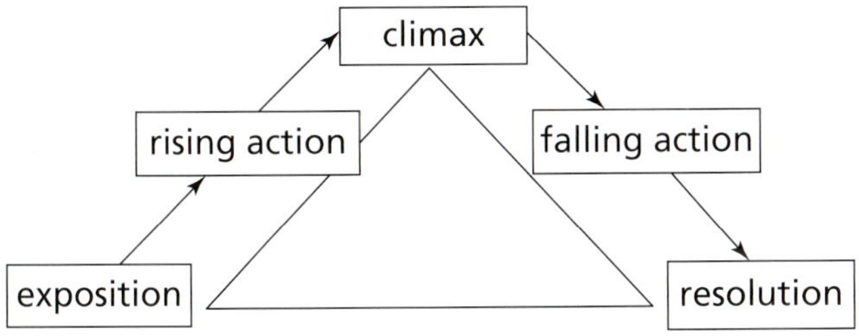

exposition	the beginning – the way things are before the 'real action' begins
rising action	the hero faces problems or obstacles that must be overcome
climax	the turning point or most dramatic moment
falling action	the events that follow on from the climax
resolution	the end of the main character's story/tying up of any loose ends for good or bad

3 Read this summary of one version of the Chinese tale 'Mulan'. Can you re-sequence the events and match each section to the stages in the pyramid?

a) Mulan's father is old and has no sons. She is washing clothes when she finds out that the army is recruiting new soldiers.

b) There is a terrible battle and Mulan fights heroically. The emperor wants to reward her, but is astonished to discover she is female!

c) Mulan asks for nothing but a horse to ride home.

d) Her father is too old and unwell to fight, so Mulan decides to join the army as his 'son' and disguises herself as a man. She leaves, carrying the sword inherited from the ancestors of the family. She fights bravely for over a decade.

e) She returns to her home town but sadly discovers that her father has passed away.

Of course, structure is equally – perhaps even more – important in poetry. Poets make a range of choices about structure to create impact or recount an experience. For example:

Structural devices	Choices poets have to make
dividing up the text as a whole	Should I keep it as one continuous 'block' of words or separate it into verses? If so, what will each line or verse focus on?
line or verse patterns	Should any of my lines or verses be repeated? If so, which and why?
sound, rhyme or rhythm patterns	Should I use a particular rhyme pattern? Should there be a regular rhythm or beat to each line, or should it change?
the overall shape	Should I create a link in language, sound or ideas between the start and end of the poem?
time	Will my poem shift in time between the present, the past and the future – or simply stick to one time or moment? If so, how will this be shown?
voice	Will the voice or perspective stay the same throughout – or will it shift to a new person, place, and so on?

Read the first two verses of Emily Brontë's poem, 'Remembrance'.

Cold in the earth—and the deep snow piled above thee,
Far, far removed, cold in the dreary grave!
Have I forgot, my only Love, to love thee,
Severed at last by Time's all-severing wave?

Now, when alone, do my thoughts no longer hover
Over the mountains, on that northern shore,
Resting their wings where heath and fern-leaves cover
Thy noble heart forever, ever more?

Emily Brontë, from 'Remembrance'

4 How many structural devices can you identify here? For example, think about:

- the repetition of particular words or phrases
- the use of rhyme
- anything else you notice.

5 Poets' use of structure is very deliberate, so you need to think about what response it creates in you. For example, the following words all appear twice in the first verse: 'cold', 'far', 'love', 'thee', 'severed/severing'. What mood or feel do these words create?

6 Both verses contain questions. What do you think the speaker is asking? What do you call this structural feature and how does it contribute to the text's effect?

Glossary

severed: cut in two with a sharp blade

Develop the skills

You have seen from the poem that structure is not just about the whole text. For example, the second line of the poem is:

'Far, far removed, cold in the dreary grave!'

The repetition of 'far' emphasises how distant and deep the burial of the loved one is. But the line could also have been structured:

'Cold in the dreary grave, far, far removed!'

7 How would this change have affected the emphasis or the power of the line?

As this shows, structure also involves word, sentence or paragraph order. Now read this opening to a novel:

> Why at the beginning of things is there always light? Dorrigo Evans' earliest memories were of sun flooding a church hall in which he sat with his mother and grandmother. A wooden church hall. Blinding light and him toddling back and forth, in and out of its transcendent welcome, into the arms of women. Women who loved him. Like entering the sea and returning to the beach. Over and over.
>
> Bless you, his mother says as she holds him and lets him go. Bless you, boy.
>
> Richard Flanagan, from *The Narrow Road to the Deep North*

this question is a general observation

this sentence shifts from the general to the specific – who, where and when

8 How do the remaining sentences of the first paragraph build on, or develop, the opening two sentences?

9 What else do you notice? Think about:

- the length and variety of sentences – why does the writer use short or minor sentences? What is their effect?
- any echoes or links between words and phrases in the text.

Apply the skills

10 Print out a copy of the poem 'Remembrance'. Using a range of coloured pens or highlighters, create a visual exploration of the structure of the text, perhaps using the same colour for linked words or phrases, or drawing arrows between similar ideas.

Check your progress:

- I can recognise aspects of structure in whole texts and within lines or sentences.
- I can identify a range of structures and comment on their effects.

Exploring viewpoint and narration

What different types of narrator do writers use?

Start thinking

Writers use a range of narrative **viewpoints** or **narrators**:

- the *first person* – stories told from the 'I' point of view: '*I* stepped onto the stage, *my* hands shaking.'
- the *third person* – stories told from the 'he/she' point of view: '*She* (or '*The girl*') stepped onto the stage, *her* hands shaking'.

The second person is used rarely in prose but often in poetry: '**You** stepped onto the stage, *your* hands shaking'.

Key terms

viewpoints: the positions from which stories are told

narrators: people telling stories

1. Think of any poem or novel you have read recently.
   - What person is it in?
   - Does it stay the same or change at any point?

Explore the skills

Here is the opening line to a short story.

> In the silence of the room the woman sat, looking across the lawn at empty windows, horizon below the sky.
>
> Maureen Ismay, from *The Bed Sitting Room*

As a reader, you may feel you are watching the woman from a distance.

Now look at these two other versions.

> In the silence of the room I sat, looking across the lawn at empty windows, horizon below the sky.

> In the silence of the room you sat, looking across the lawn at empty windows, horizon below the sky.

2. What changes have been made?
3. How does the mood or tone change in each case?

Develop the skills

What other types of narration are there? Have you come across any of these forms of narration in any stories you have read?

Type	Meaning	Example	Effect
omniscient narrator	All-seeing – the narrator knows everything about the character and the story.	'Let us picture him in his new car, shiny and expensive. How cruel Fate is! Little does he know the nasty surprise awaiting him at the office, those simple words – "You're fired!"'	The narrator is an observer who talks to the reader, watching and commenting – rather like a chess-player, moving the pieces around.
multiple narrators	many	**Chapter 1: Tony's story** Let me describe the day when I left her, and why... **Chapter 2: Fiorella** The sun was gone when I met him in the Plaza San Marco...	Provides a range of perspectives on the same event, perhaps helping the reader see that things are not always straightforward.
unreliable narrator	What is said cannot always be trusted or believed.	'You think I'm mad? Well, I can tell you I'm not. I'm as sane as you...'	Can create drama or tension as secrets are revealed, or allow the reader to get inside the head of someone evil or cunning.

4 Which would you choose if you were telling a story about a childhood friendship that falls apart in adulthood?

Apply the skills

Read this extract from a story.

> For fifteen years I'd been a gardener in New York City.
> A gardener in Manhattan? I hear you say. ***Cushy** number.*
> So some people have no ambition, so what? I liked regularity.
> One year's experience fifteen times. When I did change jobs it
> was to a garden centre. Something more stable. Out of the rain.
>
> Russell Celyn Jones, from *The Coalminer's Scarf*

Glossary

cushy: an informal word meaning 'easy' or 'comfortable'

5 Write a paragraph about the style of narration here. You could think about:

- the use of the first person and what it adds
- how close or distant the narrator sounds to the reader
- anything else that stands out.

Check your progress:

- I can understand what narration is and can identify some different styles of narration.
- I can comment on some of the effects of a range of narrative styles.

Check your progress

- I can recognise language choices writers use.
- I can understand the different sorts of characters that can be found in texts.
- I understand what 'themes' are and can identify them in some texts.
- I can recognise the way settings are used by writers for different effects.
- I can recognise how the form of plays, poems and stories differ.
- I can identify some basic conventions of well-known genres.
- I can recognise aspects of structure in whole texts and within lines or sentences.
- I can understand what narration is and can identify some different styles of narration.

- I can explain the effects of writers' language choices.
- I can explain the techniques writers use to develop characters.
- I understand and can explain some of the different ways themes are explored by writers.
- I can explain how particular words and phrases related to setting create meaning and impact.
- I can recognise different forms of writing and understand how these can influence a text's impact or meaning.
- I can explain how texts can be a mix of different genres.
- I can identify a range of structures and comment on their effects.
- I can comment on some of the effects of a range of narrative styles.

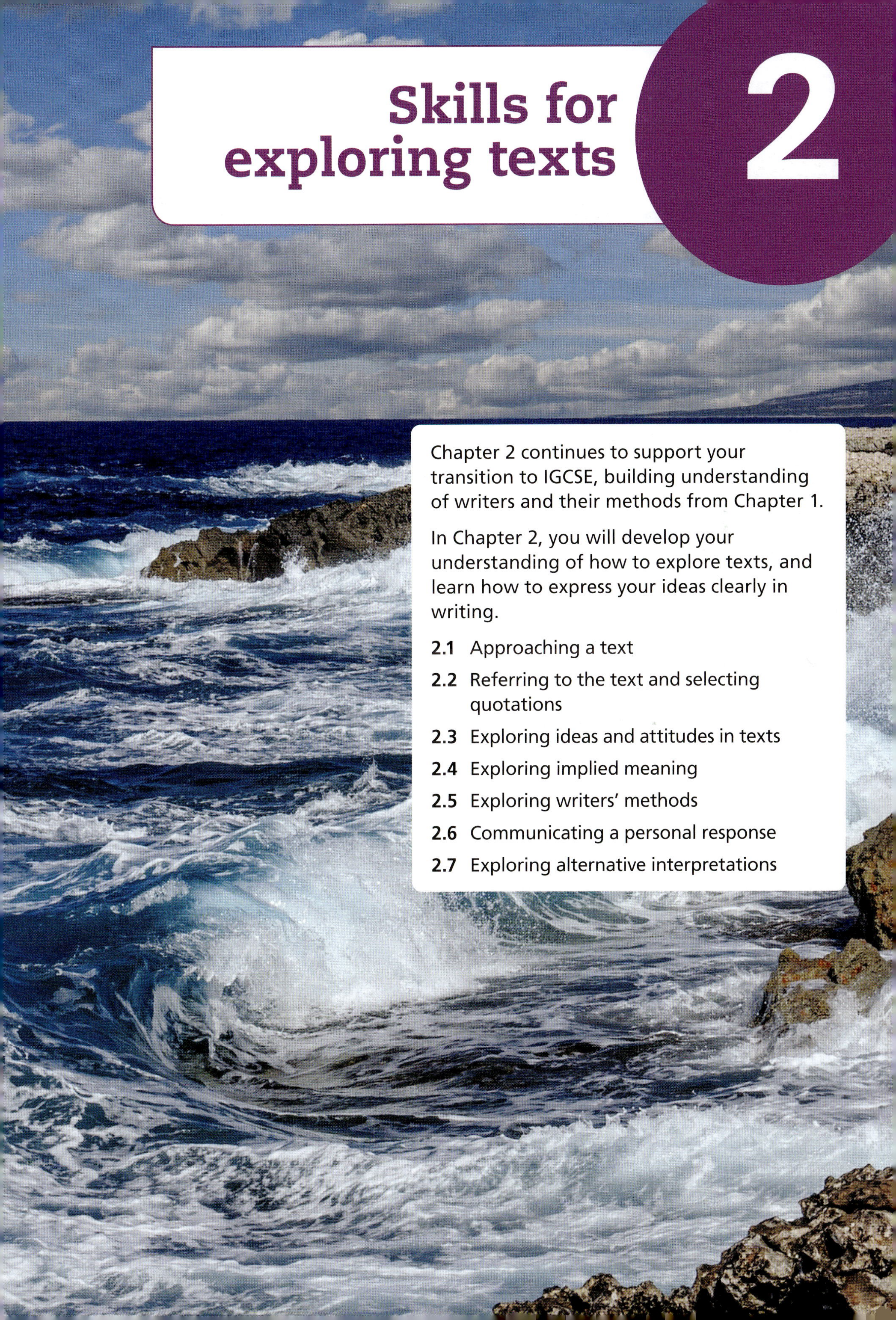

Skills for exploring texts

2

Chapter 2 continues to support your transition to IGCSE, building understanding of writers and their methods from Chapter 1.

In Chapter 2, you will develop your understanding of how to explore texts, and learn how to express your ideas clearly in writing.

Approaching a text

How do you study and understand the content of a text?

Start thinking

When you are writing about a poem, story, novel or play, you will need to demonstrate your detailed knowledge of the text.

To develop a more detailed, fuller understanding, you should:

- read the text thoroughly and deliberately
- highlight and underline key words and phrases as you read to pick out key events, ideas and language
- ensure you understand the language that is used by using a dictionary and looking up unfamiliar or challenging words
- break up the text into sections and summarise what happens in your own words.

1 Can you think of any other ways that could help you get to know a text well?

Explore the skills

Read the excerpt from 'The Tell-Tale Heart' (1843) by Edgar Allan Poe. In the story, the narrator describes how he commits the murder of an old man in the dead of night. At this point in the story, the old man is terrified by the sound of the intruder (the narrator) in his bedroom.

Glossary

tattoo: rhythmic tapping or drumming

suavity: grace, poise

[Meantime the hellish **tattoo** of the heart increased. It grew quicker and quicker, and louder and louder every instant. The old man's terror *must* have been extreme! It grew] Chunk 1
[louder, I say, louder every moment! – do you mark me well? I have told you that I am nervous: so I am. And now at the dead hour of the night, amid the dreadful silence of that old house, so strange a noise as this excited me to uncontrollable terror.] Chunk 2
[Yet, for some minutes longer I refrained and stood still. But the beating grew louder, louder! I thought the heart must burst. And now a new anxiety seized me – the] Chunk 3
[sound would be heard by a neighbour! The old man's hour had come! With a loud yell, I threw open the lantern and leaped into the room. He shrieked once – once only. In an instant I dragged him to the floor, and pulled the heavy bed over him. I then smiled] Chunk 4
[gaily, to find the deed so far done. But, for many minutes, the heart beat on with a muffled sound. This, however, did not vex me; it would not be heard through] Chunk 5
[the wall. At length it ceased. The old man was dead. I removed the bed and examined the corpse. Yes, he was stone, stone dead. I placed my hand upon the heart and held it there many minutes. There was no pulsation. He was stone dead. His eye would trouble me no more.] Chunk 6

Edgar Allan Poe, from 'The Tell-Tale Heart'

2 Read carefully and thoroughly through the text again.

3 Highlight key words or phrases that help you understand what happens.

4 Highlight and look up the meaning of any words you don't know.

Develop the skills

5 Next, break up the text into sections and summarise each section. You will see that one sample answer has decided on six chunks for this text.

Apply the skills

6 Practise applying the reading stages again, this time with a section of the story from later that night.

When I had made an end of these labours, it was four o'clock—still dark as midnight. As the bell sounded the hour, there came a knocking at the street door. I went down to open it with a light heart—for what had I *now* to fear? There entered three men, who introduced themselves, with perfect **suavity**, as officers of the police. A shriek had been heard by a neighbour during the night; suspicion of foul play had been aroused; information had been lodged at the police office, and they (the officers) had been deputed to search the premises.

Check your progress:

- I can understand how to approach reading a new text.
- I can use key strategies for reading and understanding a text thoroughly.

Referring to the text and selecting quotations

How do you choose the best references and quotations?

Start thinking

As you write about the text, you will need to make reference to it to support your ideas and demonstrate your detailed knowledge.

Reference to the text includes:

- the use of quotations
- a reference to key events or features from a text.

1 Which of these examples uses quotation and which refers to the text without quotation?

> The author also writes that when the pipe bursts, 'silver crashes to the ground / and the flow has found / a roar of tongues.' This shows how valuable the water was.

> The story is narrated from the perspective of the young girl, so we are unable to see or understand what she doesn't see.

Every point you make should be supported by one of the two types of reference.

Explore the skills

As you explore a text, you will need to gather quotations that develop your understanding of the author's tools: plot, theme, character, setting, language and structure.

Read the passage from 'The Tell-Tale Heart' on the following page. At this point in the story, before he commits the murder, the narrator creeps into his victim's bedroom.

Upon the eighth night I was more than usually cautious in opening the door. A watch's minute hand moves more quickly than did mine. Never before that night had I *felt* the extent of my own powers—of my **sagacity**. I could scarcely contain my feelings of triumph. To think that there I was, opening the door, little by little, and he not even to dream of my secret deeds or thoughts. I fairly chuckled at the idea; and perhaps he heard me; for he moved on the bed suddenly, as if startled. Now you may think that I drew back—but no.

Let's say you are answering the question: 'How does the author portray the narrator?'

Glossary

sagacity: wisdom, understanding

2 **a)** Read through the text and highlight or pick out anything that reveals the narrator's character and mood.

For example:

'I felt the extent of my own powers' – makes it sound as if he is very proud of what he is doing

b) Make a note each time of what your quote shows about the narrator.

3 In answering the question above, you may decide to make the point that the author portrays the narrator's calm pride when he approaches the crime.

a) Rank the following quotations in order, from the most relevant (1) to least relevant (6) to support this point.

b) Why have you decided to order them in this way?

- 'I *felt* the extent of my own powers'
- 'I fairly chuckled at the idea'
- 'I was more than usually cautious'
- 'Now you may think that I drew back '
- 'I could scarcely contain my feelings of triumph'
- 'I kept pushing it on steadily, steadily'

4 Read the following response to the question at the top of the page:

The author portrays the narrator as an unusual person who takes pride in his crime. For example, the author writes how he 'felt the extent of my own powers' when opening the door. He does it 'little by little' and thinks that this shows his 'sagacity'.

a) What do you notice about how the highlighted quotation fits into the flow of the sentence? (See the highlighted section.)

b) Identify other examples where a quotation fits into the flow of the sentence.

The response continues:

> The reference to 'the eighth night' and that the narrator is 'more than usually cautious' shows that he has been practising entering the room, which suggests he is patient and careful. This is emphasised by his comparison between his hand and a watch hand. The author shows the narrator's pride in his achievements, confirmed by his 'feelings of triumph'. However, his admission that he 'fairly chuckled' at such a tense moment shows his strange mental state.

5 **a)** Where do you see the writer of the response quoting from the text and where are they referring to it?

b) Look at the highlighted text. How is the writer of the response using the quotation here?

6 Use a similar approach to write a sentence integrating the quotation 'Now you may think that I drew back—but no'.

The narrator............... This suggests that..........

7 Now write a sentence about the narrator or the situation that integrates and analyses another quotation.

Develop the skills

Read another passage from the story. In this earlier excerpt, the narrator considers his decision to kill the old man.

> It is impossible to say how first the idea entered my brain; but once conceived, it haunted me day and night. Object there was none. Passion there was none. I loved the old man. He had never wronged me. He had never given me insult. For his gold I had no desire. I think it was his eye! yes, it was this! One of his eyes resembled that of a vulture—a pale blue eye, with a film over it. Whenever it fell upon me, my blood ran cold; and so by degrees—very gradually—I made up my mind to take the life of the old man, and thus rid myself of the eye forever.

8 In what ways is 'haunted' an appropriate choice of word in such a story?

9 Consider the quotations: 'One of his eyes resembled that of a vulture—a pale blue eye, with a film over it' and 'my blood ran cold'. Use the mind-maps below to map out their key meanings and **connotations**.

> **Key term**
>
> **connotations:** ideas or associations brought to mind beyond the literal or surface meaning

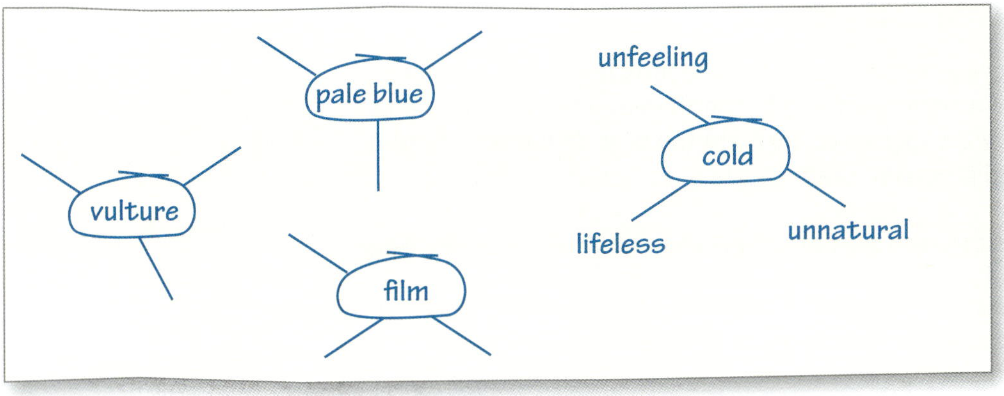

10 Choose quotations from the text that make the narrator seem irrational. Consider connotations and make notes about the effect of each.

Apply the skills

11 Write a paragraph to answer the question: **How does the author make the narrator seem mentally unstable?**

Checklist for success

✔ Include integrated quotations.

✔ Explain what each quotation suggests about the narrator.

Check your progress:

- I can choose appropriate textual references and quotations.
- I can identify and employ key strategies for making references to the text and analysing their effects in writing.

Exploring ideas and attitudes in texts

How are ideas and attitudes developed within a text?

Start thinking

As you explore a text, you will need to look beyond the surface and show your understanding of the themes, feelings, ideas and attitudes that are expressed through the plot, characters, setting, structure and language used.

You are about to read part of a short story entitled 'Madam's Sister'.

1. In the story, 'Madam' is the term of respect for the female employer. What does the title suggest by referring to her 'sister', rather than naming her?

Explore the skills

Read the following extract, the opening of a short story. The narrator, Cephas, is a security guard and odd-job-man for a professional woman in a town in Zambia. He lives with his wife in a room elsewhere in the town.

> Elina, the maid, is doing her thing of standing in a nice shaded spot on the veranda, while I stew in the heat. I carry on sweeping the paved front yard, sweat trickling down my back. The flagstones are patterned with black oil stains from the cars that park here at day's end. I pass my straw broom over these patches which refuse to be cleaned, even with water and soap. They make me look bad; lazy.
>
> 'Hey, Cephas . . . Cephas. Hey, Mr Nyambe, it's you I'm talking to. Did you hear what I said? Madam's sister, the one who lives in the UK, she's coming at the end of the week. You better move your lazy bones and clean this yard, yah? Make sure it shines London style.'
>
> My hand tightens on the broom. One: I'm not lazy. How can I be lazy, me? I'm the gardener. I'm the guard. I'm the car washer. And also the odd-job-man for all four households within the gated cluster of detached houses.
>
> Two: shine London style. I can't even begin to interpret Elina's demand. How can an oily forecourt bordered by a threadbare lawn and dusty shrubs shine like London?

contrast between Elina and Cephas, from his point of view (annotating "standing in a nice shaded spot on the veranda, while I stew in the heat.")

list emphasises the number of different jobs he has (annotating "I'm the gardener. I'm the guard. I'm the car washer.")

'Did you hear me, Cephas? I said . . .' — *Elina's insistent demands*

'Yes, yes. Okay. London style,' I say, swapping the broom for the hosepipe.

I aim a jet of water at the shrubs to wash the dust off their heat-curled leaves. Elina goes back inside, leaving me to wonder why Madam's sister is arriving at such short notice, making extra work for some of us. I also wonder what she looks like, for I have never seen her before. Is she dark, plump and pleasant like Madam? I hope so, to the last part, at least.

The sun hammers down on me as midday approaches. — *weather details and language create sense of discomfort* — I shift to stand under a tree and frown at the purple jacaranda blossoms peppering the lawn around the tree. Another task for me. But not for today. I lean my shoulder against the tree trunk, skin chaffed by the rough bark. Still, I lean against that tree, and close my eyes. Maybe I doze a little, sleeping on my feet as the hosepipe hangs loosely from my fist.

'Cephas! Cephas, come and help me in here.' — *suggests Cephas' irritation at Elina's demands*

What does Elina want now? She's worse than all the other maids put together. Always wants help with this and that but never shares her wages. I pretend not to hear her, keep my eyes closed.

Mbozi Haimbe, from 'Madam's Sister'

2 Read the sample annotations. What do we learn about Elina in the extract? Do you agree with her actions? Explain your answer, drawing on evidence from the text.

Develop the skills

Without directly making judgements, Mbozi Haimbe guides our reactions to each character through the way she presents them.

3 How does Haimbe make us feel about the character of Cephas? Annotate a copy of the text, highlighting and commenting on details that lead you to this conclusion.

Apply the skills

4 Using your annotations and notes from Questions 2 and 3, write a paragraph to answer this question:

> How does Mbozi Haimbe make the reader sympathise with Cephas in this passage?

Check your progress:

- I can identify and infer the key attitudes within a text.
- I can analyse ideas and attitudes with reference to the text.

Exploring implied meaning

What is 'implied meaning'?

Start thinking

Read this conversation between two friends:

Milo: How much do I owe you for lunch?

Rachael (waving her hand): Oh, forget it; it's nothing.

1 **a)** Write out the dictionary definitions for 'forget' and 'nothing'. Do the dictionary definitions make sense in this context?

b) What does Rachael mean, then, when she says, 'forget it; it's nothing'? How do you know?

c) What is implied by Rachael 'waving her hand'?

Explore the skills

When you write about a literary text, you need to show you not only understand the explicit meanings of literary texts, but are able to delve more deeply, looking for implicit meanings. Read the poem below.

Nettles

My son aged three fell in the **nettle** bed.
'Bed' seemed a curious name for those green spears,
That regiment of spite behind the shed:
It was no place for rest. With sobs and tears
The boy came seeking comfort and I saw
White blisters beaded on his tender skin.
We soothed him till his pain was not so raw.
At last he offered us a watery grin,
And then I took my hook and honed the blade
And went outside and slashed in fury with it
Till not a nettle in that fierce parade
Stood upright any more. Next task: I lit
A funeral pyre to burn the fallen dead.
But in two weeks the busy sun and rain
Had called up tall recruits behind the shed:
My son would often feel sharp wounds again.

Vernon Scannell

Glossary

nettle: plant native to the UK, which causes a searing rash if in contact with skin

2 **a)** What do you think the poet means when he says that 'Bed' is a 'curious name' for the grouping of nettles?

b) What words and phrases does the poet use to show us that his son felt pain?

c) What words and images does the poet use to imply the cruel intent of the nettles?

Develop the skills

3 What are the literal and implied meanings for these key words?

Key word or phrase	Literal meaning	Implied meaning in the poem
'spears'	long, sharp, knife-like weapons	The nettles are like weapons used to jab, pierce and injure people.
'White blisters'		White suggests...
'tender skin'		Tender suggests...
'pyre'		
'recruits'		

4 How does the father react to his son's pain? Why do you think he does this?

5 What do you think are the implications of the final line? Does Scannell mean his son will literally fall into the nettle bed again? Or does he mean something else?

Apply the skills

The poem is entitled 'Nettles'; however, an argument can be made that this poem isn't about nettles at all.

6 Write a paragraph explaining why this poem *is not* actually about nettles. What, then, is it implicitly about? You could use this writing frame to help you.

> On the surface, 'Nettles' seems to be about .... However, on another level it seems that the poem is about more than this. Several words have implied meanings, for example...... suggests......, and ......suggests....... Perhaps the poem's implicit meaning is that ......

Check your progress:

- I can understand the difference between literal and implied meaning.
- I can analyse language and texts beyond the surface meaning.

Exploring writers' methods

How do authors shape meaning?

Start thinking

Read the lines below, from Dennis Scott's poem 'Marrysong'.

> the shadows of her love shortened or grew
> like trees seen from an unexpected hill
>
> Dennis Scott, from 'Marrysong'

1 Consider what you have learned previously about a writer's use of language, rhythm, rhyme, form, structure and perspective.

a) Which literary techniques can you find in these lines?

b) What do you think are the key words in these lines? Why?

c) What sense of the rhythm, rhyme or structure do you get from these lines?

d) From whose perspective do you get this description?

Explore the skills

To write about literature successfully, you need to explain how and why authors use various linguistic, structural and literary techniques in their text, and what their effects are.

However, you will need to do more than just 'feature spot' – that is, just identify the author's use of similes, metaphors or rhyme scheme.

Once you identify the technique, you then need to explain its relevance to the context and discuss its effects.

Try always to answer the questions of ***why*** the author uses this technique and ***how*** it is effective: what does it make you feel, think or imagine?

2 Read the two sample responses below. Which do you think only 'feature spots' and which one discusses the *how* and *why*?

A

In 'Marrysong', Scott uses the metaphor 'that territory, without seasons, shifted / under his eye' to show the man's view of his relationship with his partner. The image creates the idea that she is almost another country and that she is unpredictable. 'Seasons' suggest regular changes, but she is 'without' those dependable alterations, but constantly changing as she 'shifted' as he watches.

B

In the poem 'Marrysong', Scott uses metaphors to describe the relationship. This is effective because it suggests the man's partner is strange. This is also imagery, because the reader can clearly imagine the woman.

Now read the whole poem.

Marrysong

He never learned her, quite. Year after year
that territory, without seasons, shifted
under his eye. An hour he could be lost
in the walled anger of her quarried hurt
or turning, see cool water laughing where
the day before there were stones in her voice.
He charted. She made wilderness again.
Roads disappeared. The map was never true.
Wind brought him rain sometimes, tasting of sea –
and suddenly she would change the shape of shores
faultlessly calm. All, all was each day new:
the shadows of her love shortened or grew
like trees seen from an unexpected hill,
new country at each jaunty, helpless journey.
So he accepted that geography, constantly strange.
Wondered. Stayed home increasingly to find
his way among the landscapes of her mind.

Dennis Scott

How do you 'learn' a person? How does this set up the rest of the poem?

Language of geography, suggesting the woman is a separate area, but 'shifted' shows that it is not stable, as we expect territories with borders to be.

Contrasting hard and soft imagery, suggesting the range of the woman's moods.

Caesuras *create short sentences and broken lines, imitating the sudden changes of direction the speaker needs to make.*

Oxymoronic *adjectives suggest the speaker's confusion.*

Key terms

caesura: a break within a line of verse created by punctuation, especially the end of a sentence.

oxymoron: an apparent contradiction in two words

3. Write a summary, in your own words, explaining literally what the relationship is like. Make sure you read and reread carefully to ensure full comprehension.

4. Now read the sample annotations, then continue to annotate your own copy of the poem, picking out language and imagery that you notice, and thinking about the effect on you.

5. Use your annotations to look for patterns of word usage. Create a table like the one below to catalogue language linked to a specific **theme** or **semantic field**.

Landscape	Weather	Journey
'territory'	'rain'	'He charted'

Key terms

theme: an idea running through a text

semantic field: a set of words or phrases that can be grouped by their meaning, linked to a particular subject, for example: 'mountain', 'valley', 'river bed' and 'pathway' are from the semantic field of landscape

Develop the skills

6. Consider all the landscape imagery. What does this semantic field tell you about the person being described?

7. The poet writes that 'he could be lost / in the walled anger of her quarried hurt.' What do you think this image means literally? What does it suggest metaphorically?

8. Explore the metaphor 'She made wilderness again. / Roads disappeared. The map was never true.' What ideas and themes does wilderness suggest? How is this connected to the disappearing roads? How does this metaphor link to the sentence 'The map was never true'?

Now read the following definitions of poetic techniques.

Feature	Meaning	Frequent effect
plosive	repetition or grouping of /b/ /p/ /t/ /d/ sounds	Creates an abrupt, sharp, sometimes shocking effect.
repetition		Creates rhythm and a sense of significance in repeated word or image; could suggest multiple meanings of the same thing.
enjambment	a continuation of a phrase beyond the end of a line of poetry	Creates a sense of continuity and fluency as the meaning runs from line to line.
anaphora	the repetition of a phrase often at the beginning of a stanza in poetry	Creates a grammatical repetition to emphasise key points.

9 Consider the phrases 'the walled anger of her quarried hurt' and 'see cool water laughing'. How do the sounds of the phrases contrast with each other? Consider the hard sounds of the 'g', 'q', 'd' and 't' in the first phrase and the soft 'ool', 'w', 'l' and 'gh' in the second. How do the sounds of the poem help us understand the images?

10 Consider the structure of the poem, looking at the single stanza, the different sentence lengths and enjambment, as well as the way the ideas unfold. How does the way the author shapes the text reflect the key ideas within the text?

11 Who is the narrator of this poem? What is the connection between the narrator and the person?

Apply the skills

12 Choose three different poetic techniques and write a paragraph to show how Dennis Scott uses these techniques to create meaning in 'Marrysong'. You can use this frame to help you.

> In 'Marrysong', Dennis Scott presents a complex relationship between a man and a woman using a number of techniques. He uses............. '.............'. This suggests....

Check your progress:

- I can identify key techniques and structural features within a text.
- I can analyse key techniques and features and explain their effects.

Communicating a personal response

How do you organise your written response to a question?

Start thinking

1 Read the following response to the poem 'Marrysong', which you read in Lesson 2.5.

> In the poem 'Marrysong', the poet talks about a relationship. 'So he accepted that geography, constantly strange.' This shows that the man wasn't sure about his relationship with the woman. The author uses a metaphor. This shows that the relationship isn't actually about geography and maps.

a) What do you think of this response?

b) What does this do well?

c) What three suggestions for improvement might you give the writer of the response?

Explore the skills

Communicating a personal response to a text involves planning, organising and writing your own ideas in a way that is clear, cohesive and even sophisticated. In doing so, you need to incorporate all the skills you have been introduced to in this chapter.

So, what should a good piece of writing about literature include?

I. A clearly stated **point** or argument linked to the question.

II. **Evidence** from the text, introduced and/or embedded.

III. **Explanation** of key words from the quotation, as well as any relevant techniques.

IV. **Links** back to the question and consideration of **effects on the reader** – your personal response.

A paragraph that follows those guidelines may look something like this, in response to the following question:

'How does Scott create a sense of the changing relationship in 'Marrysong'?'

> In 'Marrysong', Dennis Scott uses a number of techniques to communicate how the relationship between a man and a woman is constantly changing, and constantly puzzling to the man, who is the poem's speaker. He uses a metaphor to describe the woman as a 'territory without seasons', which suggests that she is like a landscape without clear and ordered changes of mood. Having established this semantic field, the changes are further emphasised by contrasting related metaphors. Scott contrasts the hard inflexibility of the 'stones in her voice' against the liquid playfulness of 'cool water laughing', also using the sounds of the words. The speaker's attempts to navigate the relationship are presented using the language of cartography: 'he charted'. His efforts are frustrated as 'The map was never true', and his changes of direction are emphasised by Scott's use of caesura in these lines.

key point identified – linked to question

relevant techniques identified

embedded quotations

clear explanations of effect on reader

2 Read the following responses to the practice question: **'How does the author powerfully portray the woman in the poem?'** Support your ideas with details from the text. [25]

First, decide which of these points best addresses the question.

3 Why did you choose the point you did? What was missing from the other responses?

A

> The author shows that she is very unpredictable when he says that she 'shifted under his eye'.

B

> The author shows that the speaker finds it difficult to follow the woman's changes, as 'The map was never true.'

C

> The author powerfully portrays the woman in the poem as unpredictable, ever-changing, but also fascinating.

4 Now read the supporting evidence from the text below.
Which evidence would support the best point from Question 3?

a.

> 'she would change the shape of shores'

b.

> For example, the author uses a metaphor to show that the 'map' of the woman 'was never true', but the single-word sentence 'Wondered' towards the end of the poem suggests that he is in awe of her.

c.

> The author writes that while he 'charted', the woman 'made wilderness again', using imagery to show how she constantly changes.

5 Again, why did you choose the evidence sentence you did? What was ineffective about the others?

Develop the skills

6 Now read the beginning of the paragraph, which combines the best point with the best evidence. Annotate the sentences with the features of an effective personal response. Some have already been done for you.

> The author powerfully portrays the woman in the poem as unpredictable, ever-changing, but also fascinating. For example, the author uses a metaphor to show that the 'map' of the woman 'was never true', but the single-word sentence 'Wondered' towards the end of the poem suggests that he is in awe of her.

words from question in opening sentence

quotations 'embedded' in the text

~~Words from the question in the opening sentence~~	The key point	Relevant technique identified
Introduced quotation	~~Quotation 'located' in the text~~	Appropriate quotation from text selected to support point

Notice that the analysis of the effect of the quotation has not yet been fully developed in this paragraph. Think about the implications of the metaphor of the 'map'. While this suggests that the woman is never the same, consider that a 'map' is made by someone to define a landscape, so the problem is also the cartographer's. This might lead to further thoughts about the verb 'Wondered'.

7 Look at the word 'Wondered'. Use the exercises below to explore how this verb indicates the speaker's feelings about the woman.

a) Define 'Wondered'. Are there different definitions of the word? What kind of thing might you wonder at?

b) Now think about 'Wondered' applied to another person. What does this imply about the other person?

c) Finally, what does the use of this word tell you about the speaker?

d) How does the use of this verb affect the reader's understanding of the relationship?

8 You are now going to complete the paragraph with an analysis of the effect of the quotation. You can use these prompts if you find them helpful.

- The verb 'wonder' can mean to feel curious about, but also implies that the woman herself is a figure of wonder …
- The different connotations of the verb 'wonder' are relevant here. 'Wondered' suggests that the speaker is puzzled and curious, but also that he finds the woman in some ways amazing … [explain how the word affects your view of both the speaker and the woman]
- This verb makes the reader think/feel …

Apply the skills

9 Improve this paragraph on 'Marrysong' from the 'Start thinking' section by re-writing it, using the structure suggested above.

Check your progress:

- I can recognise the structural features of a clearly expressed response.
- I can employ those structural features in my own response.

In the poem 'Marrysong', the poet talks about a relationship. 'So he accepted that geography, constantly strange.' This shows that the man wasn't sure about his relationship with the woman. The author uses a metaphor. This shows that the relationship isn't actually about geography and maps.

Exploring alternative interpretations

Is there only one way to read a text?

Start thinking

1 When you look at this picture, what do you see?
You will probably see one image right away, but will then see another image if you keep looking. Once you can see the two images, it is very difficult to 'unsee' either image again.

Explore the skills

Read this poem.

Between Walls
the back wings
of the

hospital where
nothing

will grow lie
cinders

in which shine
the broken

pieces of a green
bottle

William Carlos Williams

Key term

ambiguous: open to more than one interpretation

On its surface, the poem is clearly an image; however, it is rather **ambiguous**.

2 **a)** Consider the title of the poem 'Between Walls'. What image does it create and what does it suggest?

b) Make a list of words from the poem that may have negative connotations.

3 **a)** Read this sample response, which addresses the practice question: Explore the ways in which the poet creates a powerful image in this poem.

Support your ideas with details from the text. [25]

> The writer creates a powerful image in this poem by establishing a scene of desolation. For example, the title 'Between Walls' creates an image of being stuck or impeded by physical barriers, thereby creating a sense of isolation, even imprisonment. The scene takes place in the 'back wings' of the hospital, suggesting that this is a place where no one will – or even should – go, further developing that sense of isolation. Additionally, the fact that 'nothing / will grow' there shows that this is a dead place, unfit for the living. These images make the reader feel uncomfortable and uncertain.

b) What makes this response convincing and successful?

Develop the skills

4 Now make a list of words from the poem that have positive connotations. Consider words such as 'hospital', 'grow', 'shine' and 'green'.

Apply the skills

5 **a)** Read this second sample response to the same question.

> The writer creates a powerful image in this poem by establishing a scene of unconventional beauty. Initially, the title of the poem, 'Between Walls', creates the impression of a dark, lonely place – a place where nobody goes and where 'nothing will grow'. However, Williams juxtaposes this initial negativity with positive images. The fact that this scene takes place in a hospital – a place where people are made better – suggests a sense of optimism, recovery and rejuvenation. The 'green' colour of the bottle suggests ideas of plants and life, so that, even in this place where 'nothing / will grow', there is still a sense of vivacity and liveliness. The fact that the bottle 'shines' only heightens these themes of life, since the green glass is receiving its liveliness from the Sun and sunshine – just like a plant would. This verb develops the optimistic tone of the poem, in that this 'broken' bottle grows into an object of beauty and appreciation, thereby showing the reader how beauty can occur at any moment, in any place.

b) What makes this second response convincing?

The two responses interpret differently, but both are strong. As long as you have evidence and work from the text, your own personal response will be valid.

6 Which of the two sample responses do you agree with? Can you 'unsee' either of them?

Check your progress:

- I can understand that a text can be interpreted in different ways.
- I can understand that an interpretation is convincing when supported closely with textual evidence.

Check your progress

- I can understand how to approach reading a new text.
- I can choose appropriate textual references and quotations.
- I can identify and infer the key attitudes within a text.
- I can understand the difference between literal and implied meaning.
- I can identify key techniques and structural features within a text.
- I can recognise the structural features of a clearly expressed response.
- I can understand that a text can be interpreted in different ways.

- I can use key strategies for reading and understanding a text thoroughly.
- I can identify and employ key strategies for making references to the text and analysing their effects in writing.
- I can analyse ideas and attitudes with reference to the text.
- I can analyse language and texts beyond the surface meaning.
- I can analyse key techniques and features and explain their effects.
- I can employ the structural features of a clearly expressed response in my own writing.
- I can understand that an interpretation is convincing when supported closely with textual evidence.

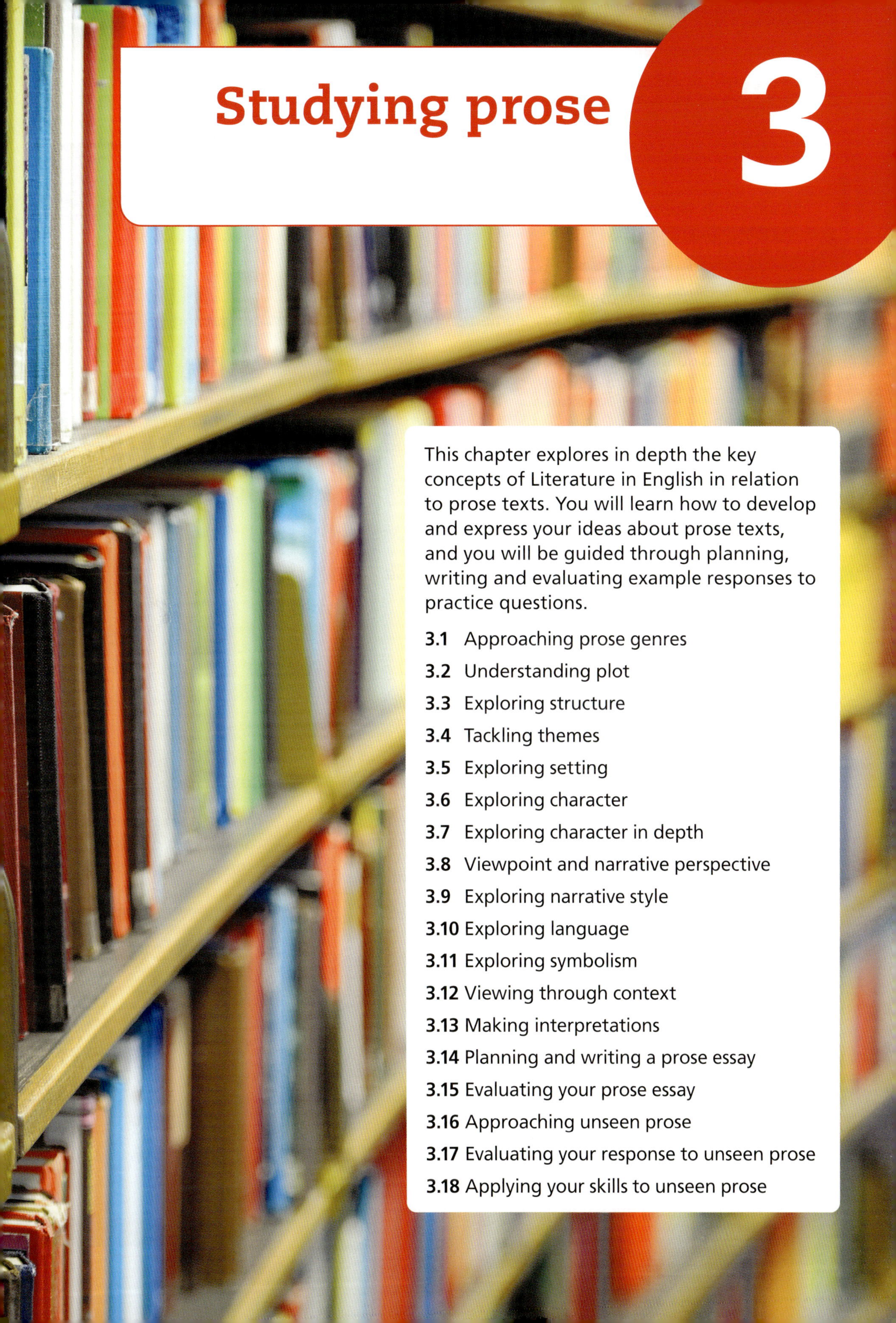

Studying prose 3

This chapter explores in depth the key concepts of Literature in English in relation to prose texts. You will learn how to develop and express your ideas about prose texts, and you will be guided through planning, writing and evaluating example responses to practice questions.

Approaching prose genres

How do writers use genre conventions?

Start thinking

There are many different prose genres, each with its own **conventions**. These conventions are made up of key elements such as plot, characters and setting.

1 **a)** Write a definition for five or more of the following genres, considering characters, events and setting.

For example:

Travelogue: Non-fiction account of the writer's experience of a journey or places visited.

Historical	Autobiography	Science fiction	Thriller
Tragedy	Romance	Biography	Dystopian

b) Which of these genres share elements?

Key term

conventions: the usual rules or expectations of a text type

Explore the skills

Authors may use conventions from more than one genre. This is known as a **hybrid** text. For example, a crime story set in the future would be a hybrid of crime fiction and sci-fi. Most prose set texts do not belong to one single genre, but contain elements of different genres, which may affect your expectations of the text.

Genre can be implied through an author's language choices.

Key term

hybrid: a text combining conventions of two or more genres

2 What genres could the following words belong to?

moon blood ethereal haunted
isolated shadow

A writer may use genre conventions in unusual ways to play with readers' expectations.

3 **a)** Write a romantic description of a person, using the words above. For example:

Her skin glowed like a full moon; I felt haunted by her radiant beauty ...

b) How does using this vocabulary affect the romantic description?

Develop the skills

You are now going to explore genre conventions in an extract.

> The Hopi country is in Arizona, next to the Navajo country, and some seventy miles north of the Santa Fé railroad. [...] It consists of a square track of greyish, unappetising desert, out of which rise three tall arid mesas, broken off in ragged, pallid rock.
>
> D. H. Lawrence, from *Mornings in Mexico*

Read the following sample notes on the text:

- describes place – place is real, not imaginary
- mainly factual – names, statistics 'seventy miles', 'three ... mesas'
- present tense 'is in Arizona'
- gives sense of what you can see – adjectives 'greyish', 'ragged', 'pallid', 'arid'
- some opinions – 'unappetising' – finds place unpleasant

4 Write a paragraph identifying the possible genre of the text and the expectations this creates. Use the notes and these sentence starters to help you:

> The extract could belong to the genre... because it features conventions like... for example, '____________' I expect a text of this genre to...

Apply the skills

Now read the extract below.

> He was an elderly man, grey-haired and deeply lined about the face, but lithe and active in movement. As he rose, he threw his cloak from him and now stood up clothed only in his war-girdle. In his hand was a club or mere of greenstone, a thong from the handle of the weapon being caught in a hoop round his thumb.
>
> William Satchell, from *The Greenstone Door*

5 Write a paragraph discussing the possible genres used and the expectations these set up. Consider characters, events and language

6 Read the first page of your prose set text. Identify any genre conventions and expectations set up.

Check your progress:

- I can understand and identify genre conventions.
- I very clearly explain how a writer uses genre conventions, carefully considering interpretations.

Understanding plot

How do prose plots work?

Start thinking

For a story to have a plot, there must be a change or conflict to be solved. A plot often has a five-part structure:

1. **Exposition**

   We are introduced to the world of the story.

   For example: *Three bears live in a house in the woods.*

2. **Rising action**

   A conflict or change is introduced to the world of the story.

   For example: *A girl called Goldilocks enters their house while they are out. The girl eats their food, sits on their chairs and lies in their beds.*

3. **Climax**

   The conflict comes to a head.

   For example: *The bears return and find Goldilocks asleep.*

4. **Falling action**

   Events follow on from the climax.

   For example: *The bears roar. Goldilocks wakes up terrified.*

5. **Resolution**

   The disturbance is resolved in some way, happily or unhappily.

   For example: *Goldilocks screams and runs away.*

Alternatively, the story may be left unresolved, that is, a **cliffhanger**.

For example: *The bears find her and roar. She screams and ...*

Key term

cliffhanger: an ending that leaves the reader in suspense

1 Following the above structure, invent the plot of a story using these pictures:

Explore the skills

A narrative can be complicated by adding further plot-twists, or a **sub-plot**. An example of sub-plot would be:

While Goldilocks is in the house, the bears climb trees looking for honey. They reach a beehive. But a bee stings the smallest bear. They quickly return home.

Key term

sub-plot: a secondary plot, running alongside the main plot

2 Add a sub-plot to your story.

Develop the skills

Stories are often told in **chronological** order (the order in which they happened). However, stories can also be **achronological** (events are told out of time order).

This may be done through a **flashback** (also called **analepsis**) or **flash-forward** (also called **prolepsis**).

Example of **analepsis** (flashback):

- *Goldilocks enters an empty house. She notices the bowls, chairs and beds are different sizes.*
- *The story cuts back to earlier in the morning, revealing three bears of different sizes waking and leaving the house.*
- *The story returns to the girl falling asleep. The bears arrive home. She flees.*

Example of **prolepsis** (flash-forward):

- *Goldilocks arrives at a house and pushes the door.*
- *The story cuts forward to her in the future, screaming in terror.*
- *The story returns to the girl exploring the empty house. She falls asleep. Three bears arrive home. She runs away, screaming.*

3 How does changing the chronology affect the reader's expectations in the story of Goldilocks?

4 What happens to your story if you alter the chronology?

Key terms

chronological: events are told in the order they occur in time

achronological: events are told in a different order from the order they occur in time

analepsis or **flashback:** the story cuts backwards in time to an event that happened earlier

prolepsis or **flash-forward:** the story cuts forward in time to an event that will happen later

Apply the skills

5 Read the first page of your set text. What, in the text, suggests this is the start of a story? Are there any clues that **foreshadow** later events?

Use these sentence starters to help:

> We can tell this is the start as... for example, '____________'
>
> We could guess the next stage of the plot would...

Key term

foreshadow: hint at events that will come later in the plot

Check your progress:

- I can understand plot structure.
- I can very clearly understand how a writer uses plot, and how chronology and sub-plots may affect a reader's expectations.

Exploring structure

How do writers use structural devices?

Start thinking

The structure of a text is the way it is put together: not just the plot, but the order of ideas and words, which control how and when information is revealed, and the lengths of sentences and paragraphs. These can all influence the way a reader receives and responds to the text.

1 Read the sentence:

- *I knew he would get me into trouble.*

Now read the same sentence with altered **syntax**:

- *He, I knew, would get me into trouble.*

How does altering the syntax change the emphasis in the sentence?

> **Key term**
>
> **syntax:** word order

2 Which of the following sentences creates more tension? Why?

A *Drops fell from the ceiling slowly, pooling in puddles the colour of blood.*

B *Drops fell from the ceiling, slowly pooling in puddles. The colour of blood.*

Explore the skills

Authors carefully control the information they give readers (how much readers are allowed to know and when) through structural devices. These include:

Structural device	Example
juxtaposition: placing ideas next to each other, often highlighting differences	She turned from the warm, sunlit avenue, blossoming with the scent of summer, into a gloomy lane, chilly as a winter's night.
revealing or **withholding** information	Andre stared through the window. It couldn't be! Yet it was! He knew that face too well. With a gasp, he fainted.
lengths of sentences or paragraphs	Ali drew a sharp breath, glancing at the door handle; there was no doubt he'd heard a noise. Click.
altering the **focus** by zooming in or out, or panning across a scene	Across the hallway was a dark doorway and through the door stood a dark chair. There sat a man in darkness, one small eye blinking in his shadowy face, dark down to its pinpoint depths.

3 How do each of the devices in the table above help to create tension in the examples?

Read the following extract from the opening of a novel:

Hale knew, before he had been in Brighton three hours, that they meant to murder him. With his inky fingers and his bitten nails, his manner cynical and nervous, anybody could tell he didn't belong – belong to the early summer sun, the cool **Whitsun** wind off the sea, the holiday crowd. They came in by train from Victoria every five minutes, rocked down Queen's Road standing on the tops of the little local trams, stepped off in bewildered multitudes into fresh and glittering air: the new silver paint sparkled on the piers, the cream houses ran away into the west like a pale Victorian water-colour; a race in miniature motors, a band playing, flower gardens in bloom below the front, an aeroplane advertising something for the health in pale vanishing clouds across the sky.

It had seemed quite easy to Hale to be lost in Brighton.

Graham Greene, from *Brighton Rock*

4 Start by thinking about what the writer focuses on in the extract.

a) Put the following topics in order:

- describes busy holiday crowd in the sun
- returns to Hale
- describes Hale's thoughts – he is nervous
- describes his fingers and manner
- describes bright, pale seafront and sky.

b) Why would the author zoom out from the description of Hale and return to him later? What effect is created by shifting the focus from Hale to the scene beyond him and back again?

c) What is emphasised by juxtaposing Hale and his 'bitten nails' with a description of 'the holiday crowd'?

Glossary

Whitsun: holiday Sunday in spring

Develop the skills

5 Explore the structure in depth:

a) The **clause** 'before he had been ... three hours' is right in the middle of the first sentence. What information does it leave us waiting for? How would the sentence be different if that clause were at the end?

b) How do the lengths of the sentences about Hale compare to the third sentence, about the crowd and Brighton? Why might the author use these sentence lengths? What are we kept waiting for?

c) What is the impact of this punctuation and repetition: 'didn't belong – belong to the early summer sun'?

Key term

clause: a supplementary part of a sentence

Apply the skills

6 How does the writer use structural devices to make this a memorable opening to the novel? In paragraphs, comment on:

- the order of topics
- sentence length
- syntax and punctuation.

Checklist for success

Follow these steps to structure your paragraphs:

- ✔ name the structural device
- ✔ clearly explain how it is used in the text
- ✔ discuss how it affects the reader's focus and responses to the text.

Check your progress:

▲ I can understand the way a writer uses structural devices, making reference to the text.

▲▲ I can very clearly understand the different ways a writer uses structural devices, thoughtfully developing my response in detail.

Tackling themes

How do I gain a sense of key themes across a whole text?

Start thinking

It is important to have an understanding of the whole when analysing prose texts. A good way to explore how a text develops as a whole is by looking at how themes are portrayed across a text.

Authors may convey themes through a number of techniques, including:

- patterns of images
- characters
- settings
- events.

A repeated image can be used to develop a theme across a text.

The following three extracts are from a short story that follows two pilots as they pit their flying skills against those of an eagle. The story explores themes of human pride, contrasted to nature's majesty.

1 **a)** Find examples of ways in which the writer associates the eagle with royalty.

b) Analyse the ways that these examples contribute to the theme of the power of nature.

c) How does the language of the third extract present the pilot's flight?

The delay and quick manoeuvre would be done with a princely detachment and consciousness of superiority, the eagle in the silence of its wings scorning the roar and fuss of the aircraft and its engine.

'You ought to pay him more respect, the most magnificent, majestic bird there is.'
The farmer was hostile to this idea of majesty.

In contrast with all his noisy manoeuvring, his juggling with engine and controls, the eagle had scorned him with its silence...

Geoffrey Dutton, from *'The Wedge-Tailed Eagle'*

2 **a)** What does Dutton suggest about the pilots in the phrase 'the roar and fuss of the aircraft' (extract 1)? Can you select a matching phrase from extract 3?

b) Analysing these examples, write a short paragraph about the way Dutton presents the theme of humanity's lack of natural grace and power.

You could begin like this:

> *Unlike the eagle, which flies with 'the silence of its wings', the pilots are shown to be struggling with their aircraft. The planes…*

Explore the skills

You are now going to explore how a character can be used to develop a theme. Read this extract from near the start of a novel:

> She was a strong, agile girl, with stiff black hair [...] The first time you saw her take her hat off you got a surprise, for on her crown three white hairs glittered among the black ones like silver wires. It was typical of Rosemary that she never bothered to pull the white hairs out.
>
> George Orwell, from *Keep the Aspidistra Flying*

3 Explore what Rosemary's appearance reveals about the theme of social expectations.

a) What do a few white hairs suggest about her age?

b) Why do the white hairs cause 'surprise'?

c) Why might a woman 'pull the white hairs out'?

d) What does it suggest about Rosemary's attitude to social expectations that 'it was typical of Rosemary that she never bothered to pull the white hairs out'?

4 Now look more closely at the language used. The author tells us the hairs 'glittered' 'like silver wires'.

a) What do you associate with glittering silver? Does this image seem positive or negative?

b) What does it suggest about the author's attitude to Rosemary's aging hair?

c) What could this imply about the author's view of social conformity?

Rosemary's character is described again towards the end of the novel, shortly after her marriage to the main character, Gordon:

> She had a touch of make-up on today, the first he had ever seen on her, and not too skilfully applied. [...] Rosemary looked twenty-eight, perhaps; Gordon looked at least thirty-five. But Rosemary had pulled the three white hairs out of her crown yesterday.

5 **a)** How has her appearance changed since the first extract?

b) What change must have taken place in her attitude to social expectations?

c) What does this change reveal about the theme of social conformity?

Develop the skills

Finally, several techniques can be combined to develop a theme across a text. Read these extracts from across the novel 'Tess of the d'Urbervilles' by Thomas Hardy:

> Then she became aware of the spectacle she presented to their surprised vision: roses at her breast; roses in her hat; roses and strawberries in her basket to the brim. She blushed, and said confusedly that the flowers had been given to her. When the passengers were not looking she stealthily removed the more prominent blooms from her hat and placed them in the basket, where she covered them with her handkerchief. Then she fell to reflecting again, and in looking downwards a thorn of the rose remaining in her breast accidentally pricked her chin.
>
> *Later in the novel:*
>
> The **swede**-field in which she and her companion were set hacking was a stretch of a hundred odd acres in one patch, on the highest ground of the farm […] The upper half of each turnip had been eaten off by the live-stock, and it was the business of the two women to grub up the lower or earthy half of the root with a hooked fork called a hacker, that it might be eaten also […] the whole field was in colour a desolate **drab** […] The sky wore, in another colour, the same likeness […] without anything […] but the two girls crawling over the surface of the former like flies.
>
> Thomas Hardy, from *Tess of the d'Urbervilles*

6 **a)** Throughout *Tess of the d'Urbervilles*, Tess is linked with plants and flowers. What connotations do plants and flowers normally have?

b) What other examples of imagery of the natural world are there in the extracts?

7 Complete the table to explore how the theme of change is presented across the text.

Glossary

swede: a root vegetable, similar to the turnip

drab: extremely dull

Techniques	Quotations	What changes?	What could this suggest about the theme of lost innocence?
Setting			
• earlier	'passengers'	The early setting is…	The settings show changing circumstances for Tess …
• later	'swede-field' 'the highest ground'	The farm gives the impression …	
Imagery of nature			
• earlier	'roses and strawberries' 'prominent blooms'	Tess is associated with flowers and fruit …	The early imagery suggests …
• later	'desolate drab' 'crawling over the surface like flies'	Later, she endures hard manual labour …	Later in the text, however …
Character of Tess			
• earlier	'became aware' 'stealthily removed' 'she fell to reflecting'	Tess seems attractive, but shy …	The fresh youth of Tess becomes …
• later	'grub up … the root' 'crawling'	By the end, she can have little thought about her appearance …	

Apply the skills

8 How does the author present change across the text? Support your ideas with details from the text. Use your notes from the table, and the model below, to write a paragraph on each technique.

The author uses imagery of nature to show significant changes in Tess's life. At the start, she is associated with natural beauty, wearing 'roses at her breast', suggesting she is uncorrupted, and full of vitality. It is interesting that she is accidentally pricked by a 'thorn of the rose', foreshadowing pain to come. This is later confirmed when Hardy uses the simile 'crawling over the surface like flies' for the life of Tess and her friend on the farm. By comparing them to insignificant creatures, Hardy shows the harsh change in Tess' life.

topic sentence identifying technique and theme

techniques used, quotations

effects of the examples and how this connects to the theme

Check your progress:

I can understand some of the ways themes are portrayed and start to explore meanings.

I can very clearly understand the ways themes are portrayed and thoughtfully explore deeper implicit meanings in detail.

Exploring setting

How do writers create and use settings?

Start thinking

Setting is the place and time in which an action or event occurs in a text. Where and when a text is set can have an impact on the reader's expectations of events, characters and themes, as well as the mood or atmosphere.

1 What mood do these settings suggest to you? Who would you expect to be in these settings? What events do you imagine taking place?

Settings can be realistic, for example a farm, or fantastical, for example a made-up country. Stories can be set in the past, present or future.

Some genres have **conventions** regarding settings. We might expect a fairy tale to take place 'once upon a time' and in a forest or castle. Sometimes, authors play with our expectations to overturn them.

Key term

conventions: the usual rules or expectations of a text type

2 How might a reader's expectations be altered by a fairy tale that began:

Once upon a Monday, in a land far away, a princess with a golden crown was wandering through a supermarket.

Explore the skills

Explore how a setting establishes key ideas about atmosphere. Read the following extract from the opening of a novel set in London.

> Implacable November weather. As much mud in the streets, as if the waters had but newly retired from the face of the earth, and it would not be wonderful to meet a Megalosaurus, forty feet long or so, waddling like an elephantine lizard up Holborn Hill. Smoke lowering down from chimney-pots, making a soft black drizzle, with flakes of **soot** in it as big as full-grown snow-flakes – gone into mourning, one might imagine, for the death of the sun.
>
> Charles Dickens, from *Bleak House*

It is useful to read the description for key information about time and place before exploring ideas more deeply.

Glossary

soot: black substance produced from burning coal as a fuel

3 **a)** What time of year is it?

b) How would you describe the weather?

c) What condition is the city in?

d) What is your feeling about the atmosphere? Does it seem pleasant? Creepy? Gloomy? Calm?

4 Now explore some of the words and phrases more carefully for their suggested meanings. Complete this table.

Quotation	Surface meaning	What it suggests about the place and the atmosphere
'Implacable November weather'	'Implacable' means unstoppable, relentless.	Sounds like the weather is an enemy or goes on and on. Perhaps people feel...
'As much mud in the streets, as if the waters had but newly retired from the ... earth'	'waters ... retired' – it looks like a prehistoric flood has just finished.	Suggests the city... People walking in the streets will feel...
'it would not be wonderful to meet a Megalosaurus'	This is strange. It normally *would* be remarkable or 'wonderful' to meet a dinosaur in the streets.	It's so muddy that...
'a soft black drizzle, with flakes of soot in it as big as full-grown snow-flakes'	Normally, we use 'drizzle' to mean a light rain. 'Snowflakes' are usually white. But here, both are applied to black soot and smoke.	The words 'drizzle' and 'snowflakes' are used...
'gone into mourning, one might imagine, for the death of the sun.'	In Victorian London, going 'into mourning' meant to wear black clothes for mourning someone's death.	Implies the city looks...

Here is a response exploring how the writer describes the setting to give the reader an impression of the city. They have used their ideas from the table to structure their paragraph:

Dickens compares the muddy streets to prehistoric earth, claiming 'it would not be wonderful to meet a Megalosaurus' in the mud. This **hyperbole** suggests the city is so incredibly filthy and slushy that it is like a world where dinosaurs are usual – they would not cause any wonder in passers-by. It also implies that the city is uncivilised, as though mankind has not developed yet.

- identifies techniques the writer has used
- selects a relevant quotation
- explains possible suggested ideas created by the technique
- for higher attainment, suggests another interpretation

Key term

hyperbole: exaggeration for effect

5 Now choose another quotation from the table and write a paragraph of your own. Use the response example and the sentence starters to help you.

Dickens describes the setting as ...	in the quotation '____________'	
The word/phrase/ technique ...	suggests ...	It also implies ...

Develop the skills

Settings can be used to develop themes. Read this further extract from the opening of *Bleak House*.

Foot passengers, jostling one another's umbrellas, in a general infection of ill-temper, and losing their foot-hold at street-corners, where tens of thousands of other foot passengers have been slipping and sliding since the day broke (if ever this day broke), adding new deposits to the crust upon crust of mud, sticking at those points tenaciously to the pavement and accumulating at compound interest.

6 As before, start by exploring the text for its surface meanings. Use these questions to help you:

a) What is now being described? How does this add to the impression of the city?

b) How do people in the city act? How do they feel?

7 Now look more carefully at the **connotations** of the words and phrases.

a) What might we usually associate with the words 'infection' and 'ill'? Why might Dickens have used these words to describe the bad mood of the pedestrians?

b) How do the phrases 'slipping and sliding', 'crust upon crust' and 'tens of thousands' add to our understanding of the atmosphere?

Exploring the way a writer uses patterns of language can help you to make connections to themes. Look at the words Dickens uses to describe the mud:

> adding new deposits to the crust upon crust of mud, sticking at those points tenaciously to the pavement and accumulating at compound interest.

The words 'deposits', 'accumulating' and the phrase 'compound interest' are all from the **semantic field** of money.

Money is an important theme in the novel *Bleak House.*

8 Why might Dickens use words to do with *money* to describe *mud*? What is he revealing about his *attitude* to money by doing this?

How do the *actions* and *feelings* of people in response to the mud add to our understanding of the link that has been made between mud and money?

Apply the skills

Now read the two extracts again.

9 Write five or more paragraphs exploring how Dickens has used the setting to convey:

- mood and atmosphere
- attitude and theme.

Checklist for success

Focus on the suggested meanings of particular words and phrases. Comment on:

✔ how he describes the weather and the mud

✔ how he describes the actions and feelings of people.

Check your progress:

▲ I can understand the way a writer uses language to convey setting and show some understanding of implicit information, making reference to the text.

▲▲ I can very clearly understand the different ways a writer uses language to convey setting, including implicit information. I can include a range of well-selected references to the text and thoughtfully develop my response in detail.

Exploring character

How do writers create characters?

Start thinking

Characters are the people in a story. In some texts, characters may narrate the story or provide a viewpoint. Writers create characters through a number of techniques, including:

- descriptions and sometimes names
- dialogue and interactions with other characters
- actions and role in the narrative.

a) Practise inferring ideas about a character created through these techniques. What do you learn about this character?

Name:	Mr Grimroar
Description:	red-faced, as if a kettle were boiling inside his brain
Dialogue:	'Get back here!'
Actions:	Stamps out of the room, slamming the door.

b) Write your ideas as a paragraph, using these sentence starters:

The name 'Grimroar' suggests ... The comparison to a boiling 'kettle' suggests he ...
The imperative 'Get back here' sounds ... His actions of 'slamming' and stamping imply he ...

Explore the skills

Explore a character description from this opening of a novel:

Jewel and I come up from the field, following the path in single file. Although I am fifteen feet ahead of him, anyone watching us from the cotton-house can see Jewel's frayed and broken straw hat a full head above my own [...] Still staring straight ahead, his pale eyes like wood set into his wooden face, he crosses the floor in four strides.

William Faulkner, from *As I Lay Dying*

We can infer several impressions of Jewel from the extract.

2 Find relevant quotations to match these impressions:

a) Jewel and the speaker have been working.

b) Jewel and the speaker feel distant.

c) Jewel is poor.

d) Jewel may be older than the speaker.

e) Jewel has fixed ideas and doesn't give much away.

f) Jewel is confident.

3 What does the name 'Jewel' suggest?

What seems **ironic** about this name?

Key term

ironic: when words and their apparent meanings are deliberately the opposite of the situation or intended meaning

4 Explore the *language* used to convey the character of Jewel. Complete the table.

Technique/key words	Quotation	Impression of Jewel and *how* the impression was formed	Further interpretations
factual measurements: **fifteen feet, a full head**	'I am **fifteen feet** ahead of him' 'Jewel's … hat **a full head** above my own'	Jewel and the speaker are …	They may be …
adjectives: **frayed** and **broken**	'_______________'	Jewel seems **poor** since his hat is **'frayed'**, suggesting it's…	A hat shields from the sun – Jewel may work long hours in 'the field'
simile repetition	'eyes **like wood** set into his **wooden** face'	The repetition of **'wood'** make us think … Suggesting his face is …	The simile implies his eyes… He may feel …
verb: **strides**	'_______________'	Makes Jewel seem …	The way he moves also implies …

Dialogue adds to our impressions of a character. Read the second extract, where Jewel keeps falling asleep at his jobs:

"If you ain't sick, what's the matter with you?"
"Nothing," Jewel said. "I'm all right."
"All right?" pa said. "You're asleep on your feet this minute."
"No," Jewel said. "I'm all right."
"I want him to stay at home to-day," ma said.
"I'll need him," pa said. "It's tight enough, with all of us to do it."

5 Add to your table about Jewel:

Technique	Quotation and key words	Impression of Jewel and *how* the impression was formed	Further interpretations
dialogue, repetition	'_______________'	Jewel repeatedly insists... Suggesting...	He may not want the others to feel... Because Pa says 'it's tight' suggesting...

Here is a response, exploring how the writer creates an impression of Jewel. They used their notes from the table to structure their paragraph.

> Faulkner's description of Jewel's 'frayed and broken straw hat' implies that he is poor, since the adjectives 'frayed' and 'broken' suggest the hat is worn out, so he is unlikely to wear it unless he can't afford a new one.

- identifies techniques
- selects a relevant, focused quotation
- gives an impression
- explains how the impression was created

6 The writer of the response could add other interpretations to develop this answer further. Use the table and these sentence starters to add another interpretation to their paragraph:

> We also know Jewel comes 'from the field' so maybe he wears the 'straw hat' to ... suggesting ...

7 Using your table and the example to help you, write three or more paragraphs of your own. Comment on the writer's use of *description* and *dialogue*.

Follow these steps to build your paragraphs:

- What has the writer used to give you an impression?
- Give a focused quotation, picking out key words and techniques.
- What impression did this give?
- How did you arrive at this impression?
- Are there other interpretations?

Develop the skills

Read the following extract from a novel. A young man visits a family's house for the first time.

He showed her a coating of black on the under side of the jar.

'That's not from the **firing**. See, I can scratch it off. It's soot, from when it was on the cook-fire last … You don't get them out whole like that very often.'

'But get them out of what, from where? I want to know all about it.'

'Maybe some day, Ma'am, I can tell you,' he said, wiping his sooty fingers on his handkerchief. His reply was courteous but final. He strapped his bag and picked up his hat, then hesitated and smiled. Taking a **buckskin** bag from his pocket, he walked over to the window-seat where the children were, and held out his hand to them, saying: 'These I would like to give to the little girls.' In his palm lay two lumps of soft blue stone, the colour of robins' eggs, or of the sea on **halcyon** days of summer.

The children marvelled. 'Oh, what are they?'

'**Turquoises**, just the way they come out of the mine, before the jewellers have tampered with them and made them look green. The Indians like them this way.'

Willa Cather, from *The Professor's House*

What do these details suggest about the young man's knowledge?

What does the mother's question suggest about her attitude to the young man?

What is your response to the young man's reply?

What do these actions indicate about him?

What effect does his acknowledgement of the children have on your response to him?

What is the effect of the description of the stones?

What does the children's response indicate?

What does the young man's explanation tell you about him and the stones?

8 Answer the questions in the annotations to explore how the young man is presented.

Apply the skills

9 Write an analysis of the character of the young man, using quotations and your ideas from the previous task.

Explore the impression you get of his:

- personality
- knowledge and expertise
- effect on other characters

Comment on the writer's use of techniques, including *description* and *dialogue*.

Glossary

firing: the process of making pottery with intense heat

buckskin: a type of soft leather

halcyon: perfect

turquoises: blue-green gemstones

Check your progress:

I can understand how a writer conveys ideas about a character, making relevant inferences.

I can very clearly understand different methods a writer uses to convey ideas about a character, and thoughtfully analyse relevant and detailed interpretations.

Exploring character in depth

How does a writer use the way a character speaks and what they say to reveal their personality?

Start thinking

A character's personality can be conveyed through the way they tell the story and what they say.

Read the extracts below taken from a novel, *North and South*, by Elizabeth Gaskell. Extract A is from Margaret's dialogue. Extract B is Nicholas Higgins speaking.

A: Margaret

'Why do you strike? ... Striking is leaving off work till you get your own rate of wages, is it not? You must not wonder at my ignorance; where I come from I have never heard of a strike.'

B: Nicholas Higgins

'See if we don't dang th' masters this time, See if they don't come, and beg us to come back at our own price. That's all.'

1. What differences do you notice between the two characters' language? Think about their use of: **a)** vocabulary **b)** the types of sentence they use.
2. Which one do you think is of higher social status? What about their language tells you this?
3. Which one is a newcomer and which knows about industrial work? How can you tell?

Explore the skills

A writer can make a character reveal things about themselves through what they say about other characters. Here Margaret talks about a different character called Mr Thornton, and she reveals something about herself:

'Oh! I hardly know what he is like... He is a tall, broad-shouldered man, about ... thirty – with a face that is neither exactly plain, nor yet handsome, nothing remarkable – not quite a gentleman; but that was hardly to be expected.'

Elizabeth Gaskell, from *North and South*

4 First, what judgements does Margaret make about Mr Thornton in the highlighted descriptions?

Now think about how the way Margaret talks about Mr Thornton actually reveals something about herself:

5 Margaret says: 'I hardly know what he is like'. What does her claimed lack of knowledge indicate about her attitude to Mr Thornton?

6 Margaret uses several **qualifiers**: 'hardly', 'neither exactly', 'nor yet', 'not quite'. Why might Margaret be so uncertain in her description of Mr Thornton?

7 Why is it important that Margaret decides that Mr Thornton is 'not quite a gentleman'? What does this suggest about Margaret's attitudes and personality?

8 Margaret asserts that it 'was hardly to be expected' that Mr Thornton would be a 'gentleman'. What does this judgement reveal about Margaret?

> **Key term**
>
> **qualifier:** a word or phrase used to modify an adjective, adverb or verb in order to specify its meaning

Develop the skills

Now read the narrator's account of Margaret's later thoughts about Mr Thornton, who is a prosperous and successful mill owner:

> Margaret's attention was thus called to her host; his whole manner, as master of the house, and entertainer of his friends, was so straightforward, yet simple and modest, as to be thoroughly dignified. Margaret thought she had never seen him to so much advantage… among his fellows, there was no uncertainty as to his position. He was regarded by them as a man of great force of character; of power in many ways… this gave a fine grand quietness to his voice and ways, which Margaret had missed before.

9 What are the key qualities that Margaret now recognises in Mr Thornton? How do they contrast with her earlier description of him?

10 Has Mr Thornton changed, or has Margaret? Summarise your ideas in a couple of sentences.

Apply the skills

11 What impression does Gaskell create of Margaret? Using your responses to the previous sections to help you, write three or more paragraphs considering: her language and dialogue; her internal thoughts; her recognition of how others view Mr Thornton.

Check your progress:

- I can comment on effects of dialogue and narrative voice, referring appropriately to the text.
- I can confidently explore how dialogue and narrative create character, integrating many well-chosen textual references.

Viewpoint and narrative perspective

How does viewpoint affect a reader's understanding of a text?

Start thinking

Narrative viewpoint is the perspective from which a story is told. Some genres have conventions regarding narrative viewpoint, for example, an autobiography is told in the first **person**.

In prose, there are several possible narrative viewpoints or persons.

> **Key term**
>
> **person:** point of view from which communication is delivered

1. Match the correct example on the right to the viewpoint on the left.

Viewpoint		Example
first person	A) **'I', 'me':** The narrator is within the story, giving their own point of view.	*We saw Kelvin beside the road.*
third person omniscient	B) **'he' 'she':** The narrator is outside the story. They seem omniscient (all-knowing), observing multiple characters and events.	*You watched Kelvin dart into the road. You didn't move.*
third person limited	C) **'he' 'she':** Again, the narrator is outside the story. However, their scope is more limited, following just one character.	*I saw Kelvin dart into the road. I screamed.*
second person	D) **'you':** Often found in advertising and poetry, this directly addresses the reader.	*Frank rounded the corner as Kelvin ran for it. Sonny screamed.*
first person plural	E) **'we', 'us':** Voicing the collective thoughts of several narrators.	*Kelvin knew he had to run. He saw Frank approaching. He heard a scream.*

2. Tell a partner about your day, using the first person.
3. Now get your partner to narrate your day, using the third person. How does this affect the telling?

Each narrative viewpoint creates different effects.

4. Complete the table, filling in the appropriate viewpoint to match the effect of writing from that perspective. The first row is done for you.

Narrative viewpoint	Effect of the viewpoint
first person	Creates a **subjective** and **biased** view of the story. Limits the narrative to events the speaker was aware of, but allows the reader to empathise with a character and understand their thoughts.
__________ person	Lets the reader follow a character's personal journey, but with more distance than first person. The writer explores different aspects of the narrative, but less fully than an omniscient speaker.
__________ person	Readers feel like they have been assigned the role of a character. Feels like the writer is addressing them directly.
__________ person	Allows the writer maximum range to describe events. Readers may know more than characters, helping to create suspense. Readers may relate less closely to characters, however.

Key terms

subjective: a personal view

biased: taking a particular side

Explore the skills

5 Read the following three extracts. For each one, discuss:

a) what person it is told in

b) what you feel is the effect of this on you as the reader.

They asked where you learned to speak English and if you had real houses back in Africa and if you'd seen a car before you came to America. They gawped at your hair. Does it stand up or fall down when you take out the braids? They wanted to know. All of it stands up? How? Why? Do you use a comb? You smiled tightly when they asked those questions.

Chimamanda Ngozi Adichie, from *The Thing Around Your Neck*

He didn't have a suitcase or even a jacket, but I knew.

My mouth opened and a roar started but it never came. And a pain in my chest, and I could hear my heart pumping the blood to the rest of me. I was supposed to cry; I thought I was. I sobbed once and that was all.

Roddy Doyle, from *Paddy Clarke Ha Ha Ha*

The car was brand new… It also appeared quite small and very expensive. As for Ali, there he was, looking so handsome and smiling like a little boy who knew he had done something so fantastic that congratulations from expected quarters were going to take place in some particularly affectionate form. He was not just expecting it. He knew he would get it.

Ama Ata Aidoo, from *Changes*

6 Explore the effects of these narrative choices.

a) Rewrite the first extract in the *first person*. How does this alter the way you feel about the narrator's feelings?

b) The second extract is a child's response to his father leaving for good. Rewrite the extract in the *third person*, using the speaker's name, Paddy. How does this alter the way you relate to the character? Is there anything he says about himself that you would not include in a third person perspective? Why?

c) Rewrite the second extract as if it were a *first person adult* perspective, recalling the event when he is grown up. What do you choose to alter?

d) The third extract describes Ali. How might he describe himself in the first person? How would he present himself from his own perspective?

Develop the skills

Some writers use multiple narrative perspectives. Read these extracts from *Anthills of the Savannah* by Chinua Achebe, describing Sam, known as His Excellency, the Head of State. The narrative follows the experiences and views of three friends from his youth, Chris, Ikem and Beatrice.

Chris

But His Excellency speaks instead. And not even to him the latest offender but still to me. And he is almost friendly and conciliatory, the amazing man. In that instant the day changes. The fiery sun retires temporarily behind a cloud; we are reprieved and immediately celebrating. I can hear in advance the many compliments we will pay him as soon as his back is turned: that the trouble with His Excellency is that he can never hurt a man and go to sleep over it.

Ikem

The Emperor may be a fool but he isn't a monster. Not yet, anyhow, although he will certainly become one by the time Chris and company have done with him. But right now he is still OK, thank God. That's why I believe that basically he does want to do the right thing. Some of my friends don't agree with me on this, I know.

Beatrice

His Excellency was a perfect host. From the head of the oval-shaped table he dispensed conviviality and put everyone their ease. Had there been just a little less eagerness on the part of the guests to agree with everything he said and laugh excessively whenever they thought he was making a joke the evening might have been quite remarkable.

Chinua Achebe, from *Anthills of the Savannah*

7 Explore the effects of the multiple narrative.

a) What details about Sam's personality do the three narrators comment on? What is implied about his character by details mentioned by more than one narrator?

b) What do Chris and Beatrice say about other people's behaviour towards Sam? What does this reveal about their own views of him?

c) What does Ikem say about Sam? How do his views differ from those of Chris and Beatrice?

d) Chris works as a government minister. How does that affect your understanding of his description of Sam?

e) Beatrice uses words such as 'perfect' and 'conviviality' in her account of Sam's behaviour. How does the third sentence of her paragraph present a different view?

Apply the skills

8 Why might the author choose to give us three different perspectives of Sam? What effects have been created?

Use your ideas from the previous task to write three or more paragraphs discussing:

- what is revealed about Sam
- similarities and differences between the narrators' views
- what can be inferred about the different narrators' concerns.

Checklist for success

Include:

✔ relevant quotations

✔ exploration of the possible effects on a reader.

Check your progress:

▲ I can identify narrative viewpoint and make inferences about the impact on a reader.

▲▲ I can very clearly and thoughtfully explore several interpretations of a writer's choice of narrative perspective.

Exploring narrative style

How do I explore an ambiguous narrative?

Start thinking

Some authors make their narratives deliberately **ambiguous**.

1. Why might an author want to create an ambiguous narrative? What experience will this give the reader?

One way of creating ambiguity is through an untrustworthy first person narrator, giving us a biased view. Another is through multiple narrators, providing different viewpoints. More unusual and complex is the use of **free indirect style**.

Explore the skills

Free indirect style allows a writer to merge the voice of a character with a third person narrative. It is easiest to understand through an example.

Read this extract from *Emma* by Jane Austen. Emma was trying to make a match between her friend Harriet and someone they both knew. Unfortunately, he thought Emma was interested in him instead.

> The hair was curled, and the maid sent away, and Emma sat down to think and be miserable. – It was a wretched business indeed! Such an overthrow of every thing she had been wishing for! – Such a development of every thing most unwelcome! – Such a blow for Harriet! [...]
>
> "If I had not persuaded Harriet into liking the man, I could have borne any thing."
>
> Jane Austen, from *Emma*

2. Reread the highlighted section.
   a) Are these Emma's thoughts or the narrator's? Where does the narrator's voice begin and end?
   b) How is this narrative different from straightforward third person narrative?

Key terms

ambiguous: suggesting more than one interpretation

free indirect style: a third person narrative where the narrator adopts the voice of a character, seeming to merge first person subjectivity with third person narration

Free indirect style has some advantages for an author.

- It creates ambiguity in the narrative.
- It can 'trick' us into accepting a character's subjective views as reality, so later events are more surprising.
- It can create irony or humour, as the third person presentation of a character's own voice gives us distance to be more judgmental about their words than a first person narrative.

3 What effects are created in the extract above? Irony? Humour? Tension? How do you think the writer wants us to feel about Emma's thoughts?

Develop the skills

Read the following extract, also by Austen. Isabella and her friend Catherine have been riding in separate carriages and have just returned to Catherine's home.

> ... the astonishment of Isabella was hardly to be expressed, on finding that it was too late in the day for them to attend her friend into the house:—
>
> "Past three o'clock!" it was inconceivable, incredible, impossible! and she would neither believe her own watch, nor her brother's nor the servant's [...] It was ages since she had had a moment's conversation with her dearest Catherine [...] with smiles of most exquisite misery, and the laughing eye of utter despondency, she bade her friend adieu...
>
> Jane Austen, from *Northanger Abbey*

4 Highlight words that seem to be Isabella's in one colour, and those that seem to be the narrator's in another. What do you notice?

5 By delivering Isabella's own words in the third person, we have more distance from them. Does this make her words more or less believable in your view?

6 Underline the **hyperbole** and **superlatives**. Do you think Isabella is sincere in her disappointment at running out of time? Why?

7 What do the **oxymorons** *'smiles of... misery'* and *'laughing... despondency'* imply about Isabella? What are her actions in these quotations? How do her actions compare to the way they are described?

Key terms

hyperbole: exaggeration

superlatives: adjectives expressing the highest degree, for example *best, most*

oxymoron: combination of opposing ideas, for example *white blackness*

Apply the skills

8 In paragraphs, explain how Austen has created an ironic and revealing character portrayal in the above narrative. Consider:

- narrative ambiguity and use of the free indirect style
- other language techniques.

Check your progress:

- I can recognise effects of ambiguity in a narrative, making appropriate reference to the text.
- I can confidently explore how narrative style creates multiple meanings, integrating many well-chosen and detailed textual references.

Exploring language

How do writers use language techniques in prose?

Start thinking

Writers use language techniques to build readers' impressions of characters, settings and events.

1 Match the technique to the most appropriate example.

Technique	Example
A. interesting verbs	Z) Delicately, she brushed her glamorous, radiant hair.
B. interesting adverbs and adjectives	Y) The rollercoaster was a roaring giant, his breath in our hair.
C. metaphor	X) The room was as dirty as a slime-filled pond.
D. extended metaphor	W) I couldn't know. No-one could know.
E. repetition	V) The room was a slimy pond.
F. personification	U) She was greedy and mean; her brother was kind.
G. simile	T) The room was a slime-filled pond, clothes scattered like weed; the damp air felt like a clammy fish.
H. listing	S) She slouched in. Scurrying away, the cat mewled. She scowled.
I. contrast	R) There were dirty cups, plates, toys, shoes and socks.

Other techniques include oxymoron, onomatopoeia, alliteration and assonance.

Use these techniques to describe a playground at break time.

A prose writer uses several techniques to build an overall impression, often in combination with structural devices, such as juxtaposition and sentence length.

2 Writers also use a range of sentence types. Write an example for each of the following. The first has been done for you.

- *minor*: sentence without a main verb, used for effect, for example, *The car in the road.*
- *declarative*: statement sentence, ending with '.'
- *interrogative*: question sentence, ending with '?'
- *exclamatory*: exclamation sentence, ending with '!'
- *imperative*: command sentence, an instruction

Explore the skills

You are now going to look more closely at a writer's use of language in an extract from a short story.

> With despair – cold, sharp despair – buried deep in her heart like a wicked knife, Miss Meadows, in cap and gown and carrying a little baton, trod the cold corridors that led to the music hall. Girls of all ages, rosy from the air, and bubbling over with that gleeful excitement that comes from running to school on a fine autumn morning, hurried, skipped, fluttered by; from the hollow class-rooms came a quick drumming of voices; a bell rang, a voice like a bird cried, 'Muriel.'
>
> Katherine Mansfield, from 'The Singing Lesson'

When you read a text for the first time, note down key information about character and setting before exploring language more deeply.

3 **a)** What building are we in?

b) What time of year is it?

c) Where is Miss Meadows going? What is she carrying? What do you infer about her role?

d) How would you describe her mood?

e) What is the mood of the girls?

4 Now explore Mansfield's language techniques more closely.

a) How does the punctuation in the highlighted part of the text emphasise the meaning?

b) What words are repeated in the extract? Why might the author repeat these words?

c) What simile in the first sentence describes how Miss Meadows is feeling? What does this simile imply about her pain?

d) What adjectives in the first sentence add to our impression of her mood?

e) What verb is used to describe how Miss Meadows moves down the corridors? What list of verbs describes the pupils' movements? What contrast is created?

f) What adjective describes the classrooms? How does this reflect Miss Meadows' mood?

g) The short story is called 'The Singing Lesson'. What sounds do we hear? How do they compare with Miss Meadows' mood?

h) How does the final simile echo a verb describing the girls earlier? What does this language pattern emphasise about the girls? How do they compare with Miss Meadows?

i) We might expect the author to use exclamatory sentences when conveying such intense emotions. What do you make of the fact that the passage is two long declarative sentences?

Looking for patterns of language is a good way to gain a sense of overview.

5 Complete the table to explore how the writer creates links and contrasts between Miss Meadows and her surroundings:

Mood of Miss Meadows		**Atmosphere of surroundings**	
Technique and quotation	**What is implied**	**Technique and quotation**	**Implied link or contrast with Miss Meadows?**
verb 'trod'	Implies Miss Meadows feels...	list of verbs: ____________	Girls' movements seem ... Contrasting with ... who ...
adjective 'cold'	Miss Meadows...	adjectives 'cold' and '____________'	Classrooms seem ...
simile '____________'	Her pain feels.... And the word 'wicked' ...	simile '____________' and verb 'fluttered'	Girls are compared to ...
____________ 'buried', 'deep'	Her feelings are ...	adjectives, noun phrases 'gleeful ____________', 'bubbling', 'rosy', '____________drumming'	Girls are described ... In comparison, Miss Meadows ...

Here is a response, exploring how the writer uses language to convey an impression of Miss Meadows and her surroundings. They used ideas from the second and fourth rows of the table to structure their paragraph, drawing quotations together in a pattern.

> Mansfield juxtaposes Miss Meadows' despair with her surroundings. The adjective 'cold' describes her despair, implying isolation and discomfort; it is then also used to describe the school: 'cold classrooms'. Her misery seems reflected in the chilly building. This is in contrast to the happy schoolgirls – they are 'rosy' – an adjective implying warmth, or happy blushes, while Miss Meadows is 'cold' and miserable. The comparison emphasises her despair and pain – like the freezing classrooms, her cold misery is at odds with the youthful liveliness of the students.

selects a relevant pattern of quotations

gives an overall impression created by the pattern of language

identifies techniques the writer has used

explains possible ideas suggested by the technique

for higher attainment, draws ideas together in an overview

6 Choose another pattern of language and write a paragraph of your own. Use the example above, and the following sentence starters to help you.

Mansfield contrasts __________ through the use of __________ in the quotations '__________' and '__________'. Together, these suggest __________ and __________ while the girls are '__________'. The use of __________ implies they __________ compared to Miss Meadows __________

Develop the skills

A writer may build on images to create a **motif**. Read this further extract from 'The Singing Lesson'.

> The Science Mistress stopped Miss Meadows.
>
> 'Good mor-ning,' she cried, in her sweet, affected drawl. 'Isn't it cold? It might be win-ter.'
>
> Miss Meadows, hugging the knife, stared in hatred at the Science Mistress [...]
>
> 'It is rather sharp,' said Miss Meadows, grimly.
>
> The other smiled her sugary smile.
>
> 'You look fro-zen,' said she [...] (Had she noticed anything?)

Key term

motif: recurring image or idea

7 Look at the three patterns developed.

a) Despair:

- What image from the first extract has become an extended metaphor? What does it imply about Miss Meadows?
- What other idea first linked with her despair has been continued from previously?
- In two colours, highlight vocabulary associated with each of these two motifs. What do you notice?

b) Ironic contrast:

- What adjectives create a contrast between the Science Mistress and Miss Meadows?
- What is the purpose of the Science Mistress' interrogative? How is her purpose at odds with Miss Meadows' mood?
- What is ironic about the dialogue 'It is rather sharp' and 'You look fro-zen'?

c) Distrust:

- What punctuation emphasises the Science Mistress' way of talking?
- What phrase implies this is fake?
- What sentence type and punctuation imply Miss Meadows' paranoia?

Apply the skills

8 Reread the two extracts. Write four or more further paragraphs exploring how Mansfield uses language to convey an impression of Miss Meadows. Explore patterns and focus on the implied meanings of particular phrases and techniques. Comment on: Miss Meadows; her surroundings; her interactions.

Check your progress:

- I can understand the ways a writer uses language, making relevant references to the text.
- I can very clearly understand the different ways a writer uses language, in close detail and across a whole text. I can respond in developed detail, integrating a wide range of well-selected textual references.

Exploring symbolism

How do writers use symbols and associations?

Start thinking

Some writers use language in a symbolic way. **Symbols** work through associated ideas – links we make between objects and abstract ideas.

Key term

symbol: something used to represent something else, for example a heart could *symbolise* love

1 What concepts might the following things symbolise?

a)

b)

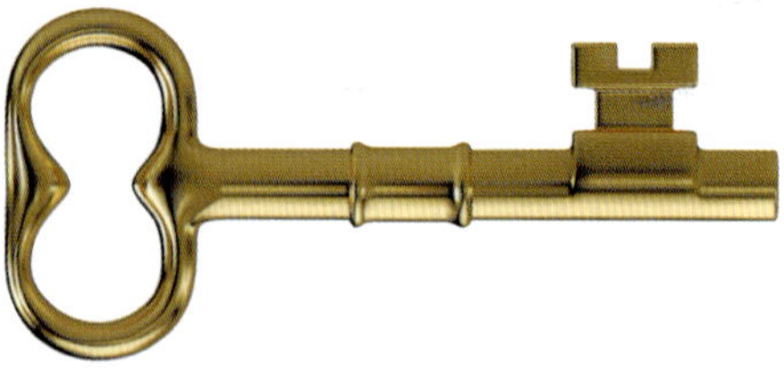

c)

2 What associations helped you make these links?

3 Thinking of symbols:

a) What is meant by the word 'civilisation'?

b) What objects could symbolise civilisation? Write your associations around a spider diagram.

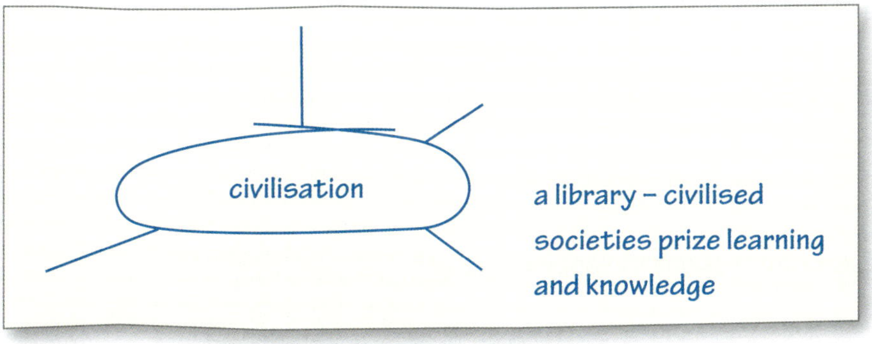

Explore the skills

Read this extract from a novel describing an upper-class community under siege, from the perspective of their leader, the Collector.

Of all the ladies who had survived [...] none now displayed greater fortitude than Louise [...]. From this pale and anaemic-looking girl who had once thought only of turning the heads of young officers, and whom the Collector had considered **insipid**, he now saw a young woman of inflexible willpower emerging. He watched her as he passed the section of the hall reserved for the sick, the wounded, and the dying. Her cotton dress was rent almost from the armpit to the hem and as she leaned forward to bring a saucer of water to the lips of a wounded man, the Collector glimpsed three polished ribs [...] modesty was one of the many considerations which no longer troubled her. She stood up, mopping her brow with the back of a skeleton wrist. The Collector moved on, [...] and stood on the steps between the Greek pillars [...]. These pillars, he could not help noticing, were dreadfully **pocked** and tattered by shot. He thought contemptuously: 'So they weren't marble after all.' He lingered for a moment sneering at the guilty red core that was revealed beneath the **stucco** of lime and sand. He hated pretence.

J. G. Farrell, from *The Siege of Krishnapur*

Glossary

insipid: unremarkable

stucco: decorative plaster

pocked: marked by a number of small holes or indentations

4 Start by exploring characters and setting:

a) What is Louise's physical condition?

b) How does she act?

c) Does she meet your expectations of an upper-class woman?

d) What does the Collector notice about Louise's appearance?

e) What is the Collector's opinion of Louise's personal qualities?

f) How is this different from what he thought about her before the siege?

g) What does the Collector notice about the appearance of the pillars?

h) How is this different from what he thought about them before the siege?

i) What is the Collector's opinion of the pillars now?

5 Explore symbols:

a) What ideas might you associate with 'Greek pillars'?

b) What does it suggest about the state of these concepts if the pillars are fake and crumbling?

6 Explore associations:

a) How is Louise's appearance comparable to a 'tattered' pillar?

b) How are her inner qualities affected by the siege, compared to those of the pillars?

Develop the skills

7 Civilisation is a key theme in the novel. Consider the Collector's views of Louise and the pillars.

a) What qualities does the Collector prize?

b) Is the *appearance* of civilisation important to him now?

c) How might the Collector define 'civilisation', in light of his experience?

Apply the skills

Now put all your findings together to complete the following task.

8 How has the writer conveyed ideas about what being civilised really means? Explore the following points, writing a paragraph on each one:

- the symbolism of the pillars
- links between Louise and the pillars; impact of the siege on both
- the Collector's views.

Use these sentence starters to help you:

> The pillars could symbolise ... because ...
> The Collector notices ... suggesting civilisation itself ...
>
> Both Louise and the pillars ... However, the siege has made the pillars ... Whereas Louise ...
>
> The Collector's attitude to Louise has changed ...
>
> Now, his view of the pillars ... The Collector now values ... suggesting his view of civilisation ...

Check your progress:

- I can understand a writer's use of symbolic language, making relevant references to the text.
- I can very clearly understand different ways a writer uses symbolic association. I can integrate a range of well-selected textual references, developing my response in considered detail.

4. How does the writer of the response link contextual information to inferences? Identify key phrases that help them join their ideas together.

5. Now consider the following literary context:

- The opera Newland goes to see is *Faust.*
- *Faust* is the story of a man who sells his soul to the devil for material things and worldly power. His fame and riches on earth come at a high price – he is eternally damned.

Why might the writer pick this opera for Newland to watch?

What connections can you make between the plot of *Faust* and the rich, upper-class Newland, who conforms to worldly expectations?

6. How does this literary context influence your ideas about Newland? Complete the paragraph.

> Newland seems concerned with status and worldly rules as he is 'perfectly aware' it is '"not the thing" to arrive early at the opera', suggesting the rich upper-classes of 1870s New York follow certain social expectations. The fact that the author chooses to make the opera Faust could be significant as...

Glossary

Pariah: in the Indian caste system, one who is considered Untouchable

Gandhi-men: followers of Mahatma Gandhi, who led the campaign for Indian Independence

Develop the skills

Read the following extract from Raja Rao's novel *Kanthapura*. Moorthy is campaigning for social reforms.

> So Moorthy goes from house to house... and – what do you think? – he even goes to the Potters' quarter and the Weavers' quarter and the Sudra quarter, and I closed my ears when I heard he went to the **Pariah** quarter. We said to ourselves, he is one of these **Gandhi-men**, who say there is neither caste nor clan nor family, and yet they pray like us and they live like us. Only they say, too, one should not marry early, one should allow widows to take husbands and a brahmin might marry a pariah and a pariah a brahmin.
>
> Raja Rao, from *Kanthapura*

7 Explore ideas about Moorthy.

a) What is the narrator's attitude towards Moorthy?

b) Consider the phrases 'what do you think?' and 'I close my ears'.

What do these suggest about the narrator's attitude to Moorthy?

c) What impression of Moorthy do you gain from the extract?

d) What do Moorthy's visits to all sections of society indicate about him?

Now consider the following contextual information:

- The extract is set in India in 1930. At that time, India was under British control as part of the British Empire.
- Traditional Hindu society in India was divided into different social groups, or castes.
- Each caste has a traditional social function or occupation. The castes form a strict hierarchy.
- Brahmins are the highest caste, often priests, while the lowest are the Pariahs or Untouchables.
- Mahatma Gandhi was an Indian lawyer and politician who led the campaign for Indian independence from British rule.
- Gandhi also worked for an end to poverty, for women's rights and to remove the idea of untouchability from the caste system.

8 How does this information affect your reading of the text?

Remember that you shouldn't use context for its own sake; you need to show how it develops your understanding of the text.

Apply the skills

9 Write three or more paragraphs, exploring how the writer has portrayed Moorthy. Comment on the meanings created in light of your contextual knowledge. Include ideas about:

- his activities
- the narrator's opinion of him
- Gandhi's ideas

Check your progress:

- I can understand the meanings of literary texts and their contexts.
- I can confidently explore texts beyond surface meanings and selectively integrate contextual readings to show deeper awareness of ideas and attitudes.

Planning and writing a prose essay

How do I plan a response to an essay question on a prose text?

Understand the task

During your course, you may have to write an essay on your prose text.

The question may be worded in a number of ways, but will always ask you to explore the writer's methods.

Sample questions:

- How does [author] make [character name] such a memorable character?
- What does [author's] writing make you feel towards [character name] at the end of the novel?
- Explore the ways in which [author] creates such a striking contrast between [character 1] and [character 2].
- In what ways...
- To what extent ...

1 Read this practice question on the short story 'Miss Brill' by Katherine Mansfield, which is widely available online.

> How far does Mansfield's writing make you sympathise with Miss Brill in 'Miss Brill'? Support your ideas with details from the text. [25]

The first thing to do is identify the key things the question is asking you to focus on. Look at the highlighting. For this question, the key focuses are:

a) your feelings of *sympathy* towards Miss Brill

b) *how* the writer makes you feel sympathy through their *writing*

c) how *far* you sympathise with Miss Brill.

Gather your ideas and evidence

The next step is to plan what to include in your response.

Remember:

- You are *not* being asked to retell the story. Focus on several key parts of the story in detail, making links that bring in your wider knowledge of the story and its context.
- You must closely explore *how* the language and structure of key parts of the story make you feel sympathy for Miss Brill and how far that sympathy extends, or how it might invite a less sympathetic response.

Here are some parts you could choose to explore that might affect the extent to which you feel sympathy for Miss Brill.

A. Miss Brill's arrival at the park. She sits alone and finds it 'disappointing' that no one talks to each other. She 'always looked forward to the conversation'.

B. Her reflections on how the park is like a theatre – it's her entertainment; she fantasises about being important to the other people.

C. The mocking comments of the young couple on the bench.

D. The ending of the story.

2 Consider what other parts of the story you can use to respond to the task. Which parts are the most interesting to explore?

Plan your response

Once you have chosen key parts to explore in detail, you can organise your ideas into an argument. There are several ways of doing this:

Focus on *parts of the story* that made you feel sympathy.

- Consider how **one part** has made you feel sympathy for Miss Brill. Build one or more analysis paragraphs around this point, making links to broader ideas.

↓

- Then move on to the **next part** of the story that made you feel sympathy. Build a further analysis paragraph around this point, making links to broader ideas.

↓

- Continue until you have covered several parts in detail, making sure you explore aspects of **language, structure and form** that made you feel sympathy.

↓

- Don't forget to explore any parts that **limit** the extent to which you feel sympathy for Miss Brill as well.

Focus on *ways* that made you feel sympathy.

- Recall writers' methods (for example, narrative perspective, dialogue and reported speech, imagery, descriptive techniques, structural devices and sentences).

↓

- Choose **one method or pattern of language** you feel is significant in the way it contributes to the extent to which you feel sympathy across your chosen parts of the story. Write an analysis paragraph on how this method or pattern of language affects your view, including references from **several parts of the story** to make your point.

↓

- Next, consider how **a second method or pattern of language** contributes to the extent to which you feel sympathy across the parts you chose. Write one or more analysis paragraphs, including **several parts of the story** to make your point.

↓

- Continue until you have covered a number of relevant writers' methods.

You can also write your essay in another way of your own.

3 Decide your approach now, and gather your ideas into your chosen form of plan.

The final step is to plan your paragraphs.

Checklist for success

Paragraphs should do the following:

- ✔ Focus on the question (here, how far you were made to feel sympathy for Miss Brill).
- ✔ Engage with the text and present your own viewpoint.
- ✔ Support ideas with understanding of the text and a range of relevant quotations.
- ✔ Explain how language/form/structure choices create an impression.
- ✔ Explore beyond surface meanings, making links to deeper ideas about character, theme or context where relevant.

4 Read the annotated paragraph on the following page. What do you notice about the paragraph structure? What is successful about the analysis paragraph?

The writer makes me feel a great deal of sympathy for Miss Brill through the conversation she overhears the couple having on the bench. The boy calls her a 'stupid old thing' with a 'silly old mug'. The insults 'stupid' and 'silly' are offensive and dismissive. The noun 'thing' suggests they don't even recognise her as a person, while the repetition emphasises that she is 'old' and therefore, as the young boy and girl see it, not needed in society anymore. The boy's rhetorical question 'who wants her?' might echo Miss Brill's own feelings, hearing this. We know she has already felt isolated as she finds it 'disappointing' earlier when no one talks. My sympathy is therefore increased by the fact that she was looking forward to listening in with a 'trembling smile', so the young couple's rudeness makes Miss Brill feel further excluded and disappointed– it is saddening to see an old woman cast aside by the younger generation.

knowledge of and quotations from the text

close analysis of language that creates sympathy

clearly reasoned argument and opinions

links to deeper understanding of character, themes and context

Write your response

5 Now plan and write your response to the following practice question in 45 minutes:

How far does Mansfield's writing make you sympathise with Miss Brill in 'Miss Brill'? Support your ideas with details from the text. [25]

Evaluating your prose essay

How should I evaluate my response?

Before you evaluate how well you have done, check the table on page 116. It will help you decide if your work falls broadly into the first or second category – or outside them.

1. Go through your own response and write annotations around it, like the example paragraph in the previous chapter.

2. Read the following, thinking about what the writer of the response has done well and what advice they might need to make more progress.

I am going to write about Miss Brill and how far the writer makes me feel sympathy for her. I feel really sorry for her because she is lonely. She sits on the park bench but nobody speaks. It says, 'They did not speak. This was disappointing, for Miss Brill always looked forward to the conversation.' The word 'disappointing' suggests she is sad about it and makes me feel sorry for her. The words 'always looked forward' make me think she often comes to sit in the park to listen to others and this why she comes to the park. This makes me sympathetic because she must be lonely with no one to talk to. The context links to this because she is called 'Miss' so she's not married. For a woman in her time to be unmarried means she doesn't feel she fits in, as she is expected to marry.

The fur at the start is different compared to the end. Miss Brill loves her fur. She says 'Little rogue!' which suggests she feels friendly to it like it's her naughty pet. So do the words 'laid it on her lap and stroked it'. It's like it's her only companion – she doesn't even have a pet, just a fur. So it is really sad for her when the couple insult it. They say "It's her fu-fur which is so funny," giggled the girl.'

Annotations:
- clear response to the task, developing a personal view
- some comment on the writer's use of language
- developing response
- some exploration beyond surface meaning
- clear knowledge of whole text – could be more clearly expressed
- some exploration beyond surface meaning
- inference used clearly to build argument

The girl is laughing at her through the verb 'giggled' which is mean. The broken word 'fu-fur' shows she is laughing so much she can't speak.

Laughing at Miss Brill's fur hurts her feelings. This makes me feel a lot of sympathy. Miss Brill notices strange old people in the park. The quote says they come from 'dark little rooms or even – even cupboards.' At the end Miss Brill is the same, her room is 'like a cupboard'. It means she's like one of those sad people in the park and didn't know it. This is irony.

> clear focus on the task

> clear knowledge of whole text; lacking focus. Awkward expression

> starting to explore deeper meanings – needs clearer explanation and focus on the task

Comment:

The response shows understanding of the text and task, and includes several relevant quotations. The writer starts to explore language and their response is reasonably developed, although clearer focus and explanation is needed in parts. They show some understanding of the deeper meanings of the text.

3 How could this sample response be improved? Using the table on page 116 and the annotations on the sample response, think about what advice you might give the writer of the response to improve their work. Write your advice in three or more bullet points.

4 Now read a second response to the same question. Think about what is an improvement on the first response.

Mansfield creates a great deal of sympathy for Miss Brill through her use of narrative form. The story is narrated in the third person limited voice, allowing us to hear Miss Brill's thoughts, but also to understand her character across time. For example, we find out that 'she usually bought a slice of honey cake ... if there was an almond it was like carrying home a tiny present'. This habit, and the excitement suggested by the simile 'tiny present' reveals she often relies on small, nice moments to look forward to and get her through her lonely days. This increases our sympathy as it suggests she is very sensitive, making her sense of rejection at the end even more painful.

> presents argument; deliberate focus on task

> close analysis of form and language

> confident response to character and task

The image of the fur is the most significant feature that makes us feel sympathy for Miss Brill. At the start, she is excited to wear the fur: she exclaims 'Dear little thing!' The word 'dear' and the exclamation suggest its value to her. She almost seems to view it as a pet: 'she could have ... laid it on her lap and stroked it'. She clearly takes care of it, keeping it in a box and giving 'it a good brush'. Furs were fashionable at the time, an expensive symbol of status. Miss Brill seems to only have this one: 'her fur', so it's probably her most fashionable, valuable item. This adds to the cruelty of the girl's mockery of it, calling it a 'fried whiting'. By comparing it to a dead fish, the girl's simile devalues the fur in the eyes of Miss Brill. At the end, she 'unclasped the necklet quickly; quickly'. The repetition of the adverb suggests she cannot bear to look at the fur anymore, making us pity her since something she once loved is spoiled for her.

One of Miss Brill's less sympathetic qualities is her eavesdropping on others, and her judgemental comments on other silent old people in the park as 'funny' and 'odd'. This is one of the sources of irony in the story as Mansfield later creates pity for Miss Brill through her silently eavesdropping on the dialogue of the couple on the bench. The boy calls her a 'stupid old thing' with a 'silly old mug'. The insults 'stupid' and 'silly' are offensive and dismissive. The noun 'thing' suggests they don't even recognise her as a person, while the repetition emphasises that she is 'old' and, as the young couple see it, not needed in society anymore. The boy's rhetorical question 'who wants her?' might echo Miss Brill's own feelings. We know she has already felt isolated as she finds it 'disappointing' earlier when no one talks. She was looking forward to listening with a 'trembling smile' so the young couple's rudeness make Miss Brill feel further excluded and disappointed, increasing my sympathy. Perhaps Mansfield makes us pity her to highlight the isolation of unmarried, elderly women in society.

Annotations:

- sustained focus on task
- integrated range of references; confident analysis
- sensitive understanding of deeper meanings
- sustained response; sensitive analysis of character and language
- evaluative response to task and text
- integrated range of references; confident analysis
- character overview
- sensitive link to context and authorial intent

The portrayal of her room at the end of the story emphasises her isolation, increasing our sympathy. Mansfield describes it as 'the little dark room – her room like a cupboard'. The adjectives 'little' and 'dark' make it sound cramped and dingy. The simile 'like a cupboard' implies she is being packed away and dismissed, just like her fur. This makes the final line more ambiguous: is the 'something crying' the fur, or Miss Brill? Like the fur, she is shut away in a box-like space, no longer fashionable, and unwanted.

sustained response; sensitive analysis of character and language

explores ambiguity

Comment:

The response shows sustained personal engagement with the task and text and a confident critical understanding, incorporating well-selected references. The writer of the response demonstrates detailed analysis, an insightful overview of the text, and appreciation of deeper implications.

5 What advice might the writer of this response need to make even more progress? Use the table on page 116 to guide your ideas.

Approaching unseen prose

How do I plan a response to an unseen prose question?

Understand the task

During your course, you may have to write a response to an unseen prose passage.

You are advised to spend around **20 minutes reading the question and text and planning your answer** before starting to write.

The text will be **literary prose,** such as an extract from a **short story, novel, autobiography or travelogue**.

The question is constructed in three parts, as annotated on the sample question below:

> Read carefully the following extract from a novel. A Victorian scientist is telling his dinner guests about a journey he took in his invention, a Time Machine, travelling millions of years into the Earth's future.

The first part tells you to carefully read the given extract and gives you some **information** about what is happening. **Read this information carefully.**

> How does the writer make this moment so memorable?

The second part is **the question itself**. It will ask **how does the writer** convey a certain **impression** in the extract, for example, of **tension, vividness, intrigue**. Therefore, you need to explore **the writer's methods.**

> To help you answer this question, you might consider:
> - how the writer portrays the Earth in this future world
> - how he conveys the feelings and experiences of the narrator
> - how he portrays the crab-like creatures.

The third part of the question gives you **three bullet points of possible areas of the extract to explore.** Use these bullet points to build your response.

Read carefully the following extract from *The Time Machine* by H.G. Wells. A Victorian scientist is telling his dinner guests about a journey he took in his invention, a Time Machine, travelling millions of years into the Earth's future.

'I stopped very gently and sat upon the Time Machine, looking round. The sky was no longer blue. North-eastward it was inky black, and out of the blackness shone brightly and steadily the pale white stars. Overhead it was a deep Indian red and starless, and south-eastward it grew brighter to a glowing scarlet where, cut by the horizon, lay the huge hull of the sun, red and motionless. The rocks about me were of a harsh reddish colour, and all the trace of life that I could see at first was the intensely green vegetation that covered every projecting point on their south-eastern face. It was the same rich green that one sees on forest moss or on the lichen in caves: plants which like these grow in a perpetual twilight.

'The machine was standing on a sloping beach. The sea stretched away to the south-west, to rise into a sharp bright horizon against the wan sky. There were no breakers and no waves, for not a breath of wind was stirring. Only a slight oily swell rose and fell like a gentle breathing, and showed that the eternal sea was still moving and living. And along the margin where the water sometimes broke was a thick incrustation of salt—pink under the lurid sky. There was a sense of oppression in my head, and I noticed that I was breathing very fast. The sensation reminded me of my only experience of mountaineering, and from that I judged the air to be more rarefied than it is now.

'Far away up the desolate slope I heard a harsh scream, and saw a thing like a huge white butterfly go slanting and fluttering up into the sky and, circling, disappear over some low hillocks beyond. The sound of its voice was so dismal that I shivered and seated myself more firmly upon the machine. Looking round me again, I saw that, quite near, what I had taken to be a reddish mass of rock was moving slowly towards me. Then I saw the thing was really a monstrous crab-like creature. Can you imagine a crab as large as **yonder** table, with its many legs moving slowly and uncertainly, its big claws swaying, its long antennae, like carters' whips, waving and feeling, and its stalked eyes gleaming at you on either side of its metallic front? Its back was corrugated and ornamented with ungainly **bosses**, and a greenish incrustation blotched it here and there. I could see the many **palps** of its complicated mouth flickering and feeling as it moved.

'As I stared at this sinister apparition crawling towards me, I felt a tickling on my cheek as though a fly had lighted there. I tried to brush it away with my hand, but in a moment it returned, and almost immediately came another by my ear. I struck at this, and caught something threadlike. It was drawn swiftly out of my hand. With a frightful qualm, I turned, and I saw that I had grasped the antenna of another monster crab that stood just behind me. Its evil eyes were wriggling on their stalks, its mouth was all alive with appetite, and its vast ungainly claws, smeared with an **algal** slime, were descending upon me.'

H. G. Wells, from *The Time Machine*

Now read this practice question on the extract:

How does the writer make this moment so memorable? Support your ideas with details from the text. [25]

To help you answer this question, you might consider:

- how the writer portrays the Earth in this future world
- how he conveys the feelings and experiences of the narrator
- how he portrays the crab-like creatures.

The first thing to do is identify the key thing the question is asking you to focus on.

Glossary

yonder: that over there

bosses: lumps

palps: mouth-parts

algal: like algae, a slimy sea-plant

Look at the highlighting in the question above. For this question, the key focuses are:

a) the *memorable* nature of this moment

b) *how* the writer uses methods to make it so memorable.

Gather your ideas and evidence

The next step is to reread the extract carefully, annotating anything that creates a very striking or memorable impression.

Remember, you are not being asked to retell the story; focus on the three suggested key ideas in the extract carefully:

- the portrayal of the Earth
- the feelings and experiences of the narrator
- the portrayal of the crab-like creatures.

Think about how these parts of the text make it very *memorable*. You must closely explore *how* the language and structure in these parts create a memorable impression.

1 Annotate the text. Consider what other parts of the extract make it memorable. Pay particular attention to the *beginning* and *end* of any extract. Have any *changes* taken place across the extract that create a memorable impression?

Plan your response

Once you have annotated the three areas of the extract for how they create a memorable impression, you can organise your ideas into an argument.

The simplest way to do this is to write one or more analysis paragraphs for each of the three bullet points suggested in the question.

If you have time, write a final paragraph on anything else that adds to the memorable impression. You could think about the passage as a whole and any changes that have taken place.

2 Decide the order in which you want to write about these memorable moments now.

3 Next, plan each section of your response.

Checklist for success

Each analytical section should:

- ✔ focus on the question (here, how this moment has been made so memorable)
- ✔ engage with the text and present your own viewpoint
- ✔ support ideas with understanding of the text and a range of relevant quotations
- ✔ explain how language/form/structure choices create an impression
- ✔ explore deeper ideas, going beyond surface meanings.

Read the example plan for the first bullet point given in the question:

What you need to cover	How the portrayal of the Earth makes this moment so memorable
• Focus on the question – how the moment is so memorable. • Engage with the text and present your own viewpoint.	• The Earth is memorable as it seems strange, almost lifeless, an alien world.
• Support ideas with understanding of the text and range of relevant quotations.	• The colours show a strange world: sky: 'deep Indian red'; sun: 'red and motionless'; rocks: 'harsh reddish colour'. • The only life is the 'rich green' of leaves. The sea is dead, covered with 'a thick incrustation of salt'. It's very still: 'motionless', 'not a breath of wind'.
• Explain how language/ form/structure choices make it so memorable.	• Red feels oppressive, reminding us of blood, or a dying sun. • Stillness and dead sea suggest Earth is almost lifeless. Adjectives: 'rich', 'thick' suggest a great deal of time has passed for plants and salt to build up.
• Explore deeper ideas, going beyond surface meanings.	• Lifeless appearance of the Earth increases shock later in the passage when crab-creature appears – 'reddish... rock' is a monster! Sun described as 'red and motionless' – also somehow monstrous? • Writer maybe makes this memorable so we think about this future – what happened? Has humanity caused this?

Write your response

4 Now plan and write your response to the following practice question in timed conditions.

> How does the writer make this moment so memorable? Support your ideas with details from the text. [25]

To help you answer this question, you might consider:

- how the writer portrays the Earth in this future world
- how he conveys the feelings and experiences of the narrator
- how he portrays the crab-like creatures.

Evaluating your response to unseen prose

How should I evaluate my response?

Before you evaluate how well you have done, check the table on page 116. It will help you decide if your work falls broadly into the first or second category – or outside them.

1. Go through your own response and write annotations around it.

2. Read the following response, thinking about what the writer has done well and what advice they might need to make more progress.

> The first thing that's so memorable is the Earth in the future is really different which is really shocking. There aren't any people and the sky looks strange, it is 'deep Indian red and starless'. Everything is red except the plants. It doesn't look like anything is alive. It says 'all the trace of life I could see at first was the intensely green vegetation'. This means that the plants are the main thing alive. The sea is completely still which is strange because normally the sea has waves but here it says 'there were no breakers and no waves'. There is repetition of the word 'no' to show there's no waves. I think the writer is making us wonder where all the life has gone to.
>
> There is a lot of tension which makes it feel scary. There is a 'huge white butterfly' which scares him with a 'harsh scream'. The word 'harsh' is an adjective and makes it sound nasty and loud. Also butterflies don't scream so it's really strange. Then it gets more scary and the narrator is really frightened by a big crab. The simile 'as large as yonder table' shows the crab is enormous which is frightening. The simile 'like carters' whips' makes the antenna sound like they can whip you and hurt you. We get scared the narrator might die.

Annotations:

- understanding of extract; some focus on task
- several relevant quotations – could be more analytical of the writer's word choice
- some language analysis
- attempts to explore deeper meanings
- some developed analysis
- relevant quotations; some language analysis
- beginning and end of this paragraph could be more focused on task; implicit understanding of task, however

He feels scared, it says the crab is a 'monster'. This makes it sound dangerous. He grabs it by mistake and it gets angry. '*Its evil eyes were wriggling on their stalks, its mouth was all alive with appetite*'. The eyes sound gross and they are wriggling on stalks like a snail. It's covered in slime, it's disgusting which means it is memorable. It wants to eat him, it says the claws '*were descending upon me*.' It ends on a cliff-hanger which makes it suspenseful. But actually we know he made it because he is telling this story at dinner.

some consideration of effects of structure and narrative form

some developed analysis and personal response; reasonable focus on task

Comment:

This sample response shows understanding of the extract and task, and includes some relevant quotations. The writer starts to explore language and their response is reasonably developed, although further exploration is needed and they could maintain clearer focus on the task with more precise expression, particularly in the middle. They show some understanding of the deeper implications.

3 How could this sample response be improved? Using the table on page 116 and the annotations on the sample response, think about what you would improve and how. Write your advice in three or more bullet points.

4 Now read a second response to the same question. Think about what is an improvement on the first response.

The portrayal of the Earth makes this moment very memorable as it seems frighteningly strange, like an alien world. The colours of the sky and land show how much the Earth has altered in the future: the sky is 'deep Indian red'; the sun is 'red and motionless'; the rocks are 'harsh reddish colour'; the sea is 'pink'. This pattern of red colours seems unnatural – more like the planet Mars than the Earth. The adjectives 'deep' and 'harsh' make the red feel oppressive and threatening, reminding us of blood, or a dying sun. The only visible life is the 'rich green' of the leaves; the sea is dead, covered with 'a thick incrustation of salt'. The stillness of the place is emphasised through negations: 'no breakers or waves', 'motionless', 'not a breath of wind'. The negativity and lack of movement feel creepy: the stillness and salt sea suggest the Earth is almost lifeless, devoid of animals and people. The adjectives 'rich' green and 'thick' layer of salt suggest a great deal of time has passed, for the plants and salt to build up so much. The Earth's still and lifeless appearance increases the shock we feel later in the passage when a crab appears right next to the narrator – the 'reddish mass of rock' is really a monster! We might revisit the description of the sun as a 'red and motionless' – is it also somehow monstrous? Perhaps the writer makes this moment memorable so we consider this bleak future of the Earth carefully – what has happened to civilisation? Has humanity caused this barren world?

The first person narrative makes the narrator's uneasy sensations more immediate and therefore more memorable for the reader. He feels a 'sense of oppression' and is 'breathing very fast' which might make us fear for him. His experiences are memorably creepy. He sees a 'thing like a huge' butterfly and hears its 'harsh scream' and 'dismal' voice. The noun 'thing' suggests life on this future Earth is indescribably strange, and the adjectives 'harsh' and 'dismal' make the cry sound terrible. It seems appalling that a butterfly can 'scream'. The scientist's sense of unease is emphasised by his shift from scientific verbs 'I noticed', 'I judged' to admitting 'I shivered', underlining his fear.

This gradually increasing sense of unease contrasts with the sudden and terrifying appearance of 'vast' crab-like creatures,

confident focus on task and understanding of text

range of well-selected references

close language analysis

confident and sustained, detailed language analysis

perceptive sense of overview; sensitive and exploratory comment

confident engagement and exploration beyond surface meanings

confident understanding of narrative form; sustained focus on task

detailed close language analysis; range of well-selected and integrated references creating a memorable impact. The narrator draws attention to their frightening size through a rhetorical question 'can you imagine a crab as large as yonder table', reminding us this story is being told on an earlier Earth, at dinner, creating a memorable juxtaposition with this strange world. The narrator is shocked by their closeness, feeling 'frightful' when an antenna is 'tickling' him, which is shocking for the reader too as seconds ago it seemed he was alone. The alliteration of 'flickering and feeling' emphasises his fixation on the crabs' mouths, which he assumes are 'alive with appetite', creating a memorable close-up visual for the reader. He calls them 'sinister' and 'evil', making a moral judgement of them, yet ironically it is he who is an alien invader in their world – he is the real 'apparition', appearing suddenly from the past on their beach. This confrontation between past and future emphasises the distance between the two worlds, creating a very memorable impression.

sustained focus on task; sense of structural overview

confident grasp of text and narrative structure

close analysis; sustained focus on task

original response; confident reading and analysis with perceptive exploration of meanings

Comment:

The response shows perceptive, sustained personal engagement with the task and extract. The analysis is detailed, incorporating well-selected references and expresses ideas with clarity and precision. The writer of the response has an overview of the extract and considers several deeper implications.

5 What advice might the writer of this response need to make even more progress? Use the table on page 116 to guide your ideas.

Applying your skills to unseen prose

How do I apply the skills I have learned to unseen prose questions?

You are now going to apply your learning to a new prose passage.

Remember to:

- highlight the key terms of the practice question
- spend about 20 minutes reading and annotating the passage
- plan your response
- write your essay.

Read carefully the following extract from a novel set in America in the nineteenth century. Thea has always had the ambition to be a music teacher.

How does the writer vividly portray Thea's attitude to music and teaching? [25]

To help you answer this practice question, you might consider:

- how the narrator portrays Thea's musical activities
- how the narrator presents the argument with Mrs Livery Johnson
- how the conversation with Ray presents Thea's thoughts.

By the time Thea's fifteenth birthday came round, she was established as a music teacher in Moonstone. The new room had been added to the house early in the spring, and Thea had been giving her lessons there since the middle of May. She liked the personal independence which was accorded her as a wage-earner. The family questioned her comings and goings very little. She could go buggy-riding with Ray Kennedy, for instance, without taking Gunner or Axel. She could go to Spanish Johnny's and sing part songs with the Mexicans, and nobody objected.

Thea was still under the first excitement of teaching, and was terribly in earnest about it. If a pupil did not get on well, she fumed and fretted. She counted until she was hoarse. She listened to scales in her sleep. Wunsch had taught only one pupil seriously, but Thea taught twenty. The duller they were, the more furiously she poked and prodded them. With the little girls she was nearly always patient, but with pupils older than herself, she sometimes lost her temper. One of her mistakes was to let herself in for a calling-down from Mrs. Livery Johnson. That lady appeared at the Kronborgs' one morning and announced that she would allow no girl to stamp her foot at her daughter Grace. She added that Thea's bad manners with the older girls were being talked about all over town, and that if her temper did not speedily improve she would lose all her advanced pupils. Thea was frightened. She felt she could never bear the disgrace, if such a thing happened. Besides, what would her father say, after he had gone to the expense of building an addition to the house? Mrs. Johnson demanded an apology to Grace. Thea said she was willing to make it. Mrs. Johnson said that hereafter, since she had taken lessons of the best piano teacher in Grinnell, Iowa, she herself would decide what pieces Grace should study. Thea readily consented to that, and Mrs. Johnson rustled away to tell a neighbor woman that Thea Kronborg could be meek enough when you went at her right.

Thea was telling Ray about this unpleasant encounter as they were driving out to the sand hills the next Sunday.

'She was stuffing you, all right, Thee,' Ray reassured her. 'There's no general dissatisfaction among your scholars. She just wanted to get in a knock. I talked to the piano tuner the last time he was here, and he said all the people he tuned for expressed themselves very favorably about your teaching. I wish you didn't take so much pains with them, myself.'

'But I have to, Ray. They're all so dumb. They've got no ambition,' Thea exclaimed irritably. 'Jenny Smiley is the only one who isn't stupid. She can read pretty well, and she has such good hands. But she don't care a rap about it. She has no pride.'

Ray's face was full of complacent satisfaction as he glanced sidewise at Thea, but she was looking off intently into the mirage, at one of those mammoth cattle that are nearly always reflected there. 'Do you find it easier to teach in your new room?' he asked.

'Yes; I'm not interrupted so much. Of course, if I ever happen to want to practice at night, that's always the night Anna chooses to go to bed early.'

Willa Cather, from *The Song of the Lark*

Checklist for success

The completed essay should:

- ✔ clearly focus on the question throughout
- ✔ progress through clear paragraphs
- ✔ support points with close reference and quotations
- ✔ explain how the writer's choices of language/form/structure affect how you understand the text
- ✔ explore the passage in depth.

Glossary

percale, shirting, lawn: different types of material used to make clothing

Check your progress:

What are the features of a *reasonably developed, relevant* personal response?

Knowledge	• You show how you know the text **well** by making reference to it and/or by quoting from it. • You make points that are **relevant** (close textual reference and/or quotation) to the task set.
Understanding	• You show a **sound** understanding of the text, reading beyond the surface to explore implicit meanings. • You **develop your ideas** on themes, characterisation or ideas.
Language and effects	• You write about **some** of the ways in which the writer uses **language, structure and form**. • You make **some exploration** of the **effects of the writer's choices** and how these effects are created.
Personal response	• You make your own honest and **considered** response to the text, appropriate to the task. • You show **some development of your own ideas** about the text and task.

What are the features of a response showing *sustained personal and evaluative engagement* with task and text?

Knowledge	• You show a **detailed** grasp of the text as a whole and a **deep** understanding of the task. • You support your **original** ideas with **carefully selected, well-integrated reference** to the text.
Understanding	• You show a **sophisticated understanding** of the implicit meaning of the ideas, characterisation and themes in the text. • You show your ability to **analyse, evaluate and interpret** the text in an **original** and **perceptive** way.
Language and effects	• You examine **in depth** the way the writer uses **language, structure and form** and you explore different **interpretations**. • You show the ability to make a **close analysis** of extracts from the text and (where appropriate to the question) respond to the writer's effects in the text as a whole.
Personal response	• You make a **convincing** response, showing deep interest, understanding and an involvement with both text and task. • You have your own individual **ideas and judgements** about the text and express them with **confidence and enthusiasm**.

Studying poetry 4

This chapter explores in depth the key concepts of Literature in English in relation to poetry. You will learn how to develop and express your ideas about poetry texts. You will also be guided through planning, writing and evaluating example responses to practice questions.

4.1 What to expect when you read a poem
4.2 Exploring themes and ideas
4.3 Exploring language
4.4 Exploring form, sound, rhyme and rhythm
4.5 Exploring structure in poetry
4.6 Exploring setting in poetry
4.7 Viewpoint and perspective
4.8 Exploring speaker, voice and character in poetry
4.9 Understanding context in poetry
4.10 Making different interpretations
4.11 Planning and writing a poetry essay
4.12 Evaluating your poetry essay
4.13 Developing an overview
4.14 Evaluating your work
4.15 Planning and writing a response to an unseen poem
4.16 Evaluating your response to an unseen poem
4.17 Applying your skills to unseen poetry

What to expect when you read a poem

What should I expect when I read a poem?

Start thinking

1 Use the mind-map below to write down what you think about when you consider poetry.

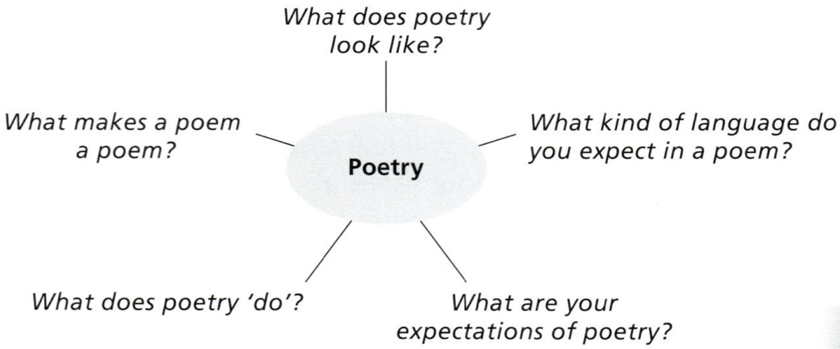

Explore the skills

While you may have different ideas, many people's conception of poetry may be something like this nineteenth century Indian poem:

A cruel throb is at my heart,
  I know not if I wake or dream,
  The past and present mingling seem–
Oh, wherefore shouldst thou thus depart,
  And leave me here without a gleam?

Govin Chunder Dutt, from 'A Cruel Throb is at My Heart'

Key term

archaic language: words no longer in everyday use, and which give the impression of coming from a historical time period

2 Look at the table below, showing classic features of poetry.

a) Circle or highlight any of the features you can identify from the five lines of the poem above.

rhyme	onomatopoeia	**archaic language**	themes of death
themes of love	metaphor	repetition	rhyme scheme
alliteration	simile	pathetic fallacy	rhythm

b) Compare these with the ideas you wrote down in your mind-map.

c) Generally, what is your impression of this poem? Does it conform to or go against your impressions of what poetry is?

Develop the skills

Read the poem to the right, published in 2005.

3 a) Take a look at the classic features of poetry listed in the table on the previous page. Do any of those apply to this text?

b) Do you think this is a poem? Why or why not?

c) What makes Tuwhare's text different from Dutt's?

d) Write two to three sentences summarising this text. What is it 'about'?

e) What makes 'Lyric' different in terms of form and organisation from just a piece of prose writing?

Lyric

I am buttoning up
the buttons of my
mouth: and now
with only one to
go — I'm whistling
you a love-song
of longing from
the wilderness —
— the throb & choke
that may only
come from the
musical palette
of my craven
heart; hear —
o, hear me!

And love my truth.

Hone Tuwhare

Apply the skills

Hone Tuwhare was a very successful and popular New Zealand poet. Though he lacked much formal education, he read widely and experimented with different styles and voices in his own poetry.

4 Reread 'Lyric'.

a) What does the speaker mean about 'buttoning up' his mouth (lines 1–5)? Imagine your own mouth with one button 'to go'. What shape would it be? How does this suggest 'whistling'?

b) Who do you think the speaker is addressing in the poem? Which words and phrases give you this idea?

c) The poem does not use rhyme or conventional stanzas. Tuwhare mainly uses dashes instead of formal punctuation. How do these aspects of structure communicate the character and voice of the speaker?

5 Write a paragraph summarising your conclusions about 'Lyric'. What makes it a poem? Consider:

- the themes and ideas
- how the language used makes it a poem
- how the structure and form make it a poem.

Check your progress:

- I can understand and identify features of poetry.
- I can clearly explain and analyse how a writer uses features of poetry to create meaning.

Exploring themes and ideas

What is poetry 'about'?

Start thinking

When reading a poem, one of the first things you should do is think: 'What is this poem about? What *themes, ideas or feelings* are being expressed here?' Poems can tackle any number of subjects: from love and hate, to life and death… even, to fruit in a fridge!

Looking at how themes, ideas or feelings are developed through a poem will give you a valuable sense of overview.

Often, the title of a poem is the first step towards understanding a poem's themes and ideas.

1 You are going to read a poem called 'When I Heard the Learn'd Astronomer'.

Before you read the poem, think about what the title might tell you and what it might lead you to expect.

'When I Heard the Learn'd Astronomer'

a) Who might be the speaker in the poem? What might their attitude be to the 'Astronomer'?

b) What does the term 'Learn'd' tell you? Is it in everyday usage?

c) What sort of occasion do you imagine might be described?

d) What sort of themes or ideas might this poem be about?

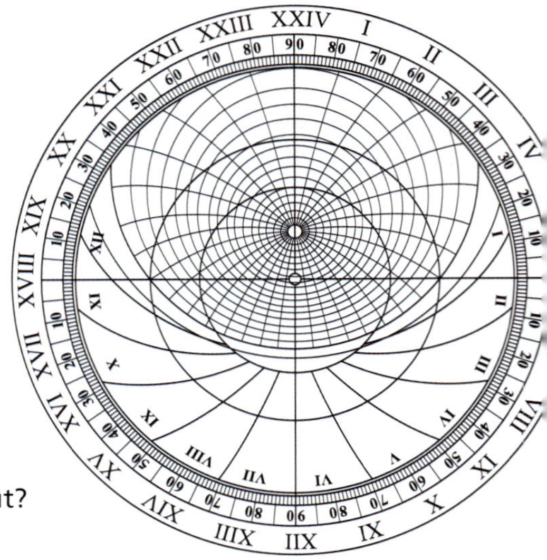

Explore the skills

Now read the poem, focusing your first reading on simply understanding what the poem is about and what ideas are introduced.

When I Heard the Learn'd Astronomer

When I heard the learn'd astronomer
When the proofs, the figures, were ranged in columns before me,
When I was shown the charts and diagrams, to add, divide, and measure them,
When I sitting heard the astronomer where he lectured with much applause in the lecture-room,
How soon unaccountable I became tired and sick,
Till rising and gliding out I wander'd off by myself,
In the mystical moist night-air, and from time to time,
Look'd up in perfect silence at the stars.

Walt Whitman

2 How does the poem meet your expectations suggested by the title? What differences did you find with what you expected?

In this poem, the poet develops the themes of space and science. However, you need to say more than this when you outline a theme.

For example, you could say:

The poem explores the relationship of humanity to the stars, and whether you understand space better by measuring and making charts, or simply by observing and feeling part of a mystical universe.

3 What other themes can you identify in the poem?

As you look more closely at the poet's language and technique, you will see how the theme develops. Writers will often build a **semantic field** of associated words to develop a theme throughout a text.

4 Complete the table below to catalogue words in the poem that fit each semantic field.

Maths, science and learning	Individual experiences, feelings, perceptions
'Learn'd'	'unaccountable'
'astronomer'	'tired and sick'

Read this example of how the associated words from the semantic field of maths, science and learning build your understanding of the theme of humanity's relationship to the stars.

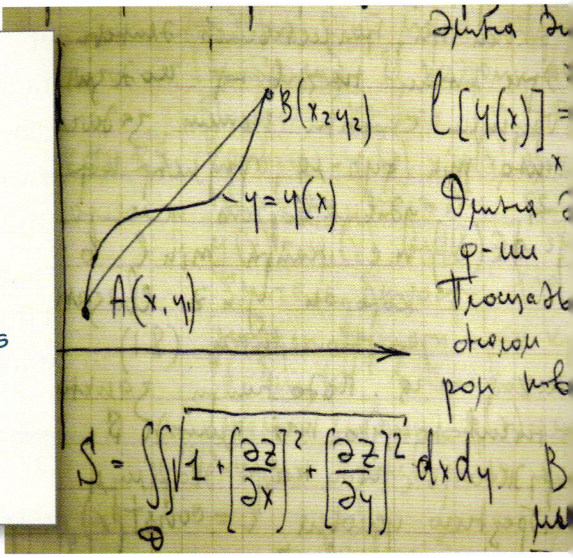

> The poem opens with the speaker sitting in a lecture theatre listening to the learn'd astronomer as he lectures. The poet creates the speaker's experience of the precise, measured, orderly world of the expert through a listing of terms from the semantic field of maths, science and learning. He is shown 'proofs', 'figures … ranged in columns' and 'charts and diagrams to add, divide and measure them'. This suggests that the learn'd astronomer is very certain of his way of understanding the stars.

5. Now write a few sentences about the effect of the poet's use of the semantic field of individual experiences, feelings and perceptions.

Develop the skills

A theme will also be developed and explored through a range of poetic techniques.

6. Read the poem again, this time aloud, highlighting the following poetic techniques and making notes about how they affect the reader (what they make you think, feel or imagine):
   - repetition of sentence starts (**anaphora**) in the first four lines
   - the effect of using a single sentence and how it develops, is punctuated and runs on (enjambment) later in the poem
   - the use of the **passive voice** and its effect in the first lines of the poem ('When I was shown …') compared with the active voice 'I wandered off' later in the poem
   - imagery, sounds and sensations.

   For example:

> The use of the passive voice in the lines, 'the figures, were ranged before me,/When I was shown the charts', makes the reader experience the speaker's lack of engagement and sense of bombardment.

Key terms

anaphora: the deliberate repetition of the first part of a sentence for effect

passive voice: a form where the subject of the sentence is acted on by the verb

7. How does the language you identified relate to the poem's themes?

8. Consider the poem's final lines. What do you think they mean? How is the idea of learning different from the experience of learning presented earlier in the poem?

Extend your notes to include how you think the techniques develop your understanding of key **themes**.

Apply the skills

Read these two opening sentences, addressing the question 'How does Whitman present the theme of learning?'

Response A

> He finds learning boring because he is told things in a boring, stuffy way. He's not interested.

Response B

> The poet presents the theme of learning by introducing and developing the contrasting themes of active learning versus passive learning, suggesting in the poem his clear preference for the former.

Response A lacks specificity, direct links to the question and a comprehensive view of the poem. How does Response B improve on the first?

9. Using Response B above as a model, write a paragraph explaining how Whitman develops the key theme of science and/or passive learning in the first half of the poem.

10. Write another paragraph explaining how Whitman develops his theme in the second half of the poem towards the idea of mysticism and learning from experience.

Check your progress:

- I can understand some of the ways thoughts, feelings and ideas are portrayed and start to explore meaning.
- I can confidently analyse how thoughts, feelings and ideas are portrayed and explore deeper implicit meanings with sensitivity.

Exploring language

Why do poets use the language they do?

Start thinking

The word 'home' is a loaded word; that is, it is full of meaning and **connotations** that go beyond its dictionary definition. Just think about this: what's the difference between a house and a home?

When this teacher thought of home once – a lovely little city in the southern US called Charleston – these words sprang to mind.

Key term

connotations: suggested meanings or associated ideas

Where I come from
The sunset hangs like a
Pomegranate, ruby-red,
In the starry-leaved sky.
It soon ripens to an alabaster peach
Pavilioned above the city's spires,
Sharp and shadowed, swallowed up
By the adjacent blackened harbour,
The water slick and smooth to your caresses
On a sultry summer's night.

1 a) When you think of home, what do you think of? Make a list of features, feelings and images.

b) Now write your own poem about your home town. Write at least 12 lines and use as many different poetic techniques as you can. It need not be flattering to your home town.

Explore the skills

Poets choose their language with great care and, as attentive and perceptive readers, we need to be extremely sensitive to the meanings each word may carry or suggest.

Word choice – denotation and connotation

When considering word choice in a poem, start with the word's *denotation* (that is, its literal meaning or dictionary definition), then think about its associative *connotations*.

Consider the word 'fist'. A 'fist' *denotes* a hand tightened into a ball. However, it *connotes* ideas of violence, aggression and animosity. Are there any additional *connotations* you can think of linked with a 'fist'?

Language techniques

Authors choose their words carefully, but they develop their meaning by using a range of language techniques.

2 Match each language technique in the left-hand column with an appropriate example on the right.

Technique	Example
1. imagery	a. The sky *brooded* in dark-grey clouds, and *sighed* a heavy wind.
2. metaphor	b. *Alone together*, I kept myself away from myself.
3. simile	c. *pink*-laced *petals*
4. personification	d. *plumed, wispy orbs*
5. alliteration	e. The peony blooms *like feathery ash*.
6. consonance / assonance	f. If we never fail, we can never *succeed*.
7. opposition & contrast	g. *the starry-leaved sky*
8. oxymoron	h. the *brittle rattle* of *sleepless dreams*

3 Read through the examples below, which use a 'fist' as a subject:

- *imagery and alliteration*: The hard, flinty fist shook in anger.
- *metaphor*: The fist – a hard, flinty rock – shook in anger.
- *simile*: The hard, flinty, rock-like fist shook in anger.

a) What impression do the adjectives 'hard' and 'flinty' add to the image of the 'fist'?

b) How does the /f/ alliteration of 'flinty' and 'fist' add to the harsh image of the 'fist'?

c) Which image of the fist do you prefer: the metaphor or the simile? Why? How are they similar? How are they different?

d) How do these techniques develop further the connotations of a fist? Do they emphasise or change them in any way?

Develop the skills

Read the poem below.

The Fist

The fist clenched round my heart
loosens a little, and I gasp
brightness; but it tightens
again. When have I ever not loved
the pain of love? But this has moved

past love to mania. This has the strong
clench of the madman, this is
gripping the ledge of unreason, before
plunging howling into the abyss.

Hold hard then, heart. This way at least you live.

Derek Walcott

'fist' used here as a metaphor; suggests violence and tension

alliteration of /l/; mimics the release of tension around the heart; the 'fist' is relaxing – perhaps falling out of love?

'pain of love' = contrast/ opposition. Usually love thought to be pleasant and joyful, not painful; narrator loves not love, but the pain it brings – why?

4 Reread the poem, this time aloud. What other words does the poet use to develop the denotations and connotations of 'fist' throughout the poem?

5 Read the annotations of the first stanza, then continue to read and annotate the word choices and language techniques you notice in the second stanza.

6 Now work closely on the poem to answer these questions:

a) How does the short, enjambed sentence, 'but it tightens / again' add tension to the first stanza?

b) The poet also develops a *semantic field* of insanity in the move from the first to the second stanza. What language demonstrates this theme?

c) Look up the word 'abyss'. What does it mean? How does it develop the ideas of violence or insanity set up earlier in the poem?

7 a) The entire poem is a *metaphor* – one object has been substituted for another. What is the 'fist' a metaphor for?

b) What do you think the *images* of a fist and insanity have to do with love?

8 Read the poem again. What do you think the final line means? How does it relate to the connotations of a 'fist'?

Apply the skills

Read the response below, which analyses how key techniques develop meaning and themes.

> In the poem 'The Fist', the poet uses the metaphor of a fist to describe his feelings of being in love. The noun 'fist' has connotations of tension and aggression, which the poet introduces when he writes 'The fist clenched around my heart'. Here, the poet compares the feelings of being in love to the violent act of a fist holding and squeezing his heart – the organ most associated with love. Initially this strikes the reader as a negative, sad, even depressing image; in fact, we feel a sense of relief when the grip 'loosens a little', the alliterative /l/ sound mimicking the 'loosening' of tension here. However, we soon learn that the narrator 'loved / the pain of love'. The contradictory feelings of 'pain' and 'love' create an interesting irony here – the poet actually enjoys the aggressive ups and downs of falling and being in love. In the first stanza at least, the metaphor of a fist is used to represent the intense, forceful, even painful emotions that being in love make him feel.

9 a) What key theme does this response focus on?

b) What language techniques does this response identify?

c) What does the response say about how each technique affects the reader?

10 Using the model above, write a second paragraph, which explains how the poet uses language techniques, such as semantic fields, imagery and metaphors, to develop the theme of love in the second and third stanzas.

Check your progress:

- I can identify the effect of language techniques and understand how they connect to the poet's ideas.
- I can convincingly analyse the effects of language techniques and show a sophisticated understanding of how they create meaning.

Exploring form, sound, rhyme and rhythm

How do form and sound affect meaning?

Start thinking

The American Modernist poet Wallace Stevens wrote that:

'poetry is words; and that words, above everything else, are, in poetry, sounds.'

For Stevens, the *sound* of words in poetry was vital to understanding the *meaning* of the poem.

1 The following techniques focus mainly on the sound words create. Match each term with its appropriate definition.

Technique	Definition
1. alliteration	a. words that imitate or reflect sounds
2. consonance/ assonance	b. repetition of the /s/ sound
3. sibilance	c. when words near each other begin with the same letter
4. onomatopoeia	d. the repetition of consonant/vowel sounds to create internal rhyme within phrases or sentences

2 Now, match the technique with an appropriate example.

Technique	Example
1. alliteration	a. The soft, sullen seas slowly churn.
2. consonance/ assonance	b. The chirps and twits of goldfinches ring through the air.
3. sibilance	c. The dark night drew nigh.
4. onomatopoeia	d. The rustling curtain swirled, then came still.

Explore the skills

Sound – particularly techniques such as alliteration, assonance, sibilance and onomatopoeia – is vital to creating a rhythm or soundscape that helps the reader identify the themes, **tone** or **atmosphere** of the poem.

Key terms

tone: the voice, attitude or feeling created by the writer's language choices

atmosphere: the mood of a text

However, the sound of words isn't the *only* way rhythm is created. Often, the **form** in which a poet decides to set the poem greatly affects word choice and rhyme – and thus, meaning.

Key terms

form: the type of poem, which may follow rules about a set number of lines, a set rhyme scheme, and a set metre or rhythm for each line

non-metrical: without a regular rhythm

3 Below are some key poetic forms. Match the form with an explanation of its specific features.

Poetic form	Definition
1. sonnet	a. a poem in which an imagined speaker addresses a silent listener
2. free verse	b. a six-line **stanza**, or the final six lines of a 14-line sonnet
3. dramatic monologue	c. a rhyming four-line stanza
4. quatrain	d. a 14-line poem, with a variable rhyme scheme, and which 'turns' in terms of tone, usually after the first eight lines
5. sestet	e. an eight-line stanza, or the first eight lines of a 14-line sonnet
6. ballad	f. **non-metrical**, non-rhyming lines that closely follow the natural rhythms of speech
7. octave	g. a popular narrative song passed down orally; it usually follows a form of rhymed (ABCB) quatrains alternating four-**stress** and three-stress lines

4 Read through the three excerpts from poems below. Which is:

a) a dramatic monologue: a poem that seems to be talking to someone else

b) a ballad: a poem that seems to begin telling a story

c) free verse: a poem that sounds like everyday speech?

Key terms

stanza: a group of lines forming a section of a poem

stresses: syllables on which the emphasis falls, creating rhythm

This is a lifeskill, and I will learn
to go back to sleep without crying.
It is normal to find myself alone
at night. It is normal to call out
and for no one to come. I will adjust.

Siân Hughes, from 'Sleep Training'

But do not let us quarrel any more,
No, my Lucrezia; bear with me for once:
Sit down and all shall happen as you wish.
You turn your face, but does it bring your heart?

Robert Browning, from 'Andrea Del Sarto'

"But they are dead; those two are dead!
Their spirits are in heaven!"
'Twas throwing words away; for still
The little Maid would have her will,
And said, "Nay, we are seven!"

William Wordsworth, from 'We are Seven'

Develop the skills

Students responding to poetry often identify key features of poetic form or a rhyme scheme, without explaining the relevance of those elements to the meaning of the poem. Whenever you're discussing poetic form or rhyme, you must demonstrate *why* it is relevant and *how* it is relevant.

5 Which of the responses below better develops *how* and *why* the poetic form is relevant?

A

The poem 'We are Seven' by Wordsworth is a ballad. It describes a conversation between the narrator and a little girl, 'the little maid', about death. She insists that she has seven siblings even though two of these are dead: 'And said, "Nay, we are seven!"'. This story makes the reader feel sad for the tragic loss, but happy that the girl gets on with her life. Moreover, the fact that the poet writes this as a ballad shows that he's creating a specific rhyme scheme – ABBA. This makes the poem flow better and helps the situation make sense.

B

In the opening lines to 'Andrea Del Sarto', the poet introduces the idea of a lover's 'quarrel' between the narrator and his wife, 'Lucrezia'. The poet writes the poem as a dramatic monologue, so that the narrator speaks directly to us. His use of direct address and the second-personal pronoun 'you' places the reader directly into the poem; in a way, we become Lucrezia, sitting down to listen to the narrator talk about his career. This immediately draws our sympathies to the narrator, who, as is common in Browning's poems, may not necessarily deserve them. For example, his use of imperatives – 'bear with me for once' and 'Sit down' – suggests a tone of control in his voice, which is contradicted by the calm and colloquial nature of his language.

6 Reread the excerpt from 'Sleep Training'. This poem is in *free verse*. Using the following notes, write a paragraph like the better response above, explaining how the form informs meaning.

- *What's it about?* The 'sleep training' of the title is a technique used with babies who cry a lot in the night. The idea is that, by ignoring their screams, parents train their child to get themselves back to sleep without help. This poem seems to be spoken by a person who is suffering and cannot sleep, but who is determined to train herself to sleep again. Is the speaker an adult or a child?
- *Form*: free verse, following the patterns of natural speech. This makes the expression of the poem feel more personal.
- *Techniques*:
  - Lines of verse *run on* – look and see where this happens and which words are emphasised. How does this affect meaning?
  - *Repetition*: find examples of words or phrases that are repeated. What tone of voice or feeling is created through the repetition?

Apply the skills

Now practise those skills with another poem; one with a conventional form. Read the poem below.

What lips my lips have kissed, and where, and why

What lips my lips have kissed, and where, and why,
I have forgotten, and what arms have lain
Under my head till morning; but the rain
Is full of ghosts tonight, that tap and sigh
Upon the glass and listen for reply,
And in my heart there stirs a quiet pain
For unremembered lads that not again
Will turn to me at midnight with a cry.

Thus in winter stands the lonely tree,
Nor knows what birds have vanished one by one,
Yet knows its boughs more silent than before:
I cannot say what loves have come and gone,
I only know that summer sang in me
A little while, that in me sings no more.

Edna St. Vincent Millay

7 **a)** What do you think the poem is about? What does it describe?

b) What *form* does this poem take? How do you know?

c) Identify and annotate the rhyme scheme. Where do you see a big change in the scheme? How might that change be relevant to *meaning as it* develops in the poem?

d) What are the poem's *tone* and *theme(s)*?

e) Identify and annotate key techniques including *metaphors*, *similes*, *imagery*, *alliteration* and *sibilance*. How do these techniques help inform the meaning?

8 Write a paragraph addressing this question:

How does the poet portray the loss and loneliness of the narrator?

Make reference to the poetic **form** as a means of understanding the theme of loneliness.

Check your progress:

- I can identify aspects of form, sound, rhyme and rhythm and explain their effects.
- I can sensitively analyse aspects of form, sound, rhyme and rhythm and confidently link them to key meaning.

Exploring structure in poetry

How does structure inform meaning?

Start thinking

Read the poem on the right aloud.

Even if you can't read it aloud, can you still *read* it? What does it say?

1. Write the poem out so that you can read it normally. How does this change its impact?

l(a

le
af
fa
ll

s)
one
l

iness

e. e. cummings

Explore the skills

The poem by e. e. cummings is an extreme example of how structure affects meaning. The way cummings has organised the poem quite literally makes it unreadable. However, that presentation – and even that inability to read to it – creates meaning.

2. The key theme is isolation and loneliness. But how does the poet express this idea?
   a) What key *image* does cummings employ?
   b) How does the poet use **enjambment** to emphasise these themes?
   c) What number does the structure of the poem resemble? Why might that be important to the poem?
   d) How does the inability to read the poem aloud reflect the key ideas within the poem?

Key term

enjambment: the continuation of a sentence without a pause beyond the end of a letter, word, line, couplet or stanza

Develop the skills

3. Look at these two responses on cummings's poem. Which do you think employs the term enjambment to the greater effect? How and why do they do this?

A

In 'l(a', the poet uses enjambment after the close parenthesis – 's) / one' – in order to develop the theme of isolation. In doing so, the poet places prominence on the word 'one' within the larger word 'loneliness'. Here, 'one' emphasises the dramatic and intense sense of loneliness the narrator feels.

B

In 'l(a', the poet uses enjambment when he goes from one line to another while still in the same sentence. He does this throughout the entire poem, breaking up one word into different parts. This creates a sense of separation, which suggests he is apart from things. This affects the reader because we feel sad for him.

Read the poem below.

caesura

Quickdraw

I wear the two, the mobile and the landline phones,
like guns, slung from the pockets on my hips. I'm all
alone. You ring, quickdraw, your voice a pellet
in my ear, and hear me groan.

You've wounded me.
Next time, you speak after the tone. I twirl the phone,
then squeeze the trigger of my tongue, wide of the mark.
You choose your spot, then blast me

through the heart.
And this is love, high noon, calamity, hard liquor
in the old Last Chance saloon. I show the mobile
to the sheriff; in my boot, another one's

concealed. You text them both at once. I reel.
Down on my knees, I fumble for the phone,
read the silver bullets of your kiss. Take this ...
and this ... and this ... and this ... and this ...

Carol Ann Duffy

enjambment

4 What are the key themes developed in this text?

5 Notice where Duffy uses enjambment. How does the poet use each instance to create tension? How does this contribute to the meaning of the poem?

6 Notice where the author uses caesuras. What effect does this have on how you read the poem?

7 What is happening in the closing lines?

Apply the skills

8 Now write a paragraph on the use of caesura in 'Quickdraw', using one or two examples.

Key term

caesura: a break within a line of verse created by punctuation, especially the end of a sentence.

Check your progress:

- I can identify key features of structure and I understand how they can create meaning.
- I can confidently analyse how structural features create meaning.

Exploring setting in poetry

What is the importance of setting within a poem?

Start thinking

Places often inspire poets, either because they believe the place tells a unique story or because the beauty or significance of the place captures their imagination.

1. Which of these famous places that form the setting and subject of a poem do you recognise?

2. a) Can you think of a place that particularly inspired or moved you? Where was it and why did it inspire you?

   b) Write a short description (about 50 words) of that place – the sights you saw, the sounds you heard, the emotions you felt. What language – or even literary techniques – have you used to convey the emotional impact of that place?

Explore the skills

Setting can be concerned with time, place and **mood**. In poetry, the setting is often important to the way a poet introduces and develops key themes and ideas.

In many cases, the setting of a poem is the subject of the poem – that is, it is what the poem is about. However, poets often use setting metaphorically to introduce more complex ideas. In this sense, as a reader, you want to be aware of the ways in which poets may use setting to move from the concrete or **literal**, to the **metaphorical** or perhaps even symbolic.

Read the following poem written in 1803, and set on Westminster Bridge in London, near the Houses of Parliament.

Key terms

mood: the feeling or atmosphere of a piece of writing

literal: the usual, basic meaning of a word or image

metaphorical: symbolic or figurative meaning of a word or image

Composed Upon Westminster Bridge, September 3, 1802

Earth has not anything to show more fair:
Dull would he be of soul who could pass by
A sight so touching in its majesty:
This City now doth, like a garment, wear
The beauty of the morning; silent, bare,
Ships, towers, domes, theatres, and temples lie
Open unto the fields, and to the sky;
All bright and glittering in the smokeless air.
Never did sun more beautifully steep
In his first splendour, valley, rock, or hill;
Ne'er saw I, never felt, a calm so deep!
The river glideth at his own sweet will:
Dear God! the very houses seem asleep;
And all that mighty heart is lying still!

William Wordsworth

3. What is the initial mood of the setting? Is it calm, peaceful, chaotic or hectic? Pick out words, phrases or images that give you this impression.

4. **a)** Wordsworth was a poet who loved nature and the rural countryside. However, in this poem he is in the middle of a major city. What emotions and thoughts are produced by this particular setting?

   b) What language does he use to celebrate the city environment?

   c) What about the rural environment?

   d) Why do you think this city environment was so moving?

5. What techniques does the poet use to show his appreciation of the setting? What effect do these techniques have on the reader and your understanding of what the poem is about? Complete the table below.

Language / Image	Technique	Effect on the reader
'All bright and glittering in the smokeless air.'	imagery, adjectives	suggests a clean, pristine environment (ironic as it's a large city?)
'A sight so touching in its majesty'		suggests a sense of grandeur and magnificence
'The river glideth at his own sweet will'	personification	
'This City now doth, like a garment, wear / The beauty of the morning'		

Develop the skills

6 Read the following poem in which the poet remembers the outdoor room or veranda, known as a sleepout, where he slept as a child in Australia. Answer questions a)–d).

The Sleepout

Childhood sleeps in a verandah room
in an iron bed close to the wall
where the winter over the railing
swelled the blind on its timber boom

and splinters picked lint off warm linen
and the stars were out over the hill;
then one wall of the room was forest
and all things in there were to come.

Breathings climbed up on the verandah
when dark cattle rubbed in a corner
and sometimes dim towering rain stood
for forest, and the dry cave hunched woollen.

Inside the forest was lamplit
along tracks to a starry creek bed
and beyond lay the never-fenced country,
its full **billabongs** all surrounded

by animals and birds, in loud crustings,
and something kept leaping up amongst them.
And out there, to **kindle** whenever
dark found it, hung the daylight moon.

Les Murray

a) Comment on the poet's use of personification in the first stanza of the poem.

b) The narrator remembers his childhood room. Look at the details he picks out to mention as the poem opens. Is the room comfortable? How do you think he feel about it ?

c) His room was exposed to the outside world. What ideas or feelings are suggested by the words highlighted in grey?

d) There is a change of tone as the poet describes the world beyond the sleepout. How do these lines present the surrounding landscape? Think about the language and the effect of the enjambment.

Glossary

billabong: a small body of water (Australian English)

kindle: spark a fire

7 What is the setting? Think about the time of day, the season, the weather and what can be seen.

8 How do the first two stanzas present the child's sleeping place on the verandah?

9 How does the third stanza present the child's experience of the night?

10 What is the setting of the last stanza? What shift in mood is there? How does the poet create this effect?

Apply the skills

11 Which response below do you think more adequately addresses the effects of the setting on the poem 'Composed Upon Westminster Bridge'? Explain why.

A

Wordsworth vividly conveys the setting in 'Composed Upon Westminster Bridge' by comparing an urban landscape with a rural one. For example, the 'Ships, towers, domes, theatres, and temples lie / Open unto the fields, and to the sky.' Here, Wordsworth creates an image where the cityscape setting shifts smoothly into the surrounding landscape, suggesting their equivalence in terms of beauty and inspiration; the fact that the city opens 'to the sky' moreover suggests to the reader that the city is a place of transcendence, or divine perfection.

B

Wordsworth shows that the city and nature are the same. Wordsworth loved nature and thought it more important, but here, he is in the city and says the city is just as good as nature. We see that the nature around the city is important, but so is the city itself. This proves then that Wordsworth thought the city setting as important as the natural setting.

12 Using the better example as a model, write a paragraph about the setting in 'The Sleepout', and how it is used to represent the poet's thoughts and feelings.

Checklist for success

Make sure you include:

- ✔ key techniques you can identify
- ✔ effects on the reader.

Check your progress:

- I can understand the way a writer uses language to convey setting and show some understanding of implicit information, making reference to the text.
- I can very clearly understand the different ways a writer uses language to convey setting, including implicit information. I can include a range of well-selected references to the text and thoughtfully develop my response in detail.

Viewpoint and perspective

In what ways does viewpoint influence meaning?

Start thinking

Just as poets agonise over language choices, they also very carefully choose the *perspective* or *viewpoint* from which a poem is narrated.

1 In the table below, match each viewpoint with an appropriate example.

Viewpoint	Example
1. first person perspective: told from the point of view of 'I', 'me', 'we' and 'us'	a. You must change your life'
2. second person perspective: told from the point of view of 'you' and 'your'	b. 'It is an ancient mariner, / And he stoppeth one of three'
3. third person perspective: told from the point of view of 'he/she', 'they' and 'them'	c. 'I wandered lonely as a cloud'

Explore the skills

The speaker and narrative perspective the poet chooses will be crucial to understanding key *themes* introduced and developed throughout the poem.

Read the opening stanzas from Samuel Taylor Coleridge's poem 'The Rime of the Ancient Mariner'. In this opening, the *third person speaker* tells the reader about an old sailor who stops a happy wedding guest ('one of three'), bewitches him with a crazed stare, and begins telling him a fantastical story. In this story he kills an albatross. Following this, his ship then gets lost at sea; his crewmates die, turn into ghosts and disappear; his ship sinks and he's rescued; and he becomes cursed to tell his tale throughout the lands forever as penance for his unprovoked crime against nature.

It is an ancient Mariner,
And he stoppeth one of three.
'By thy long grey beard and glittering eye,
Now wherefore stopp'st thou me?

The Bridegroom's doors are opened wide,
And I am next of kin;
The guests are met, the feast is set:
May'st hear the merry din.'

He holds him with his skinny hand,
'There was a ship,' quoth he.
'Hold off! unhand me, grey-beard loon!'
Eftsoons his hand dropt he.

He holds him with his glittering eye—
The Wedding-Guest stood still,
And listens like a three years' child:
The Mariner hath his will.

The Wedding-Guest sat on a stone:
He cannot choose but hear;
And thus spake on that ancient man,
The bright-eyed Mariner.

Samuel Taylor Coleridge, from 'The Rime of the Ancient Mariner'

Here, you hear the wedding guest speaking to the Ancient Mariner, having been grabbed by him. What does the wedding guest say to the old man?

What is the Ancient Mariner saying here? Does he take any notice of what the wedding guest says to him? Why or why not?

The wedding guest is speaking again. What impression of the Ancient Mariner does he have here?

How has the wedding guest's attitude towards the Ancient Mariner changed by this point?

What does this line suggest about the wedding guest? Is he able to resist listening to the Ancient Mariner's story? Why or why not?

Glossary

eftsoons: soon afterwards

2 This poem is told by a third person, omniscient – or all-knowing and seeing – speaker. Rewrite this episode in a prose paragraph or a rhymed/unrhymed poem from the first person perspective of the wedding guest. Consider:

- What is your speaker doing just before meeting the Ancient Mariner?
- What does the Ancient Mariner look like to your speaker?
- How does your speaker react to the Mariner?

Make sure you use details from the original poem in your reconstructed perspective.

3 How has the altered perspective changed your understanding of the story?

Develop the skills

Read the poem below.

Why the old woman limps

Do you know why the old woman sings?
She is sixty years old with six grandchildren to look after
While her sons and their wives are gone south to dig gold.
Each day she milks the goat, sells the milk to buy soap,
Feeds and washes the children, and tethers the goat.
In the evening she tells all stories of old at the fireside:
I know why the old woman sings.

Do you know when the old woman sleeps?
She rests with the dark, at night she thinks of
Tomorrow: she's to feed the children and graze the goat.
She's to weed the garden, water the seedling beans,
The thatch has to be mended, the barnyard cleared.
Maize pounded, chaff winnowed, millet ground, fire lit …
I do not know when the old woman sleeps.

Do you know why the old woman limps?
She goes to fetch water in the morning
   and the well is five miles away,
Goes to fetch firewood with her axe
   and the forest is five miles the other way,
Goes to the fields to look for pumpkin leaves
   leaving the goat tethered to the well tree
And hurries home to the children to cook:
I know why the old woman limps.

Lupenga Mphande

In this poem Lupenga Mphande presents an elderly lady in her daily work.

4 a) What activities does the old woman do in the poem?

b) Who else is mentioned and what is her relationship with them?

c) Who do you think is the speaker of the poem?

5 a) What is the focus on each stanza?

b) Each stanza begins by addressing the reader directly using the second person 'you'. Each time, the narrator asks a question. What are the effects of doing this, do you think?

6 a) Each stanza ends with the narrator, who speaks in the first person. Why is this, do you think?

b) What effect is created each time?

7 a) We never hear from the woman herself in the poem. What effect does this have?

b) Lupenga Mphande is known as a political activist, focusing on human rights and social and environmental justice. Does this affect your reading of the poem?

8 a) What view of the woman's life does the poem present over the three stanzas?

b) What is the tone of the poem?

c) Does it pity the old woman or celebrate her life?

Apply the skills

9 In the following response, the writer notes that Mphande's use of questions in 'Why the old woman limps':

challenges the reader, who is directly addressed, to consider key aspects of the old woman's life.

a) Do you agree?

b) Write two paragraphs about how the writer uses different perspectives and ways of addressing the reader in the poem.

Check your progress:

- I can identify viewpoint in poetry and make inferences about its impact in a poem.
- I can confidently explore the effect of viewpoint and perspective in a poem.

Exploring speaker, voice and character in poetry

Who's speaking in a poem and why does it matter?

Start thinking

Read the poem below.

I'm nobody! Who are you?

I'm nobody! Who are you?
Are you – Nobody – too?
Then there's a pair of us?
Don't tell! they'd advertise – you know!

How dreary – to be – Somebody!
How public – like a Frog –
To tell one's name – the livelong June –
To an admiring Bog!

Emily Dickinson

1 a) To whom is the **speaker** speaking in the poem?

b) Who do you think 'they' are?

c) Why do you think the speaker wants to be a 'Nobody'? What are the advantages? What are the disadvantages?

Key terms

speaker: the person in a poem who 'speaks' or describes the events

tone: the style and the opinions or ideas expressed in a piece of writing

diction: the speaker's style of expression and the wording or phrasing they use

Explore the skills

Closely linked to perspective are the concepts of poetic voice, speaker and character.

Voice encompasses the speaker's **tone**, **diction** and rhythm. This should give you an impression of the speaker's character.

2 Which of the following adjectives would you use to describe the *character* of the speaker?

self-centred	internal	self-promoting	isolated
superficial	private	introverted	extroverted

3. Reread the poem aloud. Is the speaker being playful or serious? Which words or phrases suggest a playful tone? Which suggest a serious tone?

4. Consider the line: 'Don't tell! they'd advertise – you know!'

   a) Do the exclamations and hyphen emphasise the playfulness or the seriousness of the tone?

   b) How does the hyphen change the rhythm of the phrase? If you take it away, does it change how you say the phrase – or how you interpret it?

5. How do you think the speaker voices the phrases 'Don't tell!' and 'you know!' Angrily? Flirtatiously? Quietly? Frantically?

6. Do you agree with this sample response which claims that the speaker, 'rejects the idea of fame and notoriety, and enjoys her status as a "nobody", an invisible person'?

7. Write a paragraph explaining your impression of the speaker, of her voice and character and of what you think the speaker's intentions are in this poem.

Develop the skills

Below is another poem where *voice* is a key feature of the poem: Carol Ann Duffy's 'Mrs Faust'. First, read the summary of the story of Doctor Faust (sometimes Doctor Faustus).

> Originally a German legend, the story of Dr Faust concerns a scholar who is successful, but largely dissatisfied with life. Using his interest in science and alchemy, Faust summons the Devil, and decides to sell his soul for unlimited knowledge and worldly pleasures during his life. However, in the end, the Devil comes to collect his due and carries Faust down to Hell for all eternity.

In her poem, Duffy retells the well-known story of Dr Faust, but changes the perspective and the voice to tell the Faust story from Faust's wife's *point of view*.

8. Read the excerpt from the poem below, then answer the questions in the annotations.

Mrs Faust

First things first –
I married Faust.
We met as students,
shacked up, split up,
made up, hitched up,
got a mortgage on a house,

flourished academically,
BA. MA. Ph.D. No kids.
Two toweled bathrobes. Hers. His.
We worked. We saved.
We moved again.
Fast cars. A boat with sails.
A second home in Wales.
The latest toys –
computers,
mobile phones. Prospered.
Moved again. Faust's face
was clever, greedy, slightly mad.
I was as bad.

I grew to love the lifestyle,
not the life.
He grew to love the kudos, not the wife.
[…]
I felt, not jealousy,
but the chronic irritation.
I went to yoga, t'ai chi,
Feng Shui, therapy, colonic irrigation.
[…]
He wanted more.
I came home late one winter's evening,
hadn't eaten.
Faust was upstairs in his study,
in a meeting.
I smelled cigar smoke,
hellish, oddly sexy, not allowed.
I heard Faust and the other laugh aloud.
[…]
As for me,
I went my own sweet way,
saw Rome in a day,
spun gold from hay,
had a facelift,
[…]
went to China, Thailand, Africa,
returned enlightened.
Turned 40, celibate,
teetotal, vegan,
Buddhist, 41.
Went blonde,
redhead, brunette,
went native, ape,
berserk, bananas;
went on the run, alone;
went home.

[…]
At this, I heard
a serpent's hiss
tasted evil, knew its smell,
as scaly devil's hands
poked up
right through the terracotta Tuscan tiles
at Faust's bare feet
and dragged him, oddly smirking, there and then
straight down to Hell.

Oh, well.
Faust's will
left everything –
the yacht,
the several houses,
the Lear jet, the helipad,
the loot, et cet, et cet,
the lot –
to me.

C'est la vie.
[…]
I keep Faust's secret still –
[…]
[Faust] didn't have a soul to sell.

Carol Ann Duffy

a) What impression of the speaker's character and of her relationship with Faust do you get at this point in the poem?

b) What impression of Faust does the speaker create by this point in the poem?

c) By this point in the poem, does the speaker seem different from or similar to the character introduced in the opening of the poem?

d) By the end of the poem, what do you think Mrs Faust's opinion of Mr Faust is? Is she concerned with his fate? Why or why not?

9 What adjectives would you use to describe the speaker of the poem?

a. superficial **b.** considerate **c.** cynical
d. loving **e.** doting **f.** manipulative
g. indecisive **h.** vain **i.** selfless
j. sincere **k.** materialistic **l.** unambitious

10 Following the example provided, use the table below to organise quotations around these key adjectival descriptions, as well as their effects.

Key adjectival description	Evidence	Effects
superficial	'Fast cars. A boat with sails. / A second home in Wales.'	Suggests to the reader that the speaker only likes luxurious, premier items.
cynical		
indecisive		She's had so many hairstyles and lifestyles – she's following fashionable 'trends' – that she's lost any true sense of self.
vain		

Apply the skills

11 Write a paragraph explaining why you think Duffy retells the Faust story from his wife's perspective.

- How is the story similar? How is it different?
- What do you learn of Mrs Faust as a wife? As a person? As a narrator?

Check your progress:

- I can identify key features of voice and character and link them to meaning.
- I can confidently analyse how aspects of voice and character create tone and meaning.

Understanding context in poetry

What is context and how do I write about it?

Start thinking

1 Look at the picture below.

a) What do you think is happening here?

b) Why do you think Friedrich, the artist, painted it?

c) What do you think it signifies, suggests or 'means'?

To many people looking at this painting, it probably 'means' nothing. It is just someone standing on a mountain looking at some clouds.

Often, to understand a piece of literature, just like a piece of art, we need **context** – that is, some background information that helps us understand how and why it was created.

Friedrich's 'Wanderer over a sea of fog' is considered a masterpiece of Romanticism – a style of art (in literature and painting alike) that values the role of the individual over society, the power of nature over technology, and the mystical influence of the imagination over the rational rules of science.

Key term

context: background to a text that aids in understanding the text

2 With that *context* in mind, consider these questions:

a) Why does the painting's subject have his back turned to us? Why is he in such a beautiful, but remote environment? What might his standing over the fog represent?

b) How does this contextual information help you appreciate this painting better?

Explore the skills

Cultural information can help you make sense of a poem. Read the opening from a longer poem below.

'English Girl Eats Her First Mango'

a kind of love poem

If I did tell she
hold this gold
of sundizzy
tonguelicking juicy
mouthwater flow
ripe with love
from the tropics

she woulda tell me
trust you to be
melodramatic

so I just say
taste this mango

John Agard, from 'English Girl Eats Her First Mango'

3 What do you understand about the situation in these stanzas of the poem when you read them for the first time?

John Agard was born in Georgetown, Guyana. Guyana is on the north coast of South America and is part of the Caribbean region. He moved to Britain in 1977 at the age of 28, where his poetry has won a number of awards. This poem was published in 1985. Although mangos were available in Britain then, they were not as common in the shops as they are now, and were considered to be a very exotic fruit.

4 How does this contextual information help your understanding of the poem?

5 a) How does it help you understand the speaker's way of speaking, or dialect, in the poem?

b) Are there any words that you do not recognise? Do you understand their meaning?

6 a) What impression do you get of the speaker's attitude to the mango?

b) What impression of the girl do you get from this poem?

c) What is the relationship between the speaker and the girl? Consider the **epigraph** and the language of the poem.

7 The last lines of the extract – 'so I just say / taste this mango' – are a marked contrast with the first stanza. Why do you think Agard has created this contrast?

Develop the skills

Another piece of contextual information that might affect your understanding and response to the poem concerns the voice of the speaker. Phrases like 'If I did tell she' might be judged to be grammatically incorrect. However, the pronoun '*she*' in 'If I did tell she' (rather than 'If I did tell *her*') is a feature of a dialect spoken by some Caribbean communities. This use of dialect serves to demonstrate the difference between the Caribbean speaker and his experience and that of the English girl.

8 a) How does this contextual information affect your response to the poem and its meaning?

b) Agard also creates several **neologisms** for this poem. Can you identify them? Why do you think he has invented words rather than used conventional ones? What is their effect?

9 Can you hear the ways in which Agard gives this poem an **auditory** quality?

10 In what ways do you recognise this as 'a kind of love poem'?

Key terms

epigraph: a short phrase at the beginning of a text that summarises the content or themes

neologism: a newly invented word

auditory: relating to hearing

Apply the skills

While knowing a writer's biographical information can be helpful, it can also hinder, limit or close down possible interpretations. Just like anything you write, you need to make sure that you put that information to useful purposes.

Read these two responses:

A

In 'English Girl Eats Her First Mango', John Agard writes about a girl eating a juicy tropical fruit. This is important because Agard was born in the Caribbean.

B

Agard writes with sensual appreciation of the tropical fruit in 'English Girl Eats Her First Mango'. Coming from the Caribbean, he emphasises his understanding of the pleasures of the fruit, which would be a new experience for an English girl in 1985, when the poem was written.

11 **a)** Which of these responses uses context to add to the understanding of the poem?

b) Which response helps develop a key theme?

Check your progress:

- I can understand the meanings of literary texts and their contexts.
- I can explore texts confidently beyond surface meanings and selectively integrate contextual understanding.

Making different interpretations

How can poems be interpreted in different ways?

Start thinking

1 Consider the phrase 'Stopping by woods on a snowy evening'. Which of the following interpretations of this phrase could you agree with?

- **a)** The person is stopping to warm up from the cold.
- **b)** The person is stopping because they are tired.
- **c)** The person is stopping to appreciate the natural environment.
- **d)** The person is stopping to see if anyone is following them.
- **e)** The person stopping is lonely.
- **f)** The person stopping wants to enjoy the peace and quiet.
- **g)** The person stops because they are contemplating their own mortality.
- **h)** The person stops because they are very busy but want a brief rest.
- **i)** The person is stopping because they have a flat tyre.
- **j)** None of the above.
- **k)** All of the above.

2 Why do some of these interpretations seem plausible – that is, more likely to be a valid interpretation – while others seem implausible?

3 Is it possible that two or more of these interpretations can be plausible at the same time? Why is that so?

Explore the skills

Read the poem below.

Stopping by Woods on a Snowy Evening

Whose woods these are I think I know. **A**
His house is in the village though; **A**
He will not see me stopping here **B**
To watch his woods fill up with snow. **A**

My little horse must think it queer **B**
To stop without a farmhouse near **B**
Between the woods and frozen lake **C**
The darkest evening of the year. **B**

He gives his harness bells a shake **C**
To ask if there is some mistake. **C**
The only other sound's the sweep **D**
Of easy wind and downy flake. **C**

The woods are lovely, dark and deep, **D**
But I have promises to keep, **D**
And miles to go before I sleep, **D**
And miles to go before I sleep. **D**

Robert Frost

One popular interpretation of this poem is that it is simply about a weary traveller who decides to take a much-needed respite to enjoy the natural scenery.

4 How might the highlighted language choices support this interpretation? Using the example below, create mind-maps for these highlighted phrases to tease out connotations suggesting an appreciation for the surrounding natural scene.

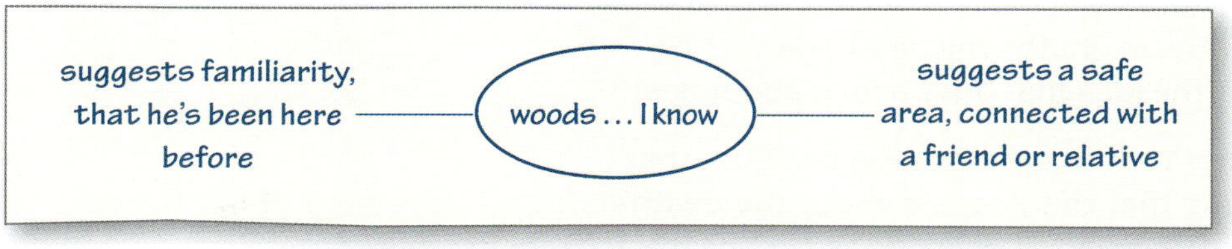

5 Which of the following adjectives do you think captures the *mood* of the poem, following this interpretation. Explain why.

a. gloomy **b.** reflective **c.** tranquil **d.** sinister **e.** relaxing

6 The rhyme scheme of the poem has been annotated for you. Note how the rhyme scheme changes, and how the rhythm of the poem swings and sways. How does the rhyme and rhythm help create a peaceful and calming *mood* to the poem?

7 What *images* or other techniques does the poet use that would help you argue that this poem is about the loveliness of a natural scene?

Another popular interpretation of this poem is that it is not about appreciating nature but about death.

8 How might the highlighted language support this alternative interpretation? Using the example provided below, create mind-maps for these phrases to tease out connotations suggesting death.

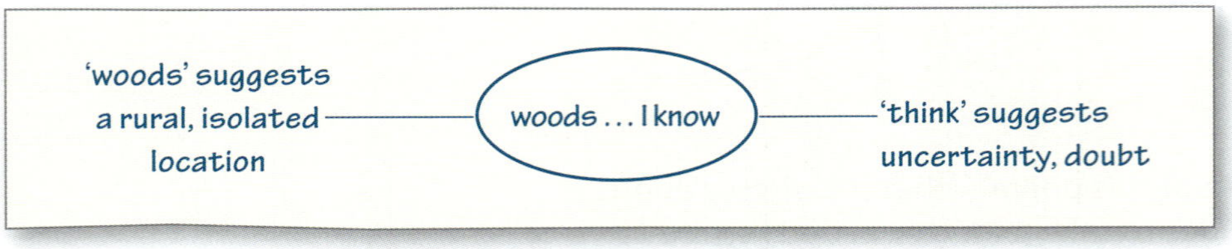

9 Which of the following adjectives do you think captures the *mood* of the poem, following this interpretation? Explain why.

a. lonely **b.** reflective **c.** depressed **d.** ominous **e.** relaxing

10 Note how the rhyme scheme changes, suggesting something's 'off', and how the rhythm swings and sways, perhaps like the speaker's thoughts. How might the *rhyme scheme* and *rhythm* of the poem support the idea that this poem is about death?

11 What *images* or other techniques does the poet use that would help you argue that this poem is about the death?

12 If this poem is about death, what do you make of the repetition of the final lines? What do they mean in this case?

Develop the skills

13 Read the following two responses, each of which begin analysing the poem a different way. For each, write the second paragraph, trying to follow a similar line of argument. Prompts have been provided for the first response to help guide you.

> The poet introduces the key theme of natural appreciation in the first stanza. For example, the narrator says how he's 'stopping here / To watch his woods fill up with snow.' Here, the poet creates a peaceful and calm image of a person observing snow fall. The alliteration of the /w/ sound in 'watch' and 'woods' emphasises this by creating an equally peaceful and calm tone – the /w/ sound perhaps onomatopoeically mimicking the soft 'whoosh' of the snow falling. Moreover, the use of the verb 'stopping' suggests rest and repose, further highlighting the peaceful scene.
>
> The poet further develops this idea of natural appreciation when he writes '______.'

a) Choose another quotation that may link to this point about the appreciation of nature, for example, 'The woods are lovely, dark, and deep'.

b) What key language or technique does Frost use in this quotation?

c) What does this key language or technique mean, suggest and/or connote?

d) What effect does this key language or technique have on the reader?

The poet introduces the key theme of death in the first stanza. For example, the narrator says how no one will 'see me stopping here' to 'watch [the] woods fill up with snow'. Here, the poet creates an image of isolation and loneliness: the narrator is alone in the forest without anyone nearby to witness his activities. Here, the verb 'stopping' suggests a cessation of activity, which introduces connotations of death; the narrator will be 'stopping' here for the rest of his life. The passivity of 'watching ... woods fill up with snow' could be symbolic of time passing away. The snow collecting on the ground is like an hourglass counting down the final moments of his life.

The poet further develops this idea of death when he writes...

Apply the skills

Believe it or not, there is one further interpretation of this poem. While it's rather silly, it only serves to prove the point that if you have the evidence to support your argument, any sensible and reasonable interpretation can be valid.

14 Find evidence and write up to two paragraphs making the case that 'Stopping by Woods on a Snowy Evening' is actually about Father Christmas or Santa Claus.

Check your progress:

- I can understand that poems can be interpreted in different ways and I can find the necessary evidence to support my interpretation.
- I can confidently express a personal interpretation of a text, supported by very clear understanding and integrated, well-selected textual references.

Planning and writing a poetry essay

How should I respond to a question on a poem I know well?

Understand the task

When you answer a question on a poem you have studied already, the first thing you should do is read the question carefully.

To start off, highlight or underline key words in the question, so you know specifically what you need to look for in the poem.

For example, look at one sample annotation of the following practice question:

Focus on authorial method; what techniques used?

Focus on characteristics; my opinion; how is the character portrayed? How is she portrayed in different ways?

> How does Duffy convey vivid impressions of Mrs Faust in these lines? Support your ideas with details from the text. [25]

'vivid' means clear, vibrant; focus on imagery, adjectives, similes and metaphors

Titular character; main character; focus must be on her as:
*protagonist – wife of Dr Faust;
*speaker – first person, female perspective
*voice/tone

1 Practise this 'engaged reading' with the following practice question:

> How does Bhatt portray Swami Anand and the speaker's attitude towards him in this poem? Support your ideas with details from the text. [25]

a) Highlight or underline all the key words in the question.

b) Annotate the question with ideas that help you understand what you need to do.

c) List all the techniques you can think of that might be relevant as you read through the poem.

Gather your ideas and evidence

After you have read the question in Question 1, highlighted or underlined key words in the question, made any appropriate notes, *then* you should reread the poem with the question in mind.

Make annotations in the margins to record your thoughts and ideas on the poet's techniques, their effects and the meanings created that clearly link to the question.

2 Practise these skills on the poem below.

Swami Anand

In Kosbad during the monsoons
there are so many shades of green
your mind forgets other colours.

At that time I am seventeen, and have just started
to wear a sari every day.
Swami Anand is eighty-nine
 and almost blind.
His thick glasses don't seem to work,
they only magnify his cloudy eyes.
Mornings he summons me
 from the kitchen
and I read to him until lunch time.

One day he tells me
"you can read your poems now"
I read a few, he is silent.
Thinking he's asleep, I stop.
But he says "continue".
I begin a long one
in which the Himalayas rise
 as a metaphor.
Suddenly I am ashamed
to have used the Himalayas like this,
ashamed to speak my imaginary mountains
to a man who walked through
 the ice and snow of Gangotri
 barefoot
a man who lived close to Kangchenjanga
 and Everest clad only in summer cotton.
I pause to apologize
but he says "just continue."

Starts with season and location – linked with growth and life. Speaker also young and growing into womanhood. Contrast with Swami – old man who seems weak with failing eyesight – contrast with later in the poem.

Glossary

swami: a Hindu title for a spiritual teacher

Later climbing through
    the slippery green hills of Kosbad,
Swami Anand does not need to lean
on my shoulder or his umbrella.
I prod him for suggestions,
ways to improve my poems.
He is silent a long while,
then, he says
    "there is nothing I can tell you
        except continue."

Sujata Bhatt

Plan your response

Drafting a quick plan helps you organise your ideas and provides a road map to develop your argument and analysis.

Generally, your response should consist of the following:

An **introduction** that:

a) addresses the key terms expressed in the question

b) links clearly to the poem's content

c) potentially provides a brief summary of the poem's main points to demonstrate your understanding.

Three or so **main body** paragraphs that:

a) develop key observations linked to the question

b) make reference to a range of quotations and techniques used within the poem

c) examine, explain and analyse *how* meaning is created through language and techniques.

A **conclusion** that:

a) summarises your key observations and explains effects on the reader.

Try this with the following practice question:

How does Bhatt portray Swami Anand and the speaker's attitude towards him in this poem? Support your ideas with details from the text. [25]

So, firstly, you need to track through the poem with the key terms of the question in mind:

- *Swami Anand and the speaker's attitude towards him* – (what feature of the poem to focus on)
- *How ...* portray – (poetic techniques and language that present the characters and their views).

Read the following sample annotation of the opening lines. As the poem opens, you may notice the age gap between the characters. Swami Anand is elderly and physically frail, which is contrasted by the later details of his past life and achievements.

3 **a)** Now continue to annotate the poem, picking out details that relate to Swami Anand himself.

b) Notice when and where the speaker's attitudes towards him are suggested.

You could track your observations using a table like this:

Key theme	Introduced: *second stanza*	Develops: *third stanza*	Develops further/ changes: *fourth stanza*
Swami Anand/ speaker's attitude	'seventeen' and 'eighty nine': age gap might suggest impatience because he is 'almost blind', emphasised by short line, and his 'thick glasses don't seem to work', a complete line 'summons': verb suggests power, authority 'I read to him' implies respect and patience	'he tells me' and 'asleep' – contrast between authority and apparent weakness But speaker respects his views and judgements on poems 'metaphor' and 'ice and snow … barefoot' – contrast between speaker's imagination and SA's physical endurance	'does not need to lean / on my shoulder or his umbrella.' – further ideas of SA's hidden strength 'prod' – she is eager for advice 'continue' – he says little, he is encouraging, emphasised by short final line

4 For each observation, think about *how* the feeling is created through poetic techniques such as language, structure, form, sound, voice or perspective. Add comments to your annotations, or to your table.

The main body of your response should follow the focus of the question in relation to how it develops as you move through the poem, from beginning to end.

Write your response

5 Using that framework, write a response to the poem using any of the practice questions above.

Checklist for success

- ✔ Have you identified the key terms of the question?
- ✔ Have you tracked through or annotated the poem with the key terms in mind?
- ✔ Have you identified key language and techniques in the poem?
- ✔ Have you identified a range of key quotations that link to the question?
- ✔ Have you created mind-maps for that key language or those key techniques to help tease out meaning?
- ✔ Have you linked your observations to the focus of the question?

Evaluating your poetry essay

How can I assess and improve my own work?

Your task

Read 'Swami Anand' by Sujata Bhatt.

How does Bhatt portray Swami Anand and the speaker's attitude towards him in this poem? Support your ideas with details from the text. [25]

Evaluating your work

Before you make an evaluation of how well you have done, check the table on page 181. It will help you decide if your work falls broadly into the first or second category – or outside them.

1. Go through your own response and, if possible, write your own brief annotations around it.
2. Now read the following response, thinking about what the writer of the response has done well and what advice they might need in order to make more progress.

Sujata Bhatt presents Swami Anand and the speaker's view of him in a number of ways. There is a gap between them, as the speaker is a young woman of 'seventeen' while Swami Anand is 'eighty-nine'. The language Bhatt chooses describes Swami Anand as an old man whose body is failing, as he is 'almost blind' and his 'thick glasses don't seem to work'. The 'thick glasses' suggest that his eyesight is very poor, yet even these 'don't seem to work'. The phrase 'and almost blind' is on a line on its own because Bhatt writes in free verse.

key quotations

some response to language

However, the speaker has asked for his advice on her poems, and when he 'summons' her to read, the verb implies his authority. Her respect for him is clear when she reads her poems to him and also when she pauses, 'Thinking he's asleep'. In a poem she uses the 'Himalayas … as a metaphor'. This shows the reader two things. She compares her use of metaphor with Swami Anand's own experience of the mountains. The

understanding of the text and some deeper implications

key quotations

language suggests great endurance in walking through 'the ice and snow ... barefoot' and living in the mountains 'clad only in summer cotton'. This shows that Swama Anand has been a strong man who has survived hardships. The speaker also shows her own perspective and feels 'ashamed' and has to 'apologize' when she compares her imagination to Swami Anand's real experience. I think this shows her respect for him. She is also eager to get his views, shown by the word 'prod'. Though he does not give her clear advice, he does encourage the speaker, telling her to 'continue' at the very end of the poem.

some use of key quotations

some response and development of language relevant response to the question

personal response

some understanding of the text

Comment:

This is a reasonably developed and relevant personal response. The writer demonstrates some thoroughness in their use of supporting evidence. They also make some response to how the poet uses language, but they don't really develop an analysis of all of the quotations used. The writer of the response also demonstrates an understanding of key ideas in the text, along with some deeper implications.

3 How could this sample response be improved? Using the table on page 181, think about what advice you might give the writer of the response to improve their work.

4 Now read a second response to the same question. As you read, think about what is an improvement on the first response.

Sujata Bhatt's presentation of Swami Anand develops through the poem and the speaker's attitude towards him at times seems to be one of pity, but proves to be one of respect.

Making 'Swami Anand' the title of the poem, with the **honorific** 'Swami', suggests respect from the start, but the reader notices the marked age gap between the speaker and the man. She is 'seventeen', at the beginning of womanhood, whereas he is 'eighty-nine'. His great age is furthered by the addition that he is 'almost blind', a detail emphasised by its inset, isolated position in the stanza. Bhatt even seems to suggest the speaker's impatience when adding that his

focused understanding of the poem's opening

Glossary

honorific: respectful title

'thick glasses don't seem to work', as 'they only magnify his cloudy eyes'. The adjectives 'thick' and 'cloudy' accentuate how poor Anand's eyesight is.

However, Bhatt creates a tone of authority when 'he summons' the speaker. Interestingly, he brings her 'from the kitchen', the traditional domain of women, again emphasised by Bhatt's use of the isolated line. In this way, he could be seen to be encouraging her to free herself from limiting female roles. The authority is also apparent in the use of the imperative when 'he tells' the speaker to read her poems. This command is also giving her the chance to find another role, as a poet.

sensitive blending of contexts with how the writer creates effects

The fourth stanza of the poem is revealing, developing both the presentation of Swami Anand himself, and the speaker's attitude to him. In a poem, the speaker has used 'the Himalayas ... / as a metaphor', and becomes acutely aware that her 'imaginary mountains' contrast with Anand's physical experience of them. Bhatt presents this by using details that make the reader feel the harsh conditions. Anand has 'walked through / the ice and the snow ... / barefoot' and lived close to Everest 'clad only in summer cotton.' In this way she portrays Anand as a man of great physical endurance in his past, creating a different perspective on the 'eighty-nine' year old. This is also apparent in the speaker's attitude, as Bhatt uses the adjective 'ashamed' to describe her feelings. The contrast between their different experiences of the Himalayas is again emphasised by the short isolated phrases 'as a metaphor' and 'barefoot' as Bhatt uses free verse.

well-selected references

Interestingly, as the two characters walk into the hills, Anand seems to regain his strength – 'he does not need to lean / on my shoulder or his umbrella' – giving the reader a final image of his strength, rather than his age. The speaker's respect and eagerness to learn from Swami Anand is also apparent in the verb in 'I prod him for suggestions'. Though Anand does not say much, his repeated command to 'continue' suggests gentle, patient encouragement. The poem, written in the first person, itself could be said to represent a result of that encouragement.

personal and evaluative engagement

Comment:

This response sustains a personal and evaluative engagement with the task and the text. The writer demonstrates a comprehensive understanding of the poem and the techniques the poet uses, using literary methods to sustain a critical understanding of the poem with individuality and insight. They also respond with sensitivity when considering the poem's language. The recognition of context, key themes, tone and verse structure demonstrates a thorough understanding of key techniques and how the author wields them to achieve her intended effects.

5 What advice might the writer of this response need to make even more progress? Use the table on page 181 to guide your ideas.

Developing an overview

How do I develop an overview and build an analysis in a poetry response?

Understand the task

This section focuses in detail on how to develop an overview and build your analysis, while working closely with the text.

One way to create a response that links your ideas together and connects them to the question, is by using *signposting* – that is, using language specific to the question and to your argument at the beginning and ending of your paragraphs.

1 Read the example introductory paragraph below on 'Mrs Faust', which begins to address the practice question:

> How does the writer convincingly portray the character of Mrs Faust in the poem? Support your ideas with details from the text. [25]

> *The writer convincingly portrays the character of Mrs Faust as materialistic, greedy and soulless. The poem retells the famous story of Dr Faust, a scientist who sells his soul to the Devil in order to obtain godlike knowledge and worldly possessions. However, Duffy chooses Faust's hypothetical wife as her narrator, and we see Faust's rise and fall from her unique perspective. Duffy shows the ways in which Mrs Faust's moral character is corrupted because of her marriage to Faust.*

a) Underline words in the introduction that reflect the language of the question.

b) Circle words that you think constitute the main ideas of an argument.

c) Double underline phrases that concisely summarise the plot of the poem.

2 Now read the ensuing first body paragraph. What language in this paragraph links back not only to the question, but also to the previous paragraph? Underline these words or phrases.

The poet introduces the idea of Mrs Faust being a materialistic, greedy and soulless character in the first stanza. For example, Duffy has the narrator say, 'I married Faust'. Here, the reader sees Mrs Faust as in control – she marries him, rather than the other way around. This is emphasised when the narrator refers to 'Two toweled bathrobes. Hers. His.' in that 'Her' bathrobe comes before the usual 'His'. This suggests her tendency to put herself first and get whatever she wants. Here, the poet demonstrates Mrs Faust's greedy nature by suggesting that she treats Faust almost as a possession himself – a trophy husband to show off with his 'PhD.'

Your body paragraphs should continue to build and link to ideas you introduced at the very opening of your response. Before you apply this approach to any poem, make sure you read and plan carefully to ensure that this approach will work to effectively address the question.

3 If you were carrying on from the paragraph above to write the second body paragraph to 'Mrs Faust', which would be the best paragraph opener?

a) *We also see Mrs Faust's character when she talks about going to 'yoga' and 't'ai chi' and see how she is only going to these activities because she 'loves the lifestyle' and doesn't have anything better to do with her life because she knows that her husband no longer loves her.*

b) *Another key idea of the poem is that of good and evil.*

c) *In the fourth stanza, the poet develops the idea of Mrs Faust's greedy and materialistic character when she writes, 'I went to yoga, t'ai chi, / Feng Shui, therapy, colonic irrigation.'*

d) *Duffy also uses short sentences, caesuras and enjambment to create effects on the reader.*

4 **a)** Why did you choose the sentence you did? How does that sentence connect with what came before?

b) Why did you reject the other ones?

Writing a conclusion can add a great dynamic and sense of purpose to your response. To have a purposeful conclusion, you need to draw an overview, together with your own personal opinions about the poem's effectiveness.

Read the example below.

> In conclusion, it's clear to me that Mrs Faust is an immoral, dishonest, and even wicked character. Duffy seems to use her to comment on the materialistic nature of modern society – of how people have come to value things and experiences over other people and even themselves. I think Duffy's portrayal of this idea is a powerful one because it shows how easily material possessions can take over your life. In this way, materialism is the Devil coming to take away your soul.

5 **a)** What broad or general idea has this response introduced to try to tie together the analysis? Highlight or circle key words that you think show this.

b) Where do you see the response offering a personal opinion? Underline these instances.

Gather your ideas and evidence

Read the question and the poem on the following page, in which the poet deals with ideas and feelings concerning love, isolation and anxiety over the passage of time.

6 Annotate:

a) where you think those ideas and feelings are conveyed

b) how those thoughts and feelings are introduced, develop or change (if indeed they do develop or change) throughout the poem

c) what key techniques you can identify.

How does the poet powerfully convey his thoughts and feelings in this poem? Support your ideas with details from the text. [25]

Bright star! would I were steadfast as thou art

Bright star! would I were steadfast as thou art—
Not in lone splendour hung aloft the night,
And watching, with eternal lids apart,
Like Nature's patient sleepless **Eremite**,
The moving waters at their priestlike task
Of pure **ablution** round earth's human shores,
Or gazing on the new soft fallen mask
Of snow upon the mountains and the moors—
No—yet still steadfast, still unchangeable,
Pillow'd upon my fair love's ripening breast,
To feel for ever its soft fall and swell,
Awake for ever in a sweet unrest,
Still, still to hear her tender-taken breath,
And so live ever—or else swoon to death.

John Keats

Glossary

Eremite: a Christian hermit or recluse

ablution: a ceremonial act of washing oneself

Plan your response

7 Use the table below to organise your own thoughts about 'Bright star!'.

Thoughts and feelings	Introduced:	Develops?	Develops further/ changes?
anxiety over the passage of time			

Write your response

8 Using the framework below, write a response to the poem, addressing the question above. Use the sentence starters provided to help build your analysis as outlined in this section, if you need to.

Introductory paragraph

> The poet powerfully conveys his ideas and feelings in this poem through the themes of love, isolation and the passage of time. The poem is about . . .

- Write the rest of the sentence summarising the poem in your own words.
- Close the introductory paragraph with a sentence that links back to the opening sentence, *highlighting* your key themes again and *signposting* the ideas you are to develop.

First body paragraph

> The poet introduces ideas of love, isolation and time in the opening lines. For example, the poet writes. . .

Second body paragraph

> The poet develops these ideas further near the middle of the poem, when he writes. . .

Third body paragraph

> However, the poet changes the tone of his feelings nearer the end when he writes. . .

Conclusion

> To conclude, I think that the poet is saying that love should be. . .

Evaluating your work

How can I assess and improve my own work?

Evaluating your response

Before you make an evaluation of how well you have done, check the table on page 181. It will help you decide if your work falls broadly into the first or second category – or outside them.

1. Go through your own response to the practice question you considered in Lesson 4.13, and write your own brief annotations around it.

> How does the poet powerfully convey his thoughts and feelings in this poem? Support your ideas with details from the text. [25]

2. Now read the following, thinking about what the writer of the response has done well and what advice they might need in order to make more progress.

> The poet conveys his thoughts and feelings in a number of ways. Firstly, he compares himself to a 'Bright star'. 'Bright' suggests being shiny, and full of light, which could suggest the way he wants his love to be. By comparing himself to a 'Bright star', the poet wants to be noticed. We know this because in the third line, the poet writes 'Not in lone splendour'. This means that he doesn't want to be alone in his 'splendour' but wants to share it, just like he wants to share his emotions. The poet also says he doesn't want to be an 'Eremite', which is a Christian hermit. A hermit is someone who lives alone, and the poet uses this simile to show his fear of being alone. Therefore, here, the poet shows feelings of wanting his love to be noticed, but also fear of being alone.
>
> This poem is a sonnet, which means it has 14 lines and a specific rhyme scheme. The rhyme scheme for this poem is ABAB CDCD in the octave, and EFEF GG in the sestet. Sonnets are also usually about love, and a major theme of this poem is love.

some thoroughness in the use of supporting evidence

missed opportunity to comment on the effects of the rhyme scheme

We see this when the poet writes, 'pillow'd upon my fair love's ripening breast.' Here, the poet says he wants to rest his head on his lover's chest for all time, therefore being with them forever. Here, he feels his lover's breast's 'soft fall and swell', a key image showing how connected they are and how connected he wants them to be. This shows his emotions to be profound in that the poet loves this person so much that he wants to spend the rest of his life with them.

some response to the writer's use of language

However, the poet also introduces the idea of death at the end – 'or else swoon to death'. Here, the poet says that if he can't be 'steadfast' like a star – that is, to be around forever – then he at least wants to be with his love until he dies. It could also suggest, however, that if he can't be with her forever, then he would rather just be dead, because he can't live without his love. This shows how powerful his emotions are, as 'swoon' suggests passing out from extreme emotion. His love is so powerful that it has the capacity to keep him alive, but it also has the ability to kill him. This is ironic as usually we think of love as a positive thing that most people want to live their life.

some understanding of the text and its deeper implications

personal response

Comment:

This is a reasonably developed and relevant personal response, although just. The writer demonstrates thoroughness in their use of supporting evidence with the use of the quotations throughout the response. They also make some response to how the poet uses language, although at times this can be quite general and sweeping rather than specific. However, there is some understanding of deeper implications.

3. How could this sample response be improved? Using the table on page 181, think about what advice you might give the writer of the response to improve their work.

4. Now read a second response to the same question. As you read, think about what has been done that is an improvement on the first response.

The speaker powerfully conveys conflicted feelings concerning his love and his fears surrounding the passage of time. He does this through his use of a central image – the 'bright star' to which the poem is addressed – and the sonnet form. The star's radiance and beauty are emphasised immediately through the adjective 'bright' placed right at the start of the poem, suggesting the powerful strength of the star's light, making it an appropriate metaphor for his desire to be strong, pure and constant in his love. The iambic rhythm of a sonnet is also immediately broken by the stress placed on this first word, 'bright', suggesting again the powerful force of the star's light, and also creating the impression that the poem is bursting from the speaker's lips, as if he is suddenly compelled to address the star because of the strength of his feelings.

However, the speaker's feelings are conflicted, as demonstrated by the fact that he almost immediately qualifies his choice of the star as an image for his commitment to his love. He thinks that a star is actually too distant and 'lone', isolated like a hermit or 'Eremite'. He uses images associated with purity, such as 'priestlike… ablution' and 'new… snow' to describe the star's 'eternal-lidded' watching. Yet these images suggest sterility as well as purity – priests bless and cleanse but they do not marry; snow is bright and white like the star itself, but cold and, as it is a 'mask', untouched and hiding the warm earth beneath. The speaker wants to have the star's constancy and 'steadfast' nature, but does not want to be cold and distant like a star, denied the touches of his lover. He feels a conflict between the purity of an eternal love and his desire to be 'pillow'd' on the 'soft' and 'ripening breast' of his lover, images suggesting embraces and fertility, as though lying with his lover in bed. The adjective 'ripening' sums up his fears – if his lover's breast is 'ripening' then at some point it must become 'ripe', but like all soft, ripe fruit, it must also then eventually start to decay. He fears to lose his lover.

confident focus on task and understanding of key writer's methods

language analysis revealing confident understanding of central ideas in the poem

detailed structural analysis

perceptive understanding of ideas, focused on the task

well-selected range of references explored perceptively and in detail

perceptive sense of overview, maintaining focus on task

detailed close language analysis; range of well-selected and integrated references; sustained focus on task

His conflicted desires, caught between an eternal yet cold and sterile love, like a distant unchanging star might feel, and a strong desire to embrace the 'fall and swell' of his lover's chest, are emphasised by the repetition of 'still, still'. This repetition suggests his desperation to keep things as they are, listening to the 'fall and swell' of his lover's breath. The repeated 'll' sounds of 'fall and swell' and 'still' create a lulling sense of continuity, like a lullaby soothing him into a comforting 'sweet unrest'. However, the 'fall and swell' of the breath itself reminds us that life is proceeding, and must end in 'death', as the final rhyming couplet emphasises. The only way the speaker can ever really gain 'still' eternity is through dying, leading him to his final feelings of impossible conflict – either attempt to remain hugging his lover forever or die.

The sonnet form itself emphasises how trapped he feels by this oxymoronic choice – rather than a single **volta** between the octet and sestet, there is this further final twist, emphasised by the caesura in the last line, as well as the two earlier rejections of his image of the star. His desire to be steadfast whilst repeatedly turning from each choice creates an overall sense of irony, which powerfully conveys his conflicted thoughts and feelings.

sustained focus on task; confident grasp of ideas; well-selected references

confident engagement; perceptive analysis of patterns of language

perceptive exploration of meanings; detailed focus on text and task

confident understanding of form

sustained focus on task; sense of overview

Comment:

The response shows perceptive, sustained personal engagement with the task and poem. The analysis is very detailed, incorporating well-selected references. The writer of the response demonstrates a critical understanding of the poem and the techniques the poet uses, as well as a clear sense of overview and the way in which meanings develop across the poem.

Key term

volta: a shift or change of direction in a poem

5 What advice might the writer of this response need to make even more progress? Use the table on page 181 to guide your ideas.

Planning and writing a response to an unseen poem

How can I organise a response to an unseen poem?

Understand the task

One big difference between tackling a question on a poem you have studied and one on an unseen poem is the amount of time you need to read, plan and prepare your response. For an unseen question, you are advised to spend 20 minutes reading and planning your response.

Take a look at the practice question below on a poem called 'Harmonium' by Simon Armitage.

> Read carefully the following poem. The narrator discusses how he and his elderly father moved an old harmonium (a church organ), which was due to be scrapped, from a church.
>
> **How does the poet's writing powerfully show the relationship between father and son?** [25]
>
> To help you answer this question, you might consider:
>
> - how the poet describes the harmonium and its history
> - how the poet describes his father
> - how the poet conveys his feelings.

Most unseen questions provide some brief **context** – or additional information – which explains the central idea of the poem. *Don't forget to read this!*

Unseen poetry questions provide bullet points after the question that help you focus your response. Treat these bullet points more as instructions rather than suggestions.

Again, the first thing you need to do is read the question carefully, highlighting or underlining key words, so you know specifically what to look for in the poem.

1 **a)** Highlight or underline all the key words in the question – *including* the context and the bullet points.

b) Annotate the question with definitions or ideas that help you understand what you need to do. Perhaps rewrite the question in your own words if you think that would be helpful.

Gather your ideas and evidence

Again, *after* you have:

1) read the question,

2) highlighted or underlined key words in the question, and

3) made any appropriate notes,

then you should read the poem.

And for the unseen poem, the routine of reading it, rereading it and then reading it again, is vital to ensure you have a solid grasp of the poem's content.

Harmonium

The **Farrand Chapelette** was gathering dust
in the shadowy porch of Marsden Church.
And was due to be bundled off to the skip.
Or was mine, for a song, if I wanted it.

Sunlight, through stained glass, which day to day
could **beatify** saints and raise the dead,
had aged the harmonium's softwood case
and yellowed the fingernails of its keys.
And one of its notes had lost its tongue,
and holes were worn in both the treadles
where the organist's feet, in grey, woollen socks
and leather-soled shoes, had pedalled and pedalled.

But its hummed harmonics still struck a chord:
for a hundred years that organ had stood
by the choristers' stalls, where father and son,
each in their time, had opened their throats
and gilded finches – like high notes – had streamed out.

Through his own blue cloud of tobacco smog,
with smoker's fingers and dottled thumbs,
he comes to help me cart it away.
And we carry it flat, laid on its back.
And he, being him, can't help but say
that the next box I'll shoulder through this nave
will bear the freight of his own dead weight.
And I, being me, then mouth in reply
some shallow or sorry phrase or word
too starved of breath to make itself heard.

Simon Armitage

Glossary

Farrand Chapelette: the brand of the organ

beatify: in the Roman Catholic church, a step towards turning someone who is already deceased into a saint; or, to make someone extremely happy

2 Read the poem and make some notes. In the first reading, you want to get a good sense of the poem's basics:

- What's happening? What is the poem 'about'?
- Who's speaking? And from what perspective and with what 'voice'?
- Where is it set? When is it set? Is it in the past or present tense?
- How is the poem organised? How many stanzas are there? To what extent may this be relevant to what the poem is about?
- Does it have a rhyme scheme and a particular rhythm?
- Is the poem written in a particular form – a sonnet perhaps?
- How might any or all of these questions help you understand the question focus?

Read the poem again. Your second reading should look to get into more detail.

3 Work through the poem closely, annotating any observations you make about the focus of the question. In this case, you need to look at:

- the *relationship* between *father* and *son*
- *how* it is *portrayed* through:
    - how the poet describes the harmonium and its history
    - how the poet describes his father
    - how the poet conveys his feelings.

When you consider *how* the relationship is portrayed, you should show how the poet's techniques (language, imagery, form, viewpoint, rhyme, and so on) create this relationship.

Read the poem again. Your third reading should be a chance to 'step back' and understand the poem as a whole.

4 **a)** How do all these poet's techniques work together to create this poem and link to the question asked?

b) Is there anything new that has sharpened or come more into focus because you've 'stepped back' from it? What is it and how does it help you address the question?

Plan your response

In your response for an unseen poem, make sure that it focuses on the question, and uses the bullet points to guide your organisation of the response. In many ways, however, it can be similar to that of a seen poem.

Generally, you can include:

- an *introductory* paragraph that provides an overview of the poem and the question focus
- three or so *main body* paragraphs where you develop your analysis, focused on the bullet points from the question. Each bullet point could be the focus of a paragraph
- a *conclusion* to draw together your ideas and your own opinions of the poem. Again, make the conclusion purposeful rather than a brief summary.

Once more, being able to trace the focus of the question through the text – noting how it is introduced in the beginning of the poem, how it develops in the middle and then how it develops further or changes by the end of the poem – is key to a strong, solid response.

You want to demonstrate that, in the short amount of time you have had with the poem, you have a healthy understanding of it and can aptly apply your analytical skills.

5 Use the table below to organise your own thoughts about 'Harmonium'.

Bullet point from the question	Observation	Poet's techniques	What this shows about the father/son relationship
how the poet describes the harmonium and its history			
how the poet describes his father			
how the poet conveys his feelings			

Write your response

You should now have a plan for your response.

6 Using this framework, write your response to 'Harmonium'.

Checklist for success

Make sure you include:

- ✔ clear points linked to the question
- ✔ a range of quotations from throughout the poem
- ✔ reference to a range of poetic techniques
- ✔ explanation of how the poetic techniques create meaning and link to the question.

Evaluating your response to an unseen poem

How can I assess and improve my own work?

Your task

Before you make an evaluation of how well you have done, check the table on page 181. It will help you decide if your work falls broadly into the first or second category – or outside them.

1. Reread the practice question on 'Harmonium' by Simon Armitage. Go through your own response and, if possible, write your own brief annotations around it.

How does the poet's writing powerfully show the relationship between father and son? [25]

To help you answer this question, you might consider:

- how the poet describes the harmonium and its history
- how the poet describes his father
- how the poet conveys his feelings.

Evaluating your work

2. Now read the following, thinking about what the writer of the response has done well and what advice they might need in order to make more progress.

The poet shows the relationship between the father and son to be centred around the harmonium, which is a church organ. The poet writes how 'for a hundred years that organ has stood / by the chorister's stalls, where father and son, / each in their time, had opened their throats'. This suggests the harmonium has been around for a long time and that it helped create a strong relationship between the father and his son. In this way, the organ represents something that kept them together. The son stops the harmonium being 'bundled off': the word 'bundled' suggests the harmonium is old and unimportant.

focus on language and its effect

The poet also describes the relationship between father and son by describing the father. He has 'smoker's fingers and dottled thumbs'. This suggests that he is old and that he smokes. Because smoking is dangerous to your health, this could also suggest that he is close to death. The father seems to realise this when he jokes that 'the next box I'll shoulder through this nave / will bear the freight of his own dead weight'. This means that the father says to his son the next time he's in the church carrying something it will be the father's coffin with his dead body inside of it. This shows the reader that the father is waiting for his death, but the fact that he jokes about it suggests he's not that bothered by it. — personal response

However, this affects the son (who is also the narrator) because he doesn't say anything or know what to say, which suggests that he is sad about the idea that his father may die soon. In this way, the poet creates a link between the organ and the father – both of which are old and falling apart. The poet uses personification saying the keys are like 'yellowed … fingernails' and this personification links the harmonium to his father. — focus on language and its effect

However, whereas the organ has previously brought fathers and sons together, this organ being taken out of the church creates a strained relationship between the narrator and his father because the narrator doesn't want his father to die. — understanding of ideas and some deeper implications

Comment:

This is a reasonably developed and relevant personal response. The writer of the response demonstrates points using supporting evidence well throughout the response, although they could have used more precise, and less lengthy, quotations to develop their arguments. More could have been done to explore the language in detail. The reference to the metaphoric link between the organ and father is well-considered, if underdeveloped. The focus on the difference in relationships the organ creates, however, in the third paragraph clearly recognises some of the deeper implications of the poem.

3. How could this sample response be improved? Using the table on page 181, think about what advice you might give the writer of the response to improve their work.

4. Now read a second response to the same question. As you read, think about what the writer has done that is an improvement on the first response.

In 'Harmonium', the poet reveals his feelings about his ageing father through his attitude towards an old church organ which was going to be thrown away. Armitage introduces his feelings about age, and how we can consider things useless if they are too old, through his description of the harmonium. The phrases 'gathering dust' and 'bundled off' suggest the organ is neglected and unvalued by its owners. The porch is 'shadowy', suggesting no-one pays it any attention in the dusty gloom. The poet contrasts the organ in the present with its history in the following stanzas. Now abandoned in darkness, it used to be touched by 'sunlight'. Although this 'sunlight' was a 'day to day' occurrence, it has a miraculous quality: it seemed to 'beatify saints and raise the dead'. The fact that the organ used to be bathed in blessing and resurrecting light makes it sound holy. But despite this glory, the light has also 'aged' the harmonium. Armitage personifies its 'yellowed ... fingernails' and 'lost ... tongue' making us sympathise with the instrument as if it is a person, and value it more for its former glory and the suffering it has undergone, repeatedly 'pedalled' by the organist. The poet seems to want to save the harmonium and demonstrate someone cares for it after its hard life, just as later in the poem he wants to hold on to his relationship with his father.

deliberate focus on task and key writer's method

close analysis of language

confident exploration of contrast and patterns of language

well-selected references; developed, detailed analysis; confident grasp of meanings conveyed

sustained focus on task

Armitage portrays the harmonium's history as valuable to him, using musical imagery to convey the instrument's importance. The warm, alliterative sound of 'hummed harmonics' and the metaphor 'struck a chord' suggest his emotional attachment to it – and particularly to the memories it evokes of 'father and son' singing in church. The final image of this stanza suggests that, for the poet, the harmonium is a symbol of harmony, both musical and metaphorical, representing shared memories between his father and himself. Like the sunlight, it is given the power of performing miracles in the reversed simile 'gilded finches – like high notes', as if birds, not music, flew from their mouths when it was played. Father and son used to sing along to the organ with the beauty and freedom of golden birds, suggesting the harmonium has the power to transform their 'day to day' voices, and relationship, into something almost magical.

confident grasp of techniques; integrated references

perceptive understanding of deeper meanings

perceptive and evaluative response to language, focused on task and text

Armitage's description of his elderly father in the last stanza draws together his impressions of his father's physical ageing with his desire to salvage and value the harmonium. His father is described as being in 'his own blue cloud', echoing the dusty shadow the harmonium stands in, while his 'smoker's fingers,' which would be yellowed by nicotine, echo the personified harmonium's 'yellowed fingernails'. Even the adjective 'dottled', suggesting hands mottled with age, echoes the earlier sound of 'treadles' and 'pedalled'. These connections suggest the poet notices his father's ageing and compares it to the decaying organ, while the smoking hints at a possible future cause of his father's death. However, his father also draws this comparison, stating in a matter-of-fact way 'the next box' the poet will carry 'will bear the freight of his own dead weight'. The **internal rhyme** of 'freight' and 'weight' and the three stresses of 'own dead weight' create a sense of finality, which the father doesn't shrink from.

However, Armitage clearly feels less able to confront his father's inevitable death, failing to 'mouth in reply' anything that could 'make itself heard'. Ironically, here, it is the poet who is most like the frail organ which has 'lost its tongue', scared to face up to the reality of losing his father. The poem as a whole can be seen as a metaphor for Armitage's desire to hang on to his ageing father, their relationship and valuable memories together, just as he wants to salvage the decaying organ for the sake of the value he places on its past.

insightful explanation of method, focused on task

integrated range of references; confident analysis; sensitive understanding of implications

close analysis of language and rhythm; carefully selected references

sustained response; evaluates patterns of language, demonstrating perceptive understanding

insightful overview

Comment:

This response sustains a detailed personal and evaluative engagement with the task and the poem throughout. The writer demonstrates a confident, critical understanding of the poem and the techniques the poet uses, sustaining an analytical understanding and incorporating well-selected references. The response demonstrates an appreciation of deeper implications as it develops and offers an insightful sense of overview.

Key term

internal rhyme: rhyme within the lines of a poem

5 What advice might the writer of the response need to make even more progress? Use the table on page 181 to guide your ideas.

Applying your skills to unseen poetry

How do I apply the skills I have learned to an unseen poem?

You are now going to apply your learning to a new poem.

Remember to:

- highlight the key terms of the question
- spend about 20 minutes reading and annotating the poem
- plan your response
- write your essay.

Read carefully the following poem. The speaker takes comfort from the natural world surrounding her.

How does the poet vividly portray the natural world? [25]

To help you answer this question, you might consider:

- how she portrays different aspects of the natural world
- how she portrays the different seasons
- the ways in which the writer presents the effects of nature on the speaker's feelings.

Solace

My window opens out into the trees
And in that small space
Of branches and of sky
I see the seasons pass
Behold the tender green
Give way to darker heavier leaves.
The glory of the autumn comes
When steeped in mellow sunlight
The fragile, golden leaves
Against a clear blue sky
Linger in the magic of the afternoon
And then reluctantly break off
And filter down to pave
A street with gold.

Glossary

solace: comfort, consolation

Then bare, gray branches
Lift themselves against the
Cold December sky
Sometimes weaving a web
Across the rose and dusk of late sunset
Sometimes against a frail new moon
And one bright star riding
A sky of that dark, living blue
Which comes before the heaviness
Of night descends, or the stars
Have powdered the heavens.
Winds beat against these trees;
The cold, but gentle rain of spring
Touches them lightly
The summer torrents strive
To lash them into a fury
And seek to break them—
But they stand.
My life is fevered
And a restlessness at times
An agony—again a vague
And baffling discontent
Possesses me.
I am thankful for my bit of sky
And trees, and for the shifting
Pageant of the seasons.
Such beauty lays upon the heart
A quiet.
Such eternal change and permanence
Take meaning from all turmoil
And leave serenity
Which knows no pain.

Clarissa Scott Delany

Checklist for success

The completed essay should:

- ✔ clearly focus on the question throughout
- ✔ progress through clear paragraphs
- ✔ support points with close reference and quotations
- ✔ explain how the writer's choices of language/form/structure affect how you understand the text
- ✔ explore the passage in depth.

Check your progress:

What are the features of a *reasonably developed, relevant personal* response?

Knowledge	• You show how you know the text **well** by making reference to it and/or by quoting from it. • You make points that are relevant (close textual reference and/or quotation) to the task set.
Understanding	• You show a **sound** understanding of the text, reading beyond the surface to explore implicit meanings. • You **develop your ideas** on themes, characterisation or ideas.
Language and effects	• You write about **some** of the ways in which the writer uses **language, structure and form**. • You make **some exploration** of the **effects of the writer's choices** and how these effects are created.
Personal response	• You make your own honest and **considered** response to the text, appropriate to the task. • You show **some development of your own ideas** about the text and task.

What are the features of a response showing *sustained personal and evaluative engagement* with task and text?

Knowledge	• You show a **detailed** grasp of the text as a whole and a **deep** understanding of the task. • You support your ideas with **relevant, well-selected, well-integrated reference to the text**, skilfully and with **flair**.
Understanding	• You support your **original** ideas with **carefully selected, well-integrated reference** to the text. • You show your ability to **analyse, evaluate and interpret** the text in an **original** and **perceptive** way.
Language and effects	• You examine in **depth** the way the writer uses **language, structure and form** and you explore different **interpretations**. • You show the ability to make a **close analysis** of extracts from the text and (where appropriate to the question) respond to the writer's effects in the text as a whole.
Personal response	• You make a **convincing** response, showing deep interest, understanding and an involvement with both text and task. • You have your own individual **ideas and judgements** about the text and express them with **confidence and enthusiasm**.

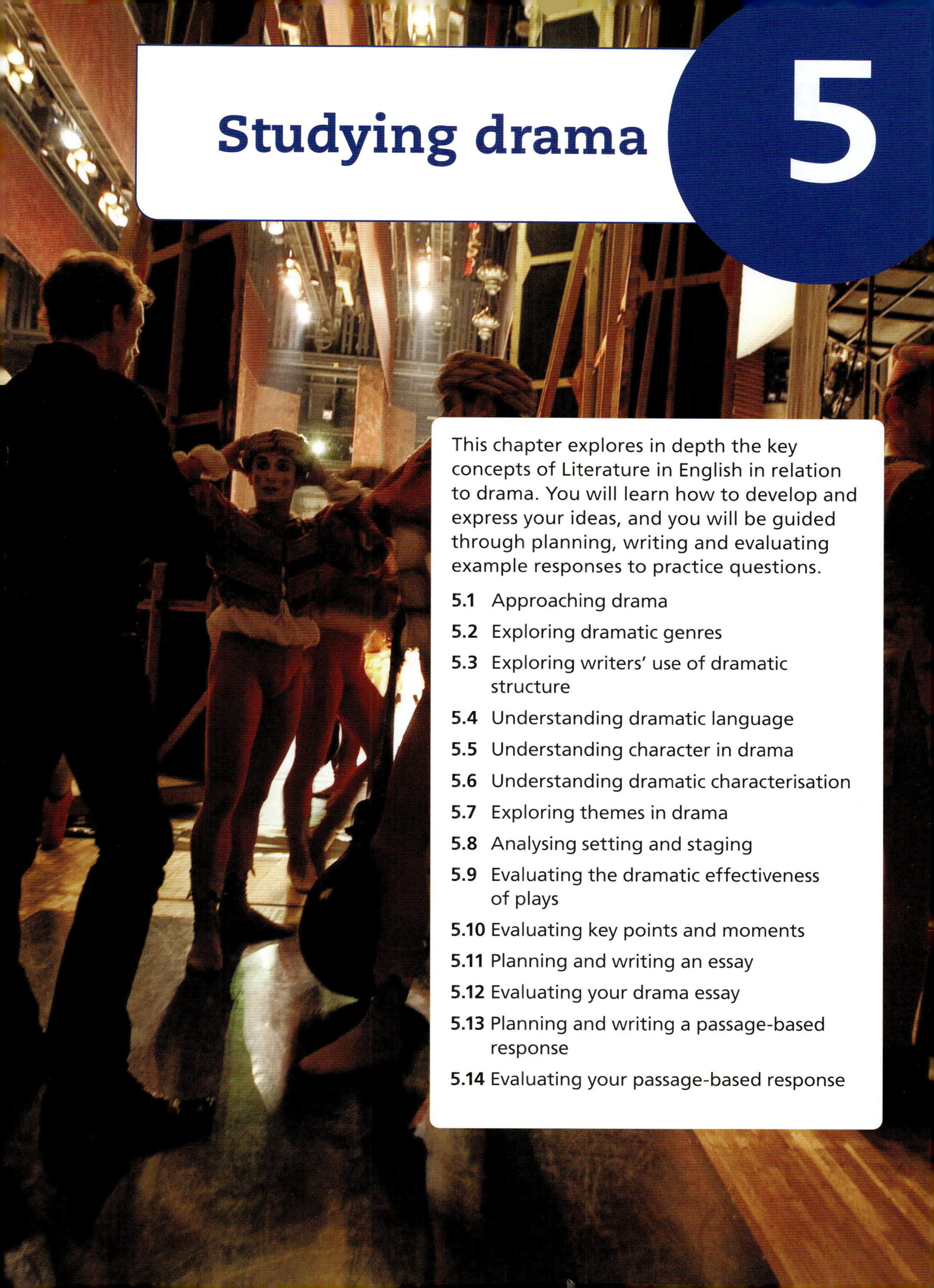

Studying drama

5

This chapter explores in depth the key concepts of Literature in English in relation to drama. You will learn how to develop and express your ideas, and you will be guided through planning, writing and evaluating example responses to practice questions.

Approaching drama

What do I need to know about the drama element of my course?

Start thinking

1 **a)** Have you seen a live drama performance – at school, perhaps, or in a theatre?'

b) What do you remember about it? Can you recall the plot or the main characters? What was the staging like – if it had any?

Explore the skills

Play scripts – plays written down – are very different from the other types of text you will study. It is important that you do not forget that plays are meant for performance so, as you study them, you need to imagine how they might look and sound on stage.

You will need to focus on:

- how characters, relationships and ideas are portrayed
- how writers create dramatic impact, tension, humour, shock or surprise.

This can be done through analysing:

- speech: what characters say, and how others react to them
- movements and gestures
- entrances and exits (how and when they arrive and leave the stage)
- the writer's stage directions (information about speech, movement, appearance and staging).

2 Which of the features above are used in this simple opening line from Shakespeare's play *Troilus and Cressida*? What does the information provided tell us?

> ***Scene VI: The battlefield***
>
> ENTER Ajax.
>
> AJAX: Troilus, thou coward Troilus, show thy head!
>
> William Shakespeare, from *Troilus and Cressida*

Key terms

staging: the **set**, **props**, lighting and design that create the space in which the play takes place

set: the objects – such as walls or furniture – that create the background for a play

props: objects that are used by actors (for example, a cup or a letter)

Develop the skills

You will need to use different sorts of skills during your course and assessment. For example, you may be asked to respond to two types of question.

Extract-based questions

You will need to learn how to focus on the way a specific moment or scene creates an impact on the audience in relation to key themes or characters.

For example, in relation to a practice question on a given passage from *Othello:*

> How does Shakespeare **make you feel sympathy for Othello** at **this moment** in the play? Support with details from the text. [25]

Questions about the whole play

Practice questions on the play as a whole or the writer's methods across the play may be more discursive – inviting you to explore ways in which a writer achieves an effect. Or you may be asked to explore the writer's presentation of a character or an idea across the play as a whole.

> In what ways does Shakespeare's portrayal of Lear add to the dramatic impact of the play? Support with details from the text. [25]

OR

> Explore the ways in which Shakespeare make Portia a strong and determined character? Support with details from the text. [25]

3 Which of these questions (possibly both?) about the whole play require you to focus on:

a) How Shakespeare's methods create a particular portrayal of a character

b) How Shakespeare's methods add to the play's impact on the audience

Apply the skills

4 Compare the opening 10–15 lines of any poem or novel you are studying with a play you have studied or are studying. What immediate differences in layout and presentation do you notice between them?

Check your progress:

- I can demonstrate knowledge of the basic requirements of the drama course.
- I can demonstrate clear critical understanding of how analysing a drama script differs from a poem or prose text.

Exploring dramatic genres

What is 'genre' and why is it important when studying plays?

Start thinking

Imagine this beginning to a story...

> Two lovers agree to meet in secret in the woods. The girl sends the boy a note arranging the time and place. However, another boy intercepts the message...

1. Discuss with a partner. Can you think of at least three different ways the story could develop?

   Think of one sad way, one funny way and one romantic way.

Explore the skills

How plays develop and end often gives us a clue to their **genre**. For example, in the story above, imagine if the first boy ended up seeing the girl and the second boy together. It is dark and he believes they are kissing. Jealous and angry, he confronts the girl and before she can explain, he does something terrible...

> Key terms
>
> **genre:** category or type of story
>
> **conventions:** standard features of a particular type of story or play
>
> **protagonist:** the leading character in a drama

Tragedy

You could call such a story a tragedy. In fact, it has many of the **conventions** of dramatic tragedy.

Main character	Often, but not always an important or noble person. He or she has a *key weakness* or *flaw* – in this case, it could be that he gets jealous too quickly, or that he is quick-tempered (or both).
Plot	The plot may contain *chance events* or *misunderstandings* that contribute to the tragedy – the first boy getting to the woods after it is dark, which means he can't see things properly. Sometimes a single, fatal error sets the **protagonist** on a path to their downfall.
Ending	In traditional tragedies, there is often a climax when the protagonist realises what they have done. Often this leads to the death of the protagonist and sometimes of others, too.

2 Can you think of any stories or plays you know that have aspects of the tragic genre?

The idea of tragedy was developed in the time of the Ancient Greeks, and can be seen in many plays, both modern and old. Shakespeare adapted Greek ideas, for example. It is not difficult to spot the conventions of tragedy in plays such as *Romeo and Juliet*, *Othello* and *King Lear.*

Comedy

As you saw from the example at the start, funny and sad plays might both begin in the same way. But the way a comedy develops and ends is often quite different.

Main character	The main character may have a weakness or flaw, but this weakness endears the character to the audience. He or she is more likely to look ridiculous or silly than sad or dangerous.
Plot	The plot may also contain misunderstandings or things that go wrong, but these are designed to make the situation silly, and the audience laugh at the characters' errors. For example, in the dark the two boys bump into each other, thinking they have met the girl…
Endings	In comedies things are sorted out, secrets uncovered and order is (usually) restored. In many traditional comedies, lovers marry.

3 Here is part of the plot of Shakespeare's play *A Midsummer Night's Dream*. What elements of both comedy *and* tragedy can be seen?

A nobleman, Egeus, is furious that his daughter Hermia refuses to marry the man he has chosen, Demetrius. Hermia says she loves someone else, Lysander. Egeus asks the King of Athens to make her follow his orders, and says if she doesn't she should die.

The king makes a judgement: if she won't marry Demetrius, she must either die or become a nun. She chooses the latter.

However, later she arranges to meet with Lysander in a local forest and they will run away. Hermia's best friend, Helena, meanwhile loves Demetrius though he says he hates her. She finds out that Hermia and Lysander are about to run away together and tells Demetrius who follows them to the forest, with Helena not far behind.

The fairies of the forest, hoping to put things right, decide to sprinkle a love potion on Demetrius's eyes so that he will love Helena, not Hermia. Unfortunately, they get the wrong man…

4 How do you think the play might end? Is it more likely to be a tragic or a happy ending? Remember to explain reasons for your views.

Develop the skills

Genres are generally very wide and – as you have seen – the divisions between them can become blurred. Often the core aspects of comedy or tragedy can still be identified in plays from whatever era, but over time other types of drama have emerged.

In the Jacobean era (under the reign of King James I of England) *revenge dramas* were popular. Plays such as *The Duchess of Malfi* by John Webster and *Titus Andronicus* and *Hamlet* by Shakespeare featured characters who are so angered by something that has happened that they commit violent, terrible acts.

Historical plays might also feature some of the elements of tragedy and comedy but, because their focus is on particular 'real' characters and political events, which are themselves of interest, they can be seen as a genre in their own right. Shakespeare's *Henry V* and Robert Bolt's *A Man for all Seasons* (about Sir Thomas More from Henry VIII's reign) or *The Madness of George III* by Alan Bennett, are good examples of this. These plays often explore what it is to be a monarch or politician and the opposition a ruler may face.

Much modern drama, especially just before and after the Second World War, began to present characters, events and ideas in a much less traditional way. Plots had no clear beginning, middle and end – and sometimes no real 'story' at all. Characters behaved in ridiculous or unpredictable ways, and weren't consistent. A movement called the 'Theatre of the Absurd' tried to reflect the fact that life was difficult to understand and often appeared meaningless.

Plays also began to reflect the everyday lives of ordinary people. The term 'kitchen-sink drama' gives an idea of where such plays were often set, and what their concerns were. The dialogue was much more like 'ordinary' conversation about money, relationships or work.

5 **a)** You are now going to read some short extracts from plays, then match them to their genres (or the ones they seem closest to). As you read each extract, consider its ingredients: does it share any conventions with the genres you have read about?

b) Write a brief sentence explaining *why* you think it most closely represents that category.

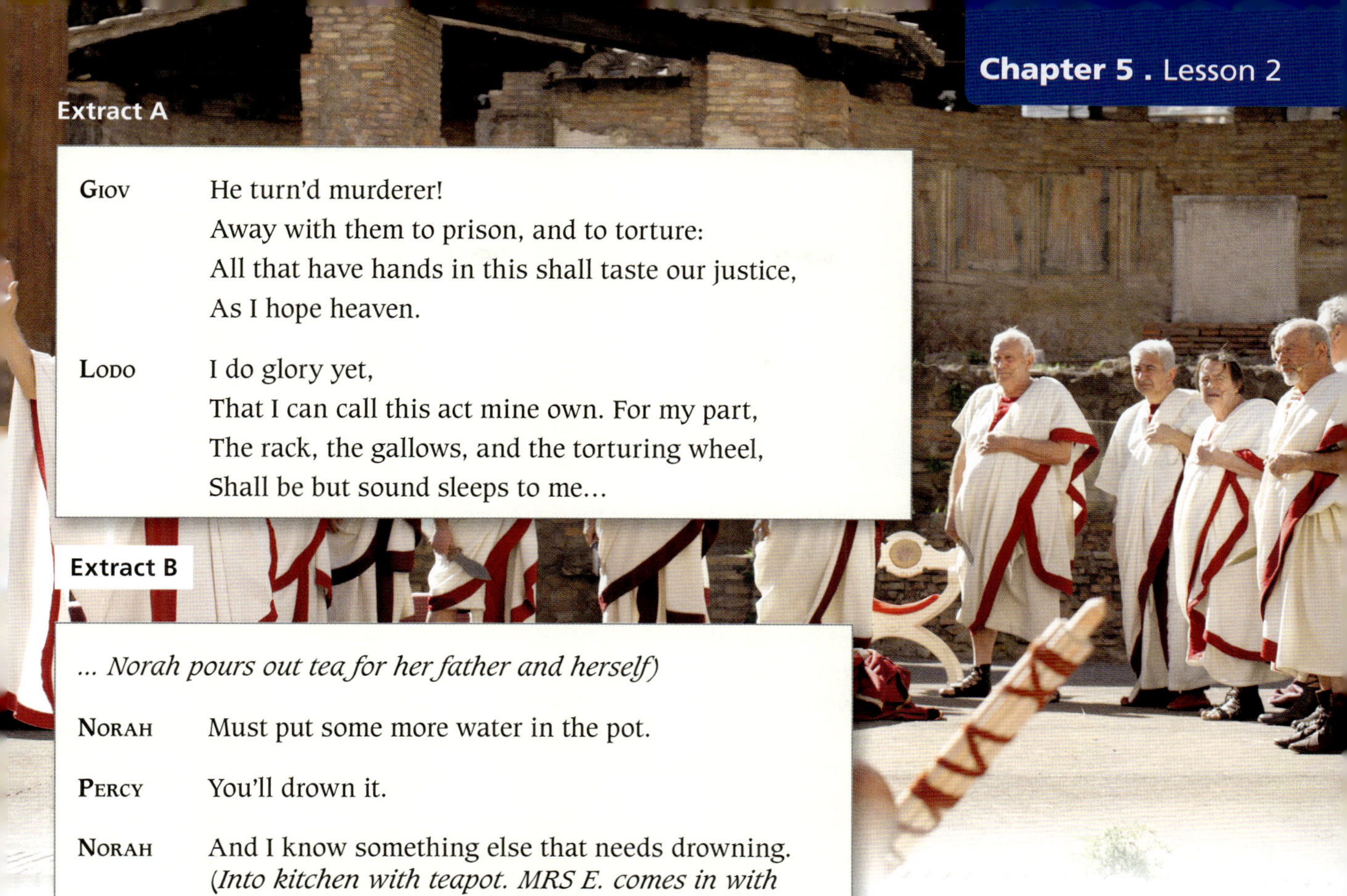

Extract A

Giov He turn'd murderer!
Away with them to prison, and to torture:
All that have hands in this shall taste our justice,
As I hope heaven.

Lodo I do glory yet,
That I can call this act mine own. For my part,
The rack, the gallows, and the torturing wheel,
Shall be but sound sleeps to me…

Extract B

… Norah pours out tea for her father and herself)

Norah Must put some more water in the pot.

Percy You'll drown it.

Norah And I know something else that needs drowning. (*Into kitchen with teapot. MRS E. comes in with plate of food, and sets it in front of PERCY.*)

Percy I said I didn't want anything.

Extract C

Decius Brutus
Caesar, all hail! Good morrow, worthy Caesar:
I come to fetch you to the senate-house.
Caesar
And you are come in very happy time,
To bear my greeting to the senators
And tell them that I will not come to-day:
Cannot, is false; and that I dare not, falser:
I will not come to-day: tell them so, Decius.

Apply the skills

6 What have you learned about 'genre' from this unit? Write a paragraph explaining what it means and how plays can be identified through their language or plot.

Check your progress:

- I can show understanding of the term 'genre' and use it correctly.
- I can demonstrate clear critical understanding of genre elements in plays and refer relevantly to how they are used.

Exploring writers' use of dramatic structure

How does the way a play is structured contribute to its effect?

Start thinking

Think for a moment about poems and novels, and how they are organised. Novels often have chapters; poems have lines and verses. But what about plays? How are they divided up – and for what reasons?

1 Look at this group of specialist words related to a play's structure. Note down what you think each refers to. Compare your explanations with a partner's.

act	entrance	exit	epilogue
scene	line	prologue	

Not all of these terms will be relevant to the play you study, but many will.

Explore the skills

Because plays were written to be performed in public spaces, people have always had strong views about what could be shown or how plays should look.

For example, the Greek writer and philosopher Aristotle established some core ideas about drama. Some later playwrights developed these into a set of rules, which they believed would make plays more truthful and realistic. They called these rules the 'unities'.

unity of **action**	plays should have **one single story** or **plot**
unity of **time**	they should take place over the course of **one full day**/night (24 hours)
unity of **place**	they should take place in **one location** or setting

2 What do you think of these rules?

Consider:

- the advantages: would the rules make plays more or less realistic?
- the disadvantages: what wouldn't be possible within these rules? How interesting would the plays be?

Like novels and stories, traditional plays followed a well-established structure. Here is the main plot of *A Midsummer Night's Dream*.

Stage	Explanation	Example
exposition	Main characters are introduced – a problem or difficulty emerges.	Hermia wants to marry a different man (Lysander) from the one her father, Egeus, has chosen (Demetrius).
rising action	The plot develops as the characters seek to resolve the situation.	Hermia and Lysander run away to the forest. An attempt by the fairies to resolve the situation with a magic potion goes wrong as Lysander now falls in love with Helena (Hermia's best friend).
climax	This is the moment of highest drama or tension.	The couples fight – the men possibly with the intention of killing each other; the best friends (the women) seeming to hate each other. Lysander tells Hermia he never loved her.
falling action	Tension drops as matters begin to be resolved or clarified.	The fairies reverse the magic, and each lover is matched to the 'right' person.
conclusion	Everything is sorted out or explained, for better or worse.	The two couples watch a humorous play together as part of a celebration of their forthcoming marriages.

3 Look at these lines from the play. Match each one to the relevant stage in the table.

a) **PUCK:** … upon thy eyes I throw / All the power this charm doth owe…

b) **THESEUS:** Here come the lovers, full of joy and mirth. / Joy gentle friends! joy and fresh days of love / Accompany your hearts!

c) **HERMIA:** I would my father looked but with my eyes.

d) **PUCK:** On the ground / Sleep sound; / I'll apply / To your eye, / Gentle lover, remedy.

e) **LYSANDER:** (*struggling with Hermia*): Hang off, thou cat, thou burr! vile thing, let loose, / Or I will shake thee from me like a serpent!

Develop the skills

The success of most plays depends on *conflict*. Conflict can be presented in a number of ways, and how that conflict develops over the course of the performance is often what engages an audience.

For example:

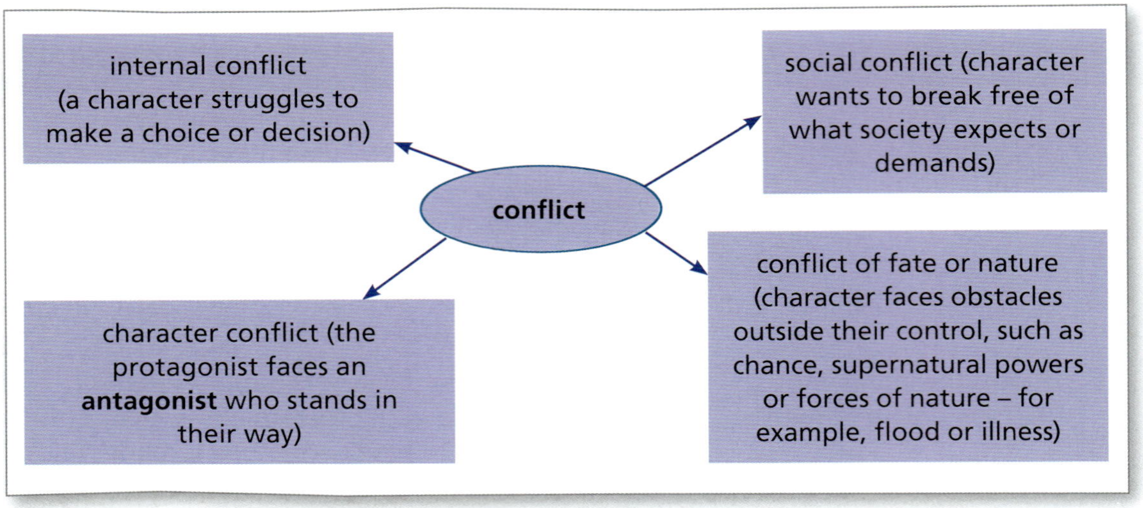

These types of conflict are often linked and combined. So, for example, a main character finds someone who opposes him or stands in his way. This might lead to inner and social conflict: What should I do? What is right? What will society think?

> **Key term**
>
> **antagonist:** a character who opposes the hero or heroine

In this dramatic version of the Cinderella story, the prince's mother (Princess Zehra) has invited people from around the kingdom to come to a party for Amir, the prince.

Princess Zehra opens envelopes. A large pile is already thickening next to her.

ZEHRA Everyone has accepted.

AMIR Since the miserable day we settled here, not one person has come to welcome us.

ZEHRA They're all coming now.

AMIR No one has invited us. This country knows nothing of hospitality.

ZEHRA There are two sides to hospitality, Amir: our hosts are not welcoming, so we must be generous guests. Every girl in the region is coming to dance and some will be beautiful.

AMIR No one is beautiful here […], they all look like boiled potatoes.

ZEHRA You must not speak like someone with a shrivelled heart.

Timberlake Wertenbaker, from *The Ash Girl*

4 a) What types of conflict can you identify from this conversation?

b) How is the conflict conveyed through what the characters say and do? For example, how does Amir describe the day they 'settled' in the country?

5 Look again at the structure grid: where in the play would you expect this scene to come?

Another structural technique to look for in plays is *contrast*. Dramatic impact is often created by:

- a change of tone or mood
- switching focus from one character to another
- moving to a new location or setting.

It would be very boring if *The Ash Girl* simply focused on Amir and his mother. How does the preceding scene from the play (below) contrast with the one you have just read? In this scene, Ruth and Judith, sisters of the ash girl, are planning to steal a key to their father's study.

Movement in the ashes. And now a figure emerges, grey, spectral, skeletally thin, a girl about seventeen.

JUDITH Ashgirl. Eyeing us.

RUTH Spying.

JUDITH Look and tell.

ASHGIRL I will tell Mother you're planning to steal the key.

They seize her arms.

RUTH You won't!

JUDITH She won't believe you.

ASHGIRL I always tell the truth.

6 Make notes on:

- who appears in the scene, and what happens
- the style of speech – and how it is different from the scene with Amir and Zehra.

7 What impact or effect does this contrast have? Think about:

- what it shows about how families treat each other (is one kinder than the other?)
- how the action is speeded up, or slowed down.

When you have finished, share your notes with a partner to get as full a picture as you can of the scene.

Apply the skills

8 Write about the conflict as shown in the scene above. Explain:

- what sort of conflict it is
- how it is shown.

Checklist for success

- ✔ Be specific about the extract you are talking about ('in this episode', 'in this dialogue between…').
- ✔ Consider its impact and where it might come in the action as a whole.
- ✔ Comment on the roles of the characters. (Is there a protagonist or antagonist? How can you tell?)

Check your progress:

- I can understand what structure is and can comment on aspects of its use.
- I can respond sensitively and in detail to how structural elements contribute to the impact of a play.

Understanding dramatic language

How does a playwright's use of dramatic language create an impact?

Start thinking

1. Look at the image on the right from a play. What do you think is happening? What is this character thinking?

Explore the skills

In plays, the only way you can tell what a character is thinking is by interpreting their movements and, more importantly, analysing what they say.

In this play extract, Anowa and her lover Kofi have run away from their village but are forced to sleep outside in a storm.

Please note that dramatists often use italics to highlight actions and ways of speaking.

KOFI You know what? Shivering like this, with all your clothes wet, you look like a chick in a puddle.

ANOWA And how about you? (*Beginning to rummage through her basket as though looking for something*)

KOFI Do you compare yourself to me? See how big I am. (*He bares his chest and spreads out his arms*)

ANOWA (*pretending to be shocked*) Ahhh! And this is why we should fear more of you. You are so tall and broad.

Ama Ata Aidoo from *Anowa*

2. What does the dialogue tell us about the lovers' relationship? Think about:
   - how Kofi talks about Anowa – the imagery he uses
   - how he talks about himself
   - how she responds to him – is she impressed?

Dramatic language is just as important as language used in poetry or novels. You will need to comment on:

- use of imagery, motifs and **symbols**
- simile and metaphor
- repetition and other patterns of language
- variety of lines or sentences.

Key terms

symbol: when an image or description represents a wider or more general idea, such as spring flowers representing new life

suspense: anxious or fearful expectation

Language can also be used in drama to heighten or release tension or to create **suspense**. One way in which playwrights do this is by using particular types of sentence in their dialogue, for example, in the way characters react to each other.

In this extract from a play version of *Treasure Island*, pirates are searching for a map, which reveals where treasure has been buried. Jim, a young boy, and his mother, who have the map, are hiding from them behind a curtain.

*The **Pirates** empty the chest onto the floor.*

BLACK DOG I don't see it!

DEATH It ain't' here no place!

HANDS Look at the linin'. It's been ripped open.
Somebody's took out the map already.

DEATH Who?

MERRY *Who?!*

BLACK DOG *Who?!*

DEATH *Who was it?*

BLIND PEW … That little pup. It's him. I'll rip his head off.
I'll pull his fingers from his hands! *I'll squeeze*
His neck until the pus runs out of his eyes!
Where is he?

*At which moment, out of fear, **Mother** makes a noise, shifting the curtains slightly.*

BLIND PEW What was that?

BLACK DOG What?

BLIND PEW I heard somethin'.

MERRY It was upstairs.

DEATH Right above us.

BLACK DOG Come on!

Ken Ludwig, adapted from *Treasure Island*

The extract starts with a very physical, visual action – the pirates emptying out the chest. But the suspense begins to build once they realise the map is missing.

3 Try acting out this scene as a group. Then, consider the following questions:

- What effect does the use of the repeated 'who' have at the start?
- How does Blind Pew's description of what he will do to Jim raise the tension even more?
- How does the noise affect the pirates' behaviour?
- How do the questions and short statements after they have heard the noise affect the mood?
- How easy was it to make the scene seem dramatic and full of suspense?

4 Write a paragraph explaining how the writer uses language to make the scene tense and dramatic. (You could also mention the writer's use of stage directions, which are relevant here.)

> Start: The short, sharp repeated question 'Who?' creates suspense through dramatic irony as the audience know that...
>
> Continue: When Blind Pew realises it is Jim who stole the map, his violent language makes the audience...

Develop the skills

On occasions, writers use **soliloquies** or **monologues** to explore a character's thoughts and **motivations**.

Later in *Anowa*, an unnamed 'Old Woman' expresses her views on Kofi and Anowa's new life, away from Yebi, where she came from.

OLD WOMAN (*closing her mouth in a heavy sigh*)
But, people of Yebi, rejoice,
For Kofi Ako has prospered
And he is your son.
Women of Nsona house,
They say Kofi Ako can stand
On his two feet to dress up fifty brides
And without moving a step
Dress up fifty more.
And where and when did this last happen
But in fables and the days of dim **antiquity**?
They say Kofi sits fat like a bullfrog in a swamp,
While *that* Anowa daily grows thin,
Her eyes popping out of her head like those of
A hungry toad in a parched grassland.
But she is the one
Who must not be allowed to step on any threshold here!
When was this infant born,
That would teach us all what to do?
Who is she to bring us new rules to live by?
It is good she said she was not coming back to Yebi.

Key terms

soliloquy: longer speech made by a character when they are on their own, which reveals their thoughts

monologue: any long speech made by a character

motivations: reasons for a character's behaviour

Glossary

antiquity: many years ago

The Old Woman uses similar imagery to compare how well Kofi and Anowa are doing.

5 What contrast does she draw between Kofi and Anowa?

6 What does this tell the audience about how things might have changed since we saw Kofi and Anowa in the storm?

Ama Ata Aidoo uses the monologue to give the audience an insight into the Old Woman's thoughts. She also seems to act as a sort of **chorus** commenting on events in general.

7 What overall impression do you get of the Old Woman from her speech?

Think of suitable adjectives you might use to describe her (kind? Thoughtful? Angry? Provocative? Cruel?)

8 What is the dramatic impact or effect of the questions she asks?

9 What is the effect of breaking up the Old Woman's speech into mostly short lines?

10 What rhythmic or rhetorical patterns can you identify in her speech?

Key term

chorus: from Greek theatre, a person or group that provides a critical commentary or explanation of the action

Apply the skills

11 Write up your ideas in about 75–100 words explaining how the writer uses language for dramatic impact and to reveal what the Old Woman thinks of Kofi and Anowa.

If there is time, swap your commentary with a partner and evaluate how well they have addressed the task, using the Checklist below.

Checklist for success

- ✔ Explain what impression you get of the Old Woman.
- ✔ Analyse the imagery she uses to describe Kofi and Anowa.
- ✔ Support what you say with well-chosen quotations from the speech.

Check your progress:

- ▲ I can make some response to the way writers use language, supporting my ideas with relevant evidence.
- ▲▲ I can respond sensitively and in detail to the way a writer achieves their effects through language.

Understanding character in drama

What do I need to know about different character types and roles and the impact they have on audiences?

Start thinking

Understanding the impact individual characters have on the action, themes and relationships within a play is key to your drama study. This understanding begins with exploring what 'character' means.

For example, look at the image on the right from Shakespeare's play *Othello*.

1 What do you know about this character? You might think about:

- his story (if you know it at all)
- what ideas or feelings you associate with him
- any well-known things he says (if you know the play).

Explore the skills

Writers create characters to make an impression on audiences. Characterisation starts in a simple way: with their names or roles listed at the front of the play.

For example:

> *Othello, the Moor, in the service of Venice*

But as the play progresses, this outline is gradually filled in so that a picture emerges.
This is achieved through:

What the character says and does	... and the impact this has on others in the play: for example, do they help/love/kill/betray someone?
How often the character appears on stage	... and in what circumstances are they appearing: for example, how often are they the 'main person' on stage? Why do they first enter the stage? How does their story end?
How the character is seen in relation to others	Are they more or less powerful? Do they come into conflict with anyone? Are they part of a family group?

2 Think about a character from a play you know or a play you are studying. Note down:

a) **one thing** the character does that is linked to the plot

b) **one event** that is going on when they first appear in the play

c) **one person** or **group** they are linked with.

Develop the skills

Such simple facts about a character may begin to tell you something about their influence on the plot or about their feelings. Or they might reveal something about a theme (for example, love or revenge).

The extent of a character's influence depends on their role in the play. Do they lead or follow events? Do events have a direct or indirect impact on them? How much of a major or minor character are they? Look at these two lists:

A major character:	A minor character:
• will be involved in the *main events* of the plot, either as someone who **instigates** them or who is profoundly affected by them • is likely to *explain* or *reveal* things about themselves, such as their *emotions*, *motives* or *worries* • is likely to have more to *say* or *do* than other characters • will be someone whose progress the audience follows closely across the play • may be a character with *authority*, *money* or *high status* (for example, a princess or the head of a family).	• may be involved in **sub-plots** • may be affected by the main plot, or contribute to it – but is unlikely to be the main person affected by it • may act as a *confidante*, *friend* or 'sidekick' to one of the main characters (either as a good or bad influence) • may reveal less of their feelings, or express them mainly in terms of how they affect the main character • may be a *poorer* character, of *lower or working class* status (such as a servant or clown).

3 a) In many cases, the division between major and minor can be quite slight. Who would you regard as the main character or characters in the play you are studying or in a play you know? Why?

b) Create a simple table for the play you chose.

Major characters		
Less important characters who have some influence on plot or themes		
Truly 'minor' characters		

Key terms

instigates: brings about or sets something in motion

sub-plots: stories that run in parallel to the main plot

It is also worth considering typical character *types*. Sometimes these are referred to as **stock characters**. For example, in many traditional or older plays you might encounter:

The tragic hero or heroine

A character, often but not always highly born (a king, princess or nobleman/woman), who has a key weakness that leads to their downfall or death (ambition, pride, vanity). They fight against their fate, but are unable to defeat it.

The passionate lover

Usually a young man or woman who falls deeply in love with one of the other main characters. Obstacles are put in their way throughout the play (his or her own pride, others' jealousy) and the play is about whether they overcome or are destroyed by them.

The best friend or 'confidante'

An adviser or guide to a main character who takes part in their adventures or troubles, and may themselves be affected by it. Sometimes their stories mirror those of the main character; at other times they stand apart.

The strict or anxious parent

A father or mother (or someone who acts in the place of a parent) who struggles with the actions and desires of their children. In comedies, they can be figures of fun; in tragedies, they may create division or conflict.

4 a) Do any of the characters from the play you know fit these 'types'? In what ways are they similar or different?

b) Are there other stock 'types' you can think of?

It can help to think of these categories, but most successful playwrights create *rounded characters* who do not always fit simply into one category. For example, in the play *Othello*, there are two main characters:

OTHELLO	*a noble soldier who loves his young wife deeply*
IAGO	*an **ensign** who serves Othello and tells him what is going on with other people*

5 Which of the above categories do they seem to fit into?

6 In the play, Othello murders his wife because he thinks she has been unfaithful. We learn that Iago has fed Othello lies about his wife because he hates him. How does this change your initial ideas about their character types?

Another important aspect when considering a character is **status**. This can take several forms.

- Social or political status: a king may have power and money through his position as ruler of a country; a father or mother may have power as the head of a family.
- Personal status: someone in a relationship may be weak or strong – for example, a man may love a woman who does not love him back.

Key term

stock characters: characters with very recognisable features or roles in stories (in fairy tales, these might be the evil stepmother or the handsome prince)

Glossary

ensign: flag bearer in the Army

Key term

status: level of power

Consider this short exchange in the play *Beauty and the Beast*, by Laurence Boswell. 'Beauty' is a humble village girl kept prisoner by the terrifying Beast.

BEAUTY	I spent the day exploring The Palace. It is like a dream.
	Beast, are you going to eat me?
BEAST	No! ... [...] ... Forever?
BEAUTY	Beast, your Palace is the most magical place I've ever known, but I can't stay here forever. I want to see my Father again and I miss my brothers and sisters.
NARRATOR 3	Beast recoiled in pain...
NARRATOR 4	It hurt him to know that Beauty was unhappy.
NARRATOR 6	Beauty changed the subject.
BEAUTY	Why do you speak so... simply, Beast?

BEAST makes a groaning sound. He is clearly embarrassed.

Laurence Boswell, from *Beauty and the Beast*

7 How is 'Beast' presented here? Make notes about:

- who should be in charge. Who actually has more power?
- how the writer characterises Beast as someone who is suffering (consider stage directions and Narrators' comments)
- how Beast's language contrasts with Beauty's.

Apply the skills

8 Now write two paragraphs explaining how Beast is presented in this scene.

- Paragraph 1: comment on the dialogue and the interplay between Beast and Beauty
- Paragraph 2: comment on other factors – stage directions, the Narrators, etc.

Check your progress:

- ▲ I can show understanding of how writers create different characters.
- ▲▲ I can demonstrate clear, critical understanding of how writers create a range of characters for different effects.

Understanding dramatic characterisation

How do playwrights create characters?

Start thinking

Characterisation is a term we use to describe the different methods through which a writer creates a character. In drama, playwrights create character through the following elements.

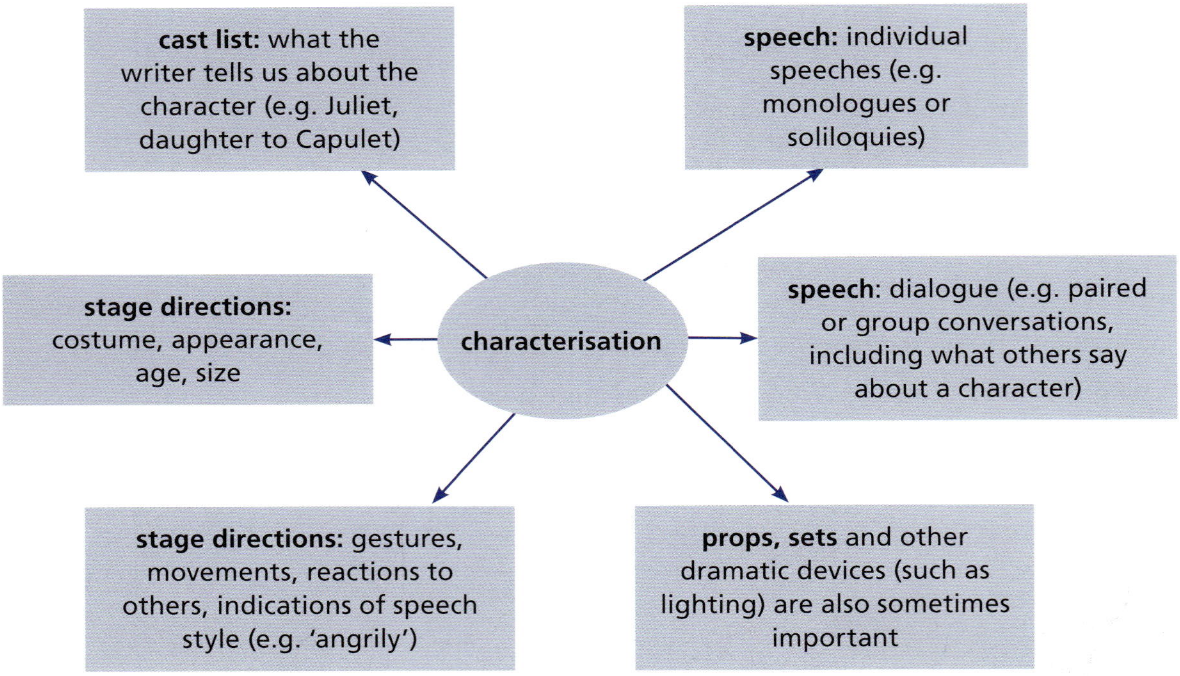

1 Select any character from a play you know or from a play you are studying. Look at their entry in the cast list, and at their first entrance or appearance in the play.

- What are you told about the character (if anything)?
- What could you analyse about the language they use at this point?
- How easy would it be to play that part based solely on this first appearance?

2 Create a grid with these headings for the main characters in the play you are studying. As you go along, or as you look back at your reading, you could fill in the relevant details.

Character names	Costume/ appearance	Notable gesture/ movement	Important individual speeches	Important dialogues with other characters	Inferences that can be drawn

Explore the skills

> **Key term**
>
> **infer:** work out from clues

Characterisation is made up of things we are told directly by the writer, and things we learn indirectly or have to **infer**.

For example, consider playwright Charlotte Jones's description of the character Mercy in her play *Humble Boy*.

Think about:

- what we are told about her appearance
- what we are told by the writer about her actions or behaviour.

> *Mercy Lott enters the garden. She is wearing black clothes with brown shoes. She is in her late fifties, a petite and timid, mousy woman. She watches Felix with concern. She approaches him, but doesn't get too close. Felix glances at her then returns his attention to the hive.*
>
> Charlotte Jones, from *Humble Boy*

3 Decide which of the highlighted sections provide:

- *direct* information about Mercy's character (look for adjectives)
- *indirect* information (look for things that suggest or support what we have been told directly, or hint at other things about Mercy).

4 On the basis of this evidence, what is the overriding impression you get of Mercy? Write a sentence summing up your thoughts.

> **Key term**
>
> **interact:** how people behave towards each other

The stage directions in *Humble Boy* are vital evidence in your understanding of Mercy's character. So far, they have been about her appearance and behaviour. But characterisation is also about how *others* **interact** with the character.

5 Reread the extract. How does the character Felix respond to Mercy?

6 Which of the following would be sensible inferences to draw from his behaviour? You could consider the idea of her status in the household.

a) Mercy is a cruel, unpleasant person who others avoid if they can.

b) Mercy is a respected friend who people can easily turn to for advice.

c) Mercy is well-meaning, but rather irrelevant and easily ignored.

Develop the skills

Speech and dialogue are central to characterisation. Dialogue is especially important when analysing relationships. In passage-based responses you will need to analyse such dialogue forensically, like a detective working through clues. Again, you should keep in mind what you are told directly and what has to be inferred.

7 Read this extract from the play *Ti-Jean and His Brothers* by Derek Walcott. You may wish to read it aloud or perform it with one or two other people. As you do so, consider your initial impressions of each character.

Ask yourself:

- How does each character behave? How does the other person respond?
- How do I feel about each character? What impact does the portrayal have on me? Is this how the playwright wanted me to feel – and, if so, how did he achieve it?

Daybreak. The hut. The MOTHER and her sons asleep. GROS JEAN rises, packs a bundle. His MOTHER stirs and watches. He opens the door.

MOTHER — You will leave me just so,
My eldest son?

GROS JEAN — Is best you didn't know.

MOTHER — Woman life is so. Watching and losing.

GROS JEAN — *Maman,* the time obliged to come I was to leave the house, go down the tall forest, come out on the high road, and find what is man work. Is big man I reach now, not no little boy again. Look this arm, but to split trees is nothing. I have an arm of iron, and have nothing I 'fraid.

MOTHER The arm which digs a grave
Is the strongest arm of all.
Your grandfather, your father,
Their muscles like brown rivers
Rolling over rocks.
Now they bury in small grass,
Just the jaws of the ant
Stronger than them now.

Derek Walcott, from *Ti-Jean and His Brothers*

8 Now, copy and complete this table about Gros Jean.

Character: Gros Jean		**What we can infer from this**
Actions	Tries to leave without the rest of the family waking ('He opens the door')	He doesn't want a scene with his mother because…
Speech	Explains why he didn't wake his mother ('Is best you didn't know')	Why is he saying it's for the best? For whom? Perhaps he feels guilty…
	Says 'Is big man I reach now'	He is saying that…
	'Look this arm, but to split trees is nothing…'	He seems to think that forest work is…

9 Based on the different elements – what he does and says – write a sentence or two about Gros Jean and how he is presented. Include at least one quotation from the extract and explain what it suggests.

10 Now complete a similar table for Gros Jean's mother. Think about what she is suggesting through lines such as:

- 'You will leave me just so, My eldest son?'
- 'Your grandfather, your father … now they bury in small grass … jaws of the ant stronger than them now.'

Apply the skills

11 How does Walcott make the relationship between son and mother memorable in this scene? Write 100–125 words.

Comment on:

- what we are told about the situation in the stage directions – and therefore the relationship
- what each character says and how the other person responds
- what you infer about the relationship from your evidence
- how the language choices the writer makes convey strong ideas about each character.

Check your progress:

- I can show understanding of some of the deeper implications in the ways writers use characterisation.
- I can demonstrate a clear, critical understanding of writers' use of characterisation, and respond sensitively to the effects created.

Exploring themes in drama

How can I recognise and write about themes in drama?

Start thinking

1 Think about work you have done on themes. Can you name any themes in books you have studied? How did you identify them?

Explore the skills

Dramatists can develop themes in different ways from poets and novelists. For example:

- Drama is a medium of spoken language, so *what* people say, *how* they say it and *how others respond* will take on extra significance.
- Drama is a physical medium: in performance, how people move, gesture, enter or leave a scene can have a big impact on meaning.
- Drama can also communicate through stage design or scene setting: these can reveal themes or ideas.

In the play *Private Peaceful*, two brothers go off to war. But the play starts when they are much younger. Look at these two very short extracts from different points in the play:

Scene 2

TOMMO I don't want to go to school!

Tommo stamps his foot and stops – Charlie stops too.

CHARLIE Piggyback? *(Tommo hops up on Charlie's back trying hard not to weep or whimper)* First day's the worst, Tommo. It's not so bad. Honest.

Scene 40

No Man's Land. The muffled sound of machine gun fire. Tommo lies in the mud.

CHARLIE Hang on, Tommo. Hang on. We'll get you out. *(Tommo is dragged into the open air by Charlie and Pete).* Thought we'd lost you.

Michael Morpurgo, from *Private Peaceful*, adapted by Simon Reade

2 What can we learn about the theme(s) of the play from these extracts? For example:

- What does the spoken language tell us about the relationship between the two brothers in both scenes?
- How do the two brothers behave? (What does Charlie do in both scenes?)
- Where do the two scenes take place?

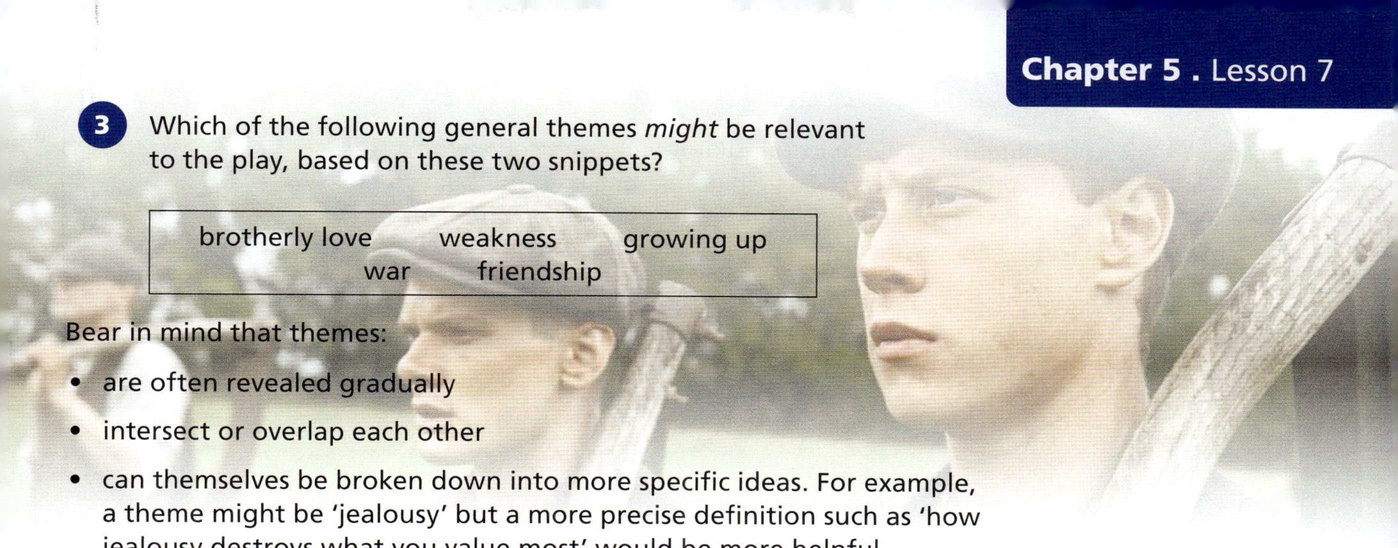

3 Which of the following general themes *might* be relevant to the play, based on these two snippets?

brotherly love	weakness	growing up
war	friendship	

Bear in mind that themes:

- are often revealed gradually
- intersect or overlap each other
- can themselves be broken down into more specific ideas. For example, a theme might be 'jealousy' but a more precise definition such as 'how jealousy destroys what you value most' would be more helpful.

4 Think again about the general themes listed above. Here are some more specific thematic ideas. Are any relevant to both extracts?

- How brotherly love survives life's challenges.
- How friends are there when you need them.
- How war ruins lives.

Develop the skills

Now read this further extract from the play and the annotations around it. The action takes place in France during the First World War. Brothers, Tommo and Charlie Peaceful, are stuck on the battlefield. Tommo is badly injured.

Glossary

magazine: a round of ammunition for a gun

TOMMO (*whispering to Charlie*): Charlie, I don't think I can make it. I don't think I can stand up.

CHARLIE It's all right. Don't you worry, we'll stay together, no matter what.

SERGEANT HANLEY Right. This is it. We're going out. Make sure you've got a full **magazine** and one up the spout. Everyone ready? On your feet. Let's go. (*nobody moves*) What in Hell's name is the matter with you lot? On your feet, damn you! On your feet!

Pause.

CHARLIE I think they're thinking what I'm thinking, Sergeant. You take us out there now and the German machine guns'll just mow us down. They've seen us go in here, and they'll be waiting for us to come out. They're not stupid. Maybe we should stay here and go back after dark. No point in going out there and getting ourselves killed for nothing, is there, Sergeant?

SERGEANT Are you disobeying my order, Peaceful?

CHARLIE No, I'm just letting you know what I think.

sergeant's angry question shows he expects to be obeyed

question emphasises disagreement between the two men

SERGEANT	And I'm telling you, Peaceful, that if you don't come with us when we go, it won't be field punishment again. It'll be a court martial for you. It'll be the firing squad. Do you hear me, Peaceful? Do you hear me? — threat – and repeated shouting
CHARLIE	Yes, Sergeant. I hear you. But the thing is, Sergeant, even if I wanted to, I can't go with you because I'd have to leave Tommo behind, and I can't do that. — Charlie's refusal

Michael Morpurgo, from *Private Peaceful,* adapted by Simon Reade

5 Each of the annotations above suggest that 'conflict' is a key theme of the play. But what *sort* of conflict is being explored in these particular lines? Is it:

- conflict between the British and the Germans
- the stupidity of war
- conflict between particular characters
- inner conflict (someone who is struggling to make a choice about what to do)?

6 Write a paragraph explaining what sort of conflict is shown, and use at least one of the highlighted annotations to support what you say.

7 Another key theme of the play, as you have seen, is 'brotherly love'. Can you find examples from the extract that indicate this? Complete the table below.

Evidence	What it tells us	What it might reveal about the theme
Tommo 'whispering to Charlie'	The fact he whispers shows Tommo only trusts his brother.	Brotherly love and trust are stronger than other ties of friendship.
Charlie: Don't you worry, we'll stay together, no matter what.	Charlie is prepared to...	
[add your own example]		
[add your own example]		

8 The writer has begun to turn their findings in the table into a paragraph about the theme. Complete it by adding your own point and evidence from the grid.

> *The theme of brotherly love is emphasised by Tommo's willingness to trust his brother rather than the other soldiers or the Sergeant. The stage direction tells the audience he is 'whispering', as if ashamed or frightened. Charlie's response is to tell him...*

Now read this speech from a play that explores a different sort of conflict. A character experiences inner conflict as he tries to decide what course of action to follow. In this scene, Hamlet has crept up on his uncle (the king) who is praying. Hamlet believes his uncle murdered his father (the old king). This is Hamlet's chance to get revenge.

The king kneels. Enter Hamlet

Now might I do it **pat**. Now he is a-praying.
And now I'll do't. And so he goes to heaven.
And so am I revenged.—That would be scanned.
A villain kills my father, and, for that,
I, his sole son, do this same villain send
To heaven.
Oh, this is hire and salary, not revenge.
He took my father grossly, full of bread,
With all his crimes broad blown, as flush as May.
And how his audit stands who knows save heaven?
But in our circumstance and course of thought
'Tis heavy with him. And am I then revenged
To take him in the purging of his soul
When he is fit and seasoned for his passage?
No.
Up, sword, and know thou **a more horrid hent**.

William Shakespeare, from *Hamlet*

9 What evidence is there in this speech of Hamlet's inner conflict? Think about:

- what happens – or what doesn't happen!
- why Hamlet cannot make up his mind to kill him
- what he says (for example, about taking revenge)
- his language (to weigh the pros and cons of murder; the use of the word 'now').

Glossary

pat: easily

Up, sword: Hamlet takes his sword away

a more horrid hent: a more violent grasp (wait for a more violent moment)

Apply the skills

10 How does Shakespeare powerfully convey Hamlet's inner conflict in this speech? Write two paragraphs.

Check your progress:

- I can demonstrate knowledge of themes through the use of supporting textual detail.
- I can respond sensitively and in detail to the ways in which writers convey themes.

Analysing setting and staging

How can a play's setting or staging help you understand its themes or impact?

Start thinking

1 Look at the following locations, which appear in some of Shakespeare's plays.

a) Can you match them to the characters most likely to be seen in them? Some might fit more than one.

b) Do you recognise the play and/or the character(s)?

Settings	Characters
a busy Italian market-place	a powerful magician
an exotic island	a moneylender
castle walls	soldiers on patrol
a forest at night-time in the summer	a nobleman about to be murdered
a dungeon in a royal prison	lovers meeting in secret

Explore the skills

Some plays (especially Shakespeare's) have very little detail about the location or setting, and provide few details about the set or design. Others provide lengthy instructions to the director. It is important to interpret what these details reveal – however little information you are given.

In Stephen Hoo's play 'Jamaica Boy' we see the same character, Ophelia, at different stages of her life. Read these two openings to the first two scenes. In the first, Christian, a **young offender**, is about to start **Community Service** for Ophelia.

Glossary

young offender: a young criminal

Community Service: a form of punishment in which the offender helps out in their local community

Scene One (Ophelia, round, in her 60s, Chris, half-Chinese, 20s)	Scene Two
PRESENT DAY LONDON/CROYDON – The back of a brick house. A back garden/allotment. A ton of mess. A shed. Ophelia is facing Christian, who has his hood up, almost totally covering his face. Ophelia is holding a file. OPHELIA: Late! CHRIS: It's ten! OPHELIA: Five past. CHRIS: (*kisses teeth*) Shut up. OPHELIA: Watch your mouth.	1960s JAMAICA – A cock crows. A Chinese dry goods store. A shop sign – LIM's DRY GOODS. A front entrance with some steps downwards. There is a small improvised makeshift area at the front, which is currently covered by blue tarpaulin. This forms a badly-attached annex. There are gas canisters, frying pans, baskets. Ophelia (aged 19) bursts out of the front of the store doors chased by Chong, who is shirtless. They kiss passionately...

Stephen Hoo, *Jamaica Boy*

2 What obvious differences can you identify in the *settings* for both scenes?

Think about:

- where they take place
- which is a domestic and which a commercial setting
- what props or objects are mentioned.

3 How is Ophelia presented differently in Scenes One and Two? Think about:

- what information the playwright gives us in the scene directions about her
- what she is saying/doing in each scene.

4 From these clues alone, you could say there has been a change in Ophelia. Write one or two sentences explaining how the setting and other stage directions/information convey this.

In the first scene, it is the 'present day' and the audience sees Ophelia standing........

However, at the start of the second scene, we are told she is........ and........

Develop the skills

Often, the mood and locations are conveyed through a character's words, rather than detailed staging.

For example, several days later, Ophelia and Christian are in her garden.

SCENE FIVE

PRESENT DAY LONDON – Traditional Chinese music blends into the sound of the inner city. Chris and Ophelia in Garden.

OPHELIA These are long lasting bulbs. Hyacinths, tulips, daffodils –
CHRIS You want them over there then?
OPHELIA They will look better here.
CHRIS Sun shines over there tho innit.
OPHELIA I suppose you're right. Maintaining a continuously flowering garden is a strategic operation. We want sixty to eighty days of colour from those bulbs.
Ophelia potters about
CHRIS Don't mess up that area please.
OPHELIA (*moving stuff*) Developing manners, I see.

5 How does this new scene change our impression of Ophelia and Christian? Think about:

- the detail about the music and sounds at the start
- what they say about the garden/flowers – and how they say it.

6 Which of these words would best describe the scene? Discuss each one with a partner and agree on at least two which match the new scene.

harsh	wild	harmonious	cosy
lively	uneasy	peaceful	

Waiting for Godot by Samuel Beckett is famous for being a play in which not very much happens. Two men are waiting for someone, and they remain in the same place throughout the play. The play is often said to be 'about' the meaning of life – what the point of it is, for example. The setting is very simple.

A country road. A tree.

Evening.

Estragon, sitting on a low mound, is trying to take off his boot. He pulls it with both hands, panting.

He gives up, exhausted, rests, tries again.
As before.
Enter Vladimir.

Estragon (*giving up again*): Nothing to be done.

Vladimir (*advancing with short, stiff strides, legs wide apart*) I'm beginning to come round to that opinion. All my life I've tried to put it from me, saying Vladimir, be reasonable, you haven't yet tried everything. And I resumed the struggle. (*He broods, musing on the struggle. Turning to Estragon.*) So there you are again.

Samuel Beckett, from *Waiting for Godot*

7 Why do you think Beckett chose to describe the opening to the play in this way?

Think about:

- what a tree brings to mind
- what the road might symbolise
- why he chose 'evening' rather than 'morning'.

Although it is not strictly related to the staging, an important stage direction is Estragon is struggling with his boot as the scene opens.

8 How does Vladimir misunderstand Estragon's comment about the boots?

Apply the skills

9 Write a paragraph about the way Beckett sets his opening scene.

Comment on:

- the particular details he provides
- the atmosphere or mood these create
- how these specific details might stand for or symbolise larger ideas.

Check your progress:

- I can demonstrate knowledge of how writers use setting and staging through the use of supporting textual detail.
- I can respond sensitively and in detail to the ways in which writers achieve effects through staging and structure.

Evaluating the dramatic effectiveness of plays

How do I write about plays and show I have engaged with them thoughtfully?

Start thinking

1 Talk for two to three minutes with a friend or partner about their favourite band or singer, using these questions as prompts.

- What do you think of his/her/their latest song?
- How was it different from or similar to their previous song – or other songs they have written?
- What makes the new song better – or not as good as the last one?

Explore the skills

In discussing the questions above, you expressed a personal opinion to begin with. This was probably straightforward – you liked or didn't like the music. However, in the second and third questions you were beginning to explore reasons – you were *evaluating* the songs. This skill is vital to your drama study.

When answering questions that require a personal response, make sure:

you **engage** with the text	This means you show interest in it, its themes, ideas and characters. The views should preferably be your own, rather than ones you repeat second-hand.
your response is an **informed** one	This means you demonstrate detailed knowledge of the play – you don't just assert things without evidence.
you consider **alternative interpretations**	This means you do not consider just one possibility but explore a range of ideas ('This might show... but it could also suggest...').
you understand that texts have **ambiguities**	You understand that not everything is crystal clear and that writers sometimes deliberately mislead or create characters whose motives are unclear or debatable.

2 Read the following extract from the play *A Slight Ache* by Harold Pinter. As you do so, think about your own response to:

- how effectively the writer creates a sense of what the characters are like
- the sort of mood or atmosphere created.

In the extract, a married couple have become aware of an old **match-seller** who stands at the end of their garden. Flora invites him into the house, and talks to him about the plants but he does not respond. He waits 'in the **hall**'.

Silence. She enters the study.

FLORA He's here.

EDWARD I know.

FLORA He's in the hall.

EDWARD I know he's here. I can smell him.

FLORA Smell him?

EDWARD I smelt him when he came under my window. Can't you smell the house now?

FLORA What are you going to do with him, Edward? You won't be rough with him in any way? He's very old. I'm not sure if he can hear, or even see. And he's wearing the oldest –

EDWARD I don't want to know what he's wearing.

FLORA But you'll see for yourself in a minute, if you speak to him.

EDWARD I shall.

[*slight pause*]

FLORA He's an old man. You won't… be rough with him?

EDWARD If he's so old, why doesn't he seek shelter... from the storm?

FLORA But there's no storm. It's summer, the longest day...

EDWARD There was a storm, last week. A summer storm. He stood without moving, while it raged about him.

Harold Pinter, from *A Slight Ache*

Now, read this practice question:

How does Pinter make you feel tension at this moment in the play?
Support your ideas with details from the text. [25]

Glossary

match-seller: (usually) a poor person who travelled around selling matches

hall: entrance space inside the front door, which leads off into different rooms

- 'To what extent' means 'how much' – so you need to make a judgement.
- '...make you...' means 'what does Pinter do' – so you need to look at techniques.
- 'tension' = 'anxious suspense' – so focus on this aspect.

3 What possible elements in the scene create tension? Begin by making notes on how Flora and Edward speak to each other.

- Do they agree/disagree?
- Do they speak lovingly or in some other way?
- Is there anything notable about the length of lines/ sentences?
- Does one character seem to have more status or control than the other?

Develop the skills

Read these two responses to the question.

A

Edward and Flora speak to each other in a stilted, cold way. However, Flora is warmer than Edward and is worried about what he might do to the old man. She says, 'You won't be rough with him?' which shows her caring side. Pinter presents Edward as blunt and unfriendly, for example when he says, 'I don't want to know what he's wearing.'

B

Pinter creates a real sense of tension from the first line through the short, blunt dialogue between Flora and Edward. To me, Flora is almost like a child, reporting back to Edward, 'He's here', but Edward seems to cut her off in an abrupt way – 'I know'. It is as if she is nervous in front of him, worried she'll anger him. However, Pinter could be suggesting he is anxious too – about a stranger coming into his house.

4 Which of these responses:

a) mentions what Pinter 'does'

b) refers to the key focus – 'tension'

c) provides evidence to support the points made

d) includes an alternative interpretation for one of the characters' behaviour?

5 Based on this assessment, which one of the two responses evaluates Pinter's skills more successfully? (Check against the features of an effective personal response on page 214.)

There are two further key skills that one of the responses demonstrates.

These are:

Skill	Example	Effect
probing, thoughtful language	The writer of the response uses words such as **'seems'**, **'almost'**, **'could be'**.	These words or phrases allow you to consider ideas as if you are thinking aloud, rather than committing to a fixed view.
interpretative comments	'**like** a child' '**as if** she is nervous… worried that…'	Using a comparison or an analogy helps the writer of the response explore what the character is like or develop a point.

Modal verbs such as 'could', 'might', 'may' are all useful if you want to think through possible interpretations.

> Key term
>
> **Modal verbs:** an auxiliary (or additional) verb that helps express levels of necessity or possibility

6 Write a further comment about Edward. You could comment on:

- how he speaks back to Flora
- what he says about the old man's smell.

As part of this, draw a comparison between Edward and something/one else, and use a verb or phrase to probe or explore an idea. Use these prompts:

> Edward is like a……………………………………………………in his behaviour towards Flora.
>
> It……………….as if………………………………………….

7 Now read the script again, and make notes about other aspects that could create tension.

For example:

- What is mysterious or strange about the match-seller (according to what we are told)?
- What do we learn about where the three characters are as this dialogue happens?
- What does Edward say about the weather the previous week?

Think carefully about each of these points and the idea of interpretation.

You need to ask yourself:

Why does Pinter reveal these *particular details* about the match-seller's movements and behaviour?

Why might Pinter have arranged his characters like this on stage? *What effect* does it create?

Why does Pinter decide that Edward will make a comment about the weather? Why might this particular type of weather be significant?

Do *all* these things create tension – or only some?

Remember – there is no set answer to this. You cannot see inside Pinter's mind, but you can try out ideas.

Apply the skills

8 Now, write a full response to the original practice question:

How does Pinter make you feel tension at this moment in the play?
Support your ideas with details from the text. [25]

Checklist for success

- ✔ Stick to the key focus of the task – Pinter's creation of tension.
- ✔ Comment on any aspects in the text that might show this.
- ✔ Support any comments you make with evidence from the text.
- ✔ Explore more than one possibility where it is appropriate.

Check your progress:

- ▲ I can make a reasonably developed and relevant personal response to a play and how it works.
- ▲▲ I can make a sustained, perceptive, convincing and relevant personal response to a play and how it works.

Evaluating key points and moments

How do I explain the effectiveness of a particular moment in a play?

Start thinking

In Lessons 5.3 and 5.9, you looked at the structure of plays, and in particular, how a new scene can reveal a character, set up a contrast or introduce new ideas. But what about the end of plays? What do you expect them to do?

Here, two students are talking about what makes the ending of William Shakespeare's *A Midsummer Night's Dream* memorable or satisfying. (The play ends with the two couples marrying each other and Oberon and Titania reconciled.)

I found the end very satisfying as it tied up all the loose ends. All the main characters are 'married off'. It was clever how Shakespeare presents this scene of married bliss.

No, I don't agree. I think it was satisfying in a different way: Demetrius really didn't want to marry Helena and it was only magic that made it happen. Shakespeare raises lots of questions about what is 'real love'. He left it *open to interpretation* so that we consider whether love is a sort of madness in which people can change affections on a whim.

1. What do you think the students mean from the phrases they use?
2. Is there a set formula that makes a play's ending 'satisfying' or 'memorable'? If so, what would be the criteria? Think about these ideas:
   - that characters surprise you with what they do or say
   - that characters are shown to be 'true' to how they have been portrayed through the play
   - that events surprise you
   - that secrets, questions or plot-lines are 'tied up' or resolved
   - that the end raises new questions or sheds further light on key themes or ideas.

Explore the skills

'Satisfying' or 'memorable' does not have to mean shocking. As an audience, we might want to see or experience:

- the *natural fulfilment of actions* taken by a character for good or bad. A character makes a decision at the start of the play – or seems to have particular views – and by the end the consequences of those views or actions come full circle. For example, in Marlowe's *Dr Faustus*, the title character makes a pact with the Devil in which he gains earthly power. At the end of the play he faces the reality of that pact – eternal damnation.
- *reconciliation or separation*: relationships that were in conflict are resolved or broken off forever. For example, in *The Crucible*, Proctor and his wife are hardly speaking; by the end of the play, the terrible events bring them together through mutual respect and love.

Endings can be memorable because they are *emotionally* satisfying. The Greeks referred to this as *catharsis*: the idea, particularly in tragedies, that audiences were taken on a rollercoaster ride of emotions as shown in the story – sadness, anger, fear, desire, despair... so that by the end of the play, they themselves were purged or cleansed of these powerful feelings.

3 What particular emotions do you think the play you are studying brings out? Can you identify any particularly powerful phrases, lines or speeches that represent or provoke these emotions?

Develop the skills

When you are exploring the dramatic effectiveness of the end of a play, there are therefore *three* stages you must go through:

Firstly, say *in what way* it is satisfying, memorable, significant or dramatic. → Secondly, explain *the effect* – which may be an emotional one. → Thirdly, explain *how it achieves this effect (or effects).* Is it simply the events that take place (someone dies, marries or leaves)? Is it the use of language or gesture? Or something else?

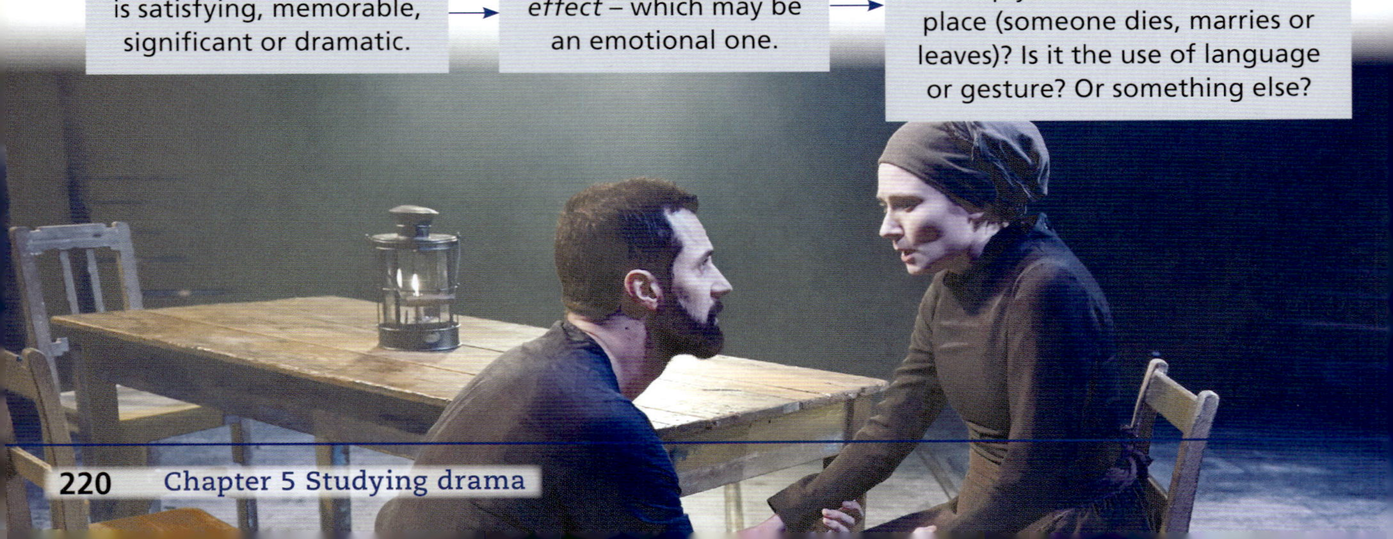

4 Read the following plot summary and extract from Shakespeare's play *King Lear*.

Think about:

- what we are shown happening – what is significant about it in the context of the play?
- the emotions this might inspire in the audience – what does it make us feel?
- how this is achieved through the language or events.

King Lear begins with the king, an old man, testing his daughters to say who loves him best – for which they will be rewarded. Two of the daughters flatter him; the third, Cordelia, who is truthful, does not. She is banished from the kingdom. The play then descends into civil war and Lear loses his throne to his evil daughters. He is finally reconciled with Cordelia, but at the end of the play she is murdered by Lear's enemies. He brings her body on to the stage, hoping she is still alive...

LEAR And my poor fool is hanged. No, no, no life?
Why should a dog, a horse, a rat have life,
And thou no breath at all? Thou'lt come no more,
Never, never, never, never, never.
Pray you, undo this button. Thank you, sir.
Do you see this? Look on her! Look. her lips!
Look there. Look there.
He dies.

EDGAR He faints. My lord, my lord!

KENT Break, heart; I prithee break.

William Shakespeare, from *King Lear*

5 In what way is this scene memorable or satisfying?

Write a paragraph explaining:

- how the scene brings the main character 'full circle' (you could consider how tragedies often begin with characters making a terrible error or feature protagonists who have a fatal flaw in their personality)
- how the emotional impact is created (you could consider Lear's actions, what he says to and about Cordelia, and the manner in which he says it).

Apply the skills

6 Consider the play you are studying. Make detailed notes on how the final scene – it can be the whole scene or the last 2–3 pages of it – could be described as 'satisfying' 'memorable' or 'significant'.

Use the grid below:

Feature	In what way	Key lines	Effect
resolves problems, mysteries or reveals secrets			(for example, satisfies our need for the truth to be shared)
character rewarded or reconciled			(for example, creates sense of joy/happiness?)
character punished/dies or learns hard lesson			(for example, creates emotional impact?)
embeds or further explores themes or key ideas (i.e. vanity is dangerous)			

7 When you have finished, write a response to this practice question:

> Explore the ways in which the author of the play you are studying makes the final scene (or the very last section of it) so memorable. Support with details from the text. [25]

Remember: 'memorable' is a term you can explain in different ways, according to how you think the author has created impact on the audience.

Checklist for success

- ✔ Consider the shape and action of the play as a whole and how it leads up to this point.
- ✔ Consider emotional, thematic and dramatic impact.

Check your progress:

- ▲ I can make a reasonably developed personal response to a play, commenting on how a writer creates key moments.
- ▲▲ I can make a sustained, perceptive, convincing and relevant personal response to a play and how a writer achieves key effects.

Planning and writing an essay

How should I respond to a discursive-style question on the whole of a play I have studied?

Understand the task

You may opt to write an extract-based or discursive response to your chosen drama set text.

The question may be worded in a number of ways, but it will always ask you to think about *the ways in which* a writer creates a *particular* effect; for example, the feelings the playwright makes you have about a character in the play or how a key idea or theme is developed. You will need to explore the writer's methods (their use of language, structure, form, genre or staging).

Read this practice question on William Shakespeare's *A Midsummer Night's Dream*.

> How does Shakespeare depict the idea that magic can be cruel in the play? Support with details from the text. [25]

Step 1

The first thing to do is to highlight the key elements in the question you need to address.

Key element in question	What you have to do
'magic can be cruel'	**Understand** and **interpret** this phrase: it means tricks and pretences can be nasty and spiteful
How does Shakespeare depict	You are being asked **to consider the methods Shakespeare uses to create this impact.**
'the play'	You must focus on the text **as a whole.** Do not simply focus on one scene or character.

1 Looking at the question on the previous page, which of these explanations best describe what you need to do?

A I must look at one particular relationship and see if it fits the key idea mentioned.

B I need to consider a key theme or idea and how relevant it is to the play as a whole.

C I have to say whether I like or dislike the play as a whole and why.

D I must look at a key scene from the play and analyse whether it involves this theme.

For the next stage, you will need to be familiar with the overall plot of *A Midsummer Night's Dream* and, as a minimum, have read Act 2 Scene 1, Act 3 Scene 2 and the start of Act 4 Scene 1.

2 Now, go through the same process with the play you are studying. 'Decode' each of the following questions in the same way.

a) Explore two moments in the play where the playwright vividly creates suspense for the audience.

b) What do you find particularly memorable about the writer's portrayal of *[add name of character]* in the play?

Gather your ideas and evidence

Step 2

You must now generate ideas and gather evidence in order to construct an effective response to the task, whatever viewpoint you have.

Remember:

- You are not being asked to re tell the events of the play.
- Focus on several key scenes or moments of the play in detail, making links that bring in your wider knowledge of the play and its context.
- You must closely explore how the *language and structure* of key parts of the play demonstrate that it is about how 'magic' can be 'cruel'.

Here are some scenes you could choose to explore:

- Egeus suggesting Lysander has 'bewitched' Hermia (1, i)
- Hermia having a terrible dream (2, ii)

- Puck using the magic potion on both Lysander and Demetrius who fall in love with Helena – she is convinced they are mocking her (3, ii)
- Hermia feeling betrayed by Helena; they argue bitterly as a result of the magic potion's effect on the men (3, ii)
- Lysander and Demetrius also arguing and fighting as a result of the effects of the potion (3, ii)
- Titania being disgusted by the knowledge she fell in love with a half-man, half-donkey (4, i)

3 Which other scenes in the play contain 'cruel magic'? Would any of these provide an alternative viewpoint – that magic brings joy and happiness?

4 You now need to add evidence to support your ideas. Here are three quotations from the play. Can you link them to the points above?

HELENA:	O spite! O hell! I see you all are bent To set against me for your merriment.

TITANIA (*to Oberon*):	How came these things to pass? O, how mine eyes do loathe his visage now!

HERMIA (*awaking*):	[....] Ay me, for pity! what a dream was here! Lysander, look how I do quake with fear. Methought a serpent eat my heart away...

5 Now find your own quotations from the play that show:

- Oberon's thoughts about punishing Titania
- Bottom looking ridiculous and frightening away his friends.

Plan your response

Step 3

Once you have chosen key scenes to explore in detail, you can organise your ideas into a balanced argument.

There are several ways to do this.

Method A

Focus on *parts of the play* that you believe show 'cruel magic'.

Consider how **one part** presents a magic that is harmful or spiteful. Build one or more **language/structure/form** analysis paragraphs around this point, making links to broader ideas.

↓

Then move on to the **next part** of the play that presents further examples of magic's damage. Build a further **language/structure/form** analysis paragraph around this point, making links to broader ideas. (For example, you might balance your point by considering how magic leads to a positive outcome.)

↓

Continue until you have covered several parts in detail, making sure you explore aspects of **language, structure and form** that demonstrate the theme in action.

Method B

Focus on *ways* that 'cruel magic' are presented.

Consider how the **structure** contributes to the theme across your chosen parts. Write an analysis paragraph including **several parts of the play** to make your point.

→

Next, consider how **language choices** contribute to the strength of 'cruel magic' as a key idea across the parts you chose. Write a number of analysis paragraphs exploring different techniques, including **several parts** to make your points.

You can also write your essay in another way of your own.

Whatever approach you take, you will need to develop an *overview* of the argument or discussion. In other words: you have a *general perspective* on the *whole play and the writer's treatment of the key idea from the question.* You are able to *maintain your focus* to develop this overall viewpoint throughout your essay.

6 The following is the beginning of a plan based on the different points in the play that show the ways magic creates cruel behaviour or leads to harmful or frightening thoughts. Copy the table and select three further examples from the list on pages 224–225 to add to the plan. Where there is contrasting evidence (that it is not 'hateful'), you could mention this too.

Paragraph 1	Introduction – explain what 'cruel magic' means and briefly mention some of the cruel things that happen.
Paragraph 2	Explain why Oberon's treatment of Titania is cruel.
Paragraph 3	
Paragraph 4	
Paragraph 5	
Paragraph 6	Conclusion – restate my overall view but don't list all my points again.

Write your response

Once you have your overall outline, you must bring together a response that:

- shows detailed knowledge of the plot, setting, characters and themes
- demonstrates deeper appreciation of themes, key ideas, contexts and the writer's intentions or motivation
- shows knowledge of the writer's methods – language choices, form, structure, staging
- engages with the play, and responds thoughtfully and personally to its ideas and characters.

Look at this sample paragraph, based on the second paragraph in the plan above.

> Shakespeare depicts the cruelty of magic at the heart of the play through Oberon's spiteful plan for revenge on his Queen, Titania, which has a domino-effect on the other characters. At the end of Act 2 Scene 1 he says, 'with the juice of this I'll streak her eyes, / And make her full of hateful fantasies'. However, it is not only her who suffers, but the lovers too. The adjective 'hateful' is interesting because it is not clear whether it means she will hate what she experiences or the fantasies will make her look bad. This reflects on a more general unpleasantness in the play when women seem punished for being independent – like Hermia with her father.

Starts with clear reference to the task wording and main issue and links back to it at the end

knowledge of and quotations from the text

close analysis of language that explores main idea

links to deeper understanding of character, themes and context

7. Write your own analytical paragraph, taking a further point from the plan. Use the quotation by Helena from page 225 when she believes Lysander and Demetrius are pretending to be in love with her.

8. Swap your paragraph with a partner. Using the Checklist below, assess how well they have completed the task.

Checklist for success

- ✔ Start with a topic sentence:

  Another time when magic creates cruelty is when…
- ✔ Add the relevant quotation.
- ✔ Analyse its effect.
- ✔ Add further comments if you can, linking it to other points in the play.

9. Now, write the whole essay in response to the practice question:

How does Shakespeare depict the idea that magic can be cruel in the play? Support with details from the text. [25]

Evaluating your drama essay

How should I evaluate my response?

Evaluate your response

Before you evaluate how well you have done, check the table on page 240. It will help you decide if your work falls broadly into the first or second category – or outside them.

1. Go through your own response and write annotations around it, like the example paragraph in the previous lesson.
2. Read the following response, thinking about what has been done well and what advice might need to be given to the writer to make more progress.

> My essay is about how magic can be cruel in the play and all the examples of this. The first example of this is when Hermia wakes up and finds out that Lysander has run off – 'Ay me for pity! What a dream was here!'. This is at the end of Act 2 Scene 2. When she says 'What a dream!' it means she had a nightmare, and she then goes on to say that a snake ate her heart. It is really cruel that the potion made Lysander abandon her in a cold, dark forest at night. I think that Hermia gets a rough deal because her father also treats her in a hateful way. It must seem like a bad dream that her father cannot accept the man she loves but fathers had control over their daughters so it is not that surprising.
>
> Another very cruel event that Shakespeare depicts is the way Helena is treated. She has not done anything wrong except to love Demetrius and he has been very nasty to her.

- reasonable response to the task, developing a personal view
- knowledge of text, but not expressed very fluently
- some comment on the writer's use of language, but missed opportunity to comment on the symbolism of the serpent
- developing response but expression still limited
- knowledge of context but doesn't really lead to much exploration of the theme

He told her earlier, 'I am sick when I do look on thee' (Act 2 Scene 1) so how is she supposed to feel when Demetrius and Lysander both tell her they adore her later? It might sound nice but actually she finds it very disturbing: 'Can you not hate me, as I know you do, But you must join in souls to mock me too?' She is saying they have teamed up to make fun of her.

I also think that Shakespeare shows how Oberon treats Titania in a very unpleasant way. Yes, they are not humans, but why does he punish her just because of a child she took as a servant? Titania is forced to kiss Bottom who has become an animal – 'And kiss thy fair large ears, my gentle joy' (Act 4 Scene 1). The fact she is kissing his 'large ears' makes her look ridiculous and even Oberon takes pity on her in the end.

So, Shakespeare shows lots of ways characters are damaged by magic but he eventually depicts them all happily married so perhaps the magic is not so cruel after all.

some knowledge of whole text linking two different parts

inference used to build argument

starting to explore deeper meanings about structure/ genre but undeveloped

Comment:

The response shows a reasonably developed understanding of the text and task, and includes a number of relevant quotations. There is some exploration of language and some links are made between different parts of the play. However, there needs to be more reference to the methods Shakespeare uses.

3 How could this sample response be improved? Using the table on page 240, think about what advice you might give the writer of the response to improve their work.

4 Now read a second response to the same question. Think about what has been done that is an improvement on the first response.

Although this appears to be a comedy, Shakespeare's introduction of a number of disturbing, even cruel episodes and ideas is really unpleasant. The 'hateful fantasies' which Oberon intends to bring to Titania's dreams in fact emerge much earlier, in Egeus's own treatment of his daughter. He believes Lysander has 'bewitched' Hermia with 'feigning voice' in Act 1 Scene 1. Not only does Shakespeare introduce ideas about pretence and disguise, it also suggests that Egeus is the one 'bewitched' – otherwise why would he demand the right to 'dispose of her' as he wishes, or for her to be killed, if she refuses? This patriarchal society is not surprisingly one that Hermia wishes to escape.

clear argument and focus on task

good range of references relevant to task

confident response making inference from text

fluent reference to context but linked to task

However, the forest in which she plans to meet Lysander becomes yet another place where Shakespeare creates a world of cruel magic. Her true love is himself 'bewitched' by the magic potion intended for Demetrius and Hermia is left alone in the wood, dreaming of a 'serpent' that eats at her heart. Shakespeare's reference to the symbolic serpent reminds the audience of the Garden of Eden in which Eve was tempted to eat the apple from the tree. It sounds as if Hermia, like Eve, is being punished for wanting something she should not have.

The spiteful magic that afflicts Hermia, is applied to Helena too. She has already suffered the indignity of knowing that Demetrius, who once loved her 'dissolved', when Hermia showed him some affection (Act 1 Scene 1). Shakespeare's use of the verb 'dissolved' suggests that Demetrius is a vacant, empty man who is inconstant and weak. But worse is to come. First he tells her he is 'sick' when he looks at her and will abandon her to the 'mercy of wild beasts' (Act 2 Scene 2). Then, he miraculously seems to fall in love with her. It is no surprise that she does not believe his adoring words, and it seems rather unbelievable that by the end of the play, they are presented as a happy couple – after all, it is only the magic that keeps them together: audiences may wonder how this relationship may develop (or not) after the play ends.

Yet it is difficult to argue that 'hateful' magic is the only force in the play. Shakespeare also depicts Bottom's dream as a wonderful one. His Garden of Eden is Titania's bower filled with 'purple grapes', 'green figs' and fans made from the wings of 'painted butterflies' (Act 3 Scene 1). This is surely paradise.

Nevertheless, Shakespeare shows that the lovers and Titania have to suffer quite severely through the damaging illusions to achieve the happiness and resolution we see at the end.

fluent link made to later part of text

confident contextual interpretation showing real engagement with task

integrated range of references; confident analysis

character overview with thoughtful response

thoughtful exploration of ambiguous relationship

confident expression of alternative ideas

clear summative final paragraph, which returns to the key focus

Comment:

This is a sustained personal response to the task and text, which demonstrates a confident critical understanding, with fluent use of references. The analysis is detailed and more profound issues are explored as appropriate.

5 What advice might this writer need to make even more progress? Use the table on page 240 to guide your ideas.

Planning and writing a passage-based response

How do I plan a response to a passage-based question on a play?

Understand the task

During your course, you may be asked to respond to a passage-based question.

The question may be worded in a number of ways, but will always ask you to think about *the ways* a writer creates or reveals a character's feelings or explores a key idea in the given extract. Therefore, you need to explore *the writer's methods*. For example, follow these steps:

Step 1

Read the given extract carefully.

1 Read this extract from *The Ash Girl*, a retelling of the Cinderella story, by Timberlake Wertenbaker.

Silence. A movement towards darkness.

Ashgirl remains alone.

A shadow falls suddenly across the walls. Sadness enters, moves and tests the room for a dominant place.

SADNESS The sudden hush of dusk is a good time.

Animals fall silent, ready for the night, and humans feel alone…

(*Whispers.*) Ashgirl…

Behind a curtain, sometimes in the corner, I am the shadow cast against the wall.

Ashgirl…

It's not even a sound, it's a ripple in the air, a chill in the light, a voice they hear and do not hear.

Ashgirl…

Ashgirl stops working for a moment.

Young girls are easiest, but I can seep into boys too, anyone… I'm the icicle in the heart, the one who makes the world so dark you wish you weren't in it. Sadness… Stretch out your hand to touch something: all you feel is an invisible layer of cold ash covering all.

Call for help: I'll muffle your voice. Dream of relief: I'll shrink your thoughts to dust. Don't even try to move…

Ashgirl…

Ashgirl I'll sew through the night and make these dresses memorable.

Sadness No one will thank you.

Ashgirl The dresses will dance at the ball.

Sadness But… never you… you stay alone.

Ashgirl droops for a moment.

Sadness I probe, I test, study the defences and slide through the crack. An unquieted doubt, a fear, the unguarded thought…

(*to Ashgirl*) No one cares what you do, no one cares for you…

Ashgirl My father was proud of my sewing, even more proud of my writing.

Sadness He abandoned you, no one's there for you. Ashgirl, listen…

Owl appears at the window.

Owl Ashgirl?

Ashgirl Owl!

Sadness I hate owls!

Owl Who were you talking to? I heard a voice I didn't like.

Ashgirl I may have been talking to myself.

Owl There's a disturbance in the air…

Sadness You listened to me, Ashgirl. I found the breach. I won't let you go now.

Sadness moves away.

Timberlake Wertenbaker, from *The Ash Girl*

2 Read the task and identify the key aspects the question wants you to focus on. For example, read this practice question on the extract above:

> How does Wertenbaker make this scene so moving and emotional? Support with details from the text. [25]

Look at the highlighting. For this question, the key focuses are:

a) the emotion this scene makes the audience feel

b) *how* the writer makes it like this through her use of language, structure and dramatic techniques in general.

Gather your ideas and evidence

Step 2

The next step is to plan what to include in your response.

Remember:

- You are not being asked to re-tell the story. Focus on several parts of the extract in detail, not forgetting the beginning and end.
- You must closely explore how the language and dramatic structure of key parts of the extract make the audience feel sad or emotional.

Here are some parts you could choose to explore:

A. the stage directions at the start of the scene

B. the things Sadness says and what they evoke

C. how Ashgirl acts and responds

3 What other elements of the scene could you also comment on? Which parts are the most interesting to explore?

Plan your response

Step 3

Once you have chosen key parts to explore in detail, you can organise your ideas into an argument. There are several ways to do this:

a) Focus on *parts of the extract* that convey a moving or emotional mood.

- Consider how *the start of the extract* conveys a downbeat mood. Build one or more *language/dramatic structure/form* analysis paragraphs around this point, making links to broader ideas.
- Then move on to the *next part* of the extract, that in which 'Sadness' speaks and explains her methods. Build a further *language/dramatic structure/form* analysis paragraph around this point, making links to broader ideas.
- Continue until you have covered several parts in detail *including the end*, making sure you explore aspects of *language, dramatic structure and form* that convey the sad and emotional tone of the scene.

b) Focus on *ways* that convey a moving or emotional mood:

- Consider how the *structure of the extract* introduces a sad tone, and builds sympathy for Ash Girl, and how this changes when Owl appears. Write an analysis paragraph including *several parts of the extract* to make your points.
- Next, consider how *imagery and figurative language* convey the sad tone across your chosen parts. Write an analysis paragraph including *several parts of the extract* to make your points.
- Next, consider how *other language choices or character dialogue* convey the emotive tone. Write an analysis paragraph including *several parts of the extract* to make your points.

You can also write your essay in another way of your own.

Step 4

Decide your approach now.

4 The final step is to plan your paragraphs, thinking about how to address the required skills.

Checklist for success

Paragraphs should:

- ✔ show a clear focus on the question (here, how the scene is made moving and emotional)
- ✔ give a clearly argued viewpoint
- ✔ support ideas with clear knowledge of the text and range of relevant quotations
- ✔ clearly explain how language/form/structure choices create sadness or an emotive mood; explore interpretations
- ✔ make links to deeper ideas about themes or setting/context where relevant.

5 Read the annotated paragraph:

The writer creates a sad, downbeat tone from the opening to the scene. The stage directions 'Silence' and a 'movement towards darkness' (probably a lighting direction) both set the scene for the entrance of 'Sadness'. The nouns 'Silence' and 'darkness' create a sense of loneliness – 'Darkness' is both literal and metaphorical, suggesting depressed feelings as well as lack of light, and this is emphasised by the stage direction, which states that Ash Girl 'remains alone'. 'The shadow' that falls across the wall as 'Sadness' enters could suggest a ghostly figure who invades the stage and brings feelings of gloom. The audience can't help but wonder if the shadowy figure will damage Ash Girl in some way, and this creates a further emotional connection with her.

Annotations:

- clearly reasoned argument; strong focus on the question
- knowledge of and quotations from the text
- close analysis of language that creates the core mood/tone
- links to deeper understanding of character, themes and context

6 How has the answer covered the objectives? What do you notice about their paragraph structure?

Write your response

7 Now plan and write your response to the following practice question in 45 minutes:

> How does Wertenbaker make this scene so moving and emotional? Support with details from the text. [25]

Evaluating your passage-based response

How should I evaluate my response?

Before you evaluate how well you have done, check the table on page 240. It will help you decide if your work falls broadly into the first or second category – or outside them.

1. Go through your own response and write annotations around it, like the example paragraph in the previous lesson.
2. Read the following response, thinking about what has been done well and what advice might need to be given to the writer in order to make more progress.

Response A

The writer makes this scene moving and emotional in lots of ways, and one of the main ways is through the description of 'Sadness'. The way this character moves and speaks creates a gloomy and unpleasant tone, which is bound to make you feel sorry for poor Ash Girl.

For a start, Sadness is described as a 'shadow.' This is not a very nice thing and makes you think of a death, Grim Reaper type character. This makes it seem like Ash Girl is in danger so you want to protect her. Also, it says, Sadness 'tests the room for a dominant place'. The word 'dominant' means having power so this also adds to us feeling anxious for Ash Girl. What will Sadness do or make Ash Girl do?

Another important thing is the way they speak to each other. It is very tense and it is like Sadness is really trying to hurt Ash Girl. When Ash Girl says she will make dresses all night long, Sadness says 'No one will thank you'. This suggests it will all be for nothing – she might as well not have bothered because her sisters and her mother don't care. This really stresses how awful the situation is for Ash Girl.

It is the same in lots of other fairy tales when a poor girl is deprived of love and kindness.

I also think the way Sadness describes herself and what she does to girls and boys really makes the audience sympathise with Ash Girl. She makes herself sound like something that really goes deep into people, 'I'm the icicle in the heart, the one who makes the world so dark you wish you weren't in it.'

Annotations:

- focus on task
- relevant evidence drawn from extract
- attempt to analyse language but rather stilted expression
- attempt at interpretation but undeveloped
- further support for point
- beginning to develop point and explain effect
- contextual reference but doesn't really add to analysis
- point with supporting evidence

The 'icicle in the heart' is a powerful metaphor that suggests a stabbing power. it , makes you wonder if depression will destroy Ash Girl even though you know the story is supposed to end happily.

To sum up, I think making 'Sadness' a character makes the scene even more emotional. This is because sadness is really a threat to Ash Girl. The way she talks and moves creates a gloomy, sad tone and makes you feel lots of sympathy for Ash Girl.

language analysis but could be linked to wider points

better attempt at interpretation linked to context

ending reiterates main argument without adding anything

Comment:

There are some reasonably developed points made here with relevant use of quotations. There are attempts to analyse in detail, and in places to interpret language but these remain rather undeveloped.

3 How could this sample response be improved? Using the table on page 240, think about what advice you might give the writer of the response to improve their work.

4 Now read a second response to the same question. Think about what is an improvement on the first response.

Response B

The writer's use of both dramatic structure and powerful language are key factors in creating a moving and emotional mood in this scene, which is only lifted by the appearance of Owl as a contrast to Sadness at the end.

The imagery used by Wertenbaker is particularly powerful. 'Sadness' describes the impact of her presence on stage, and on people as a 'shadow cast against the wall' and a 'chill in the light.' The imagery here suggests a sense of impending doom, a gathering darkness and the word 'chill' suggests iciness – as if happy feelings are frozen or smothered. Later, this is linked to the metaphorical 'icicle in the heart', a sensory description that conveys the sharp pain of loneliness or sadness, which can penetrate deep into your whole being. Such descriptions cast a very gloomy mood over the stage.

This threatening mood is further stressed by Sadness's cruel words and cold approach to someone who might be lonely or depressed. The statement and reply she uses hammers home the message that there is no way out: 'Call for help: I'll muffle your voice.' Again, this idea of smothering silence is emphasised. For the audience who know Ash Girl is already isolated and alone, this can only create more sympathy for her situation.

A similar structure can be seen when Ash Girl finally finds her voice and attempts to stress her right to be heard and recognised. When she says she'll sew all night long and 'make these dresses memorable', 'Sadness' replies bluntly, 'No one will thank you'. The use of the second person 'you' in this dialogue almost makes Sadness seem like a 'bad angel' on her shoulder, telling her to give up.

long, single sentence paragraph establishes overview

clear point made with supporting evidence

detailed and developed analysis of language

excellent wider link indicating knowledge of text

new language point linked to speech structure

sustained focus on task

develops comment on language structure

detailed language analysis with deeper interpretation

This personification of sadness continues with the verbs she uses to describe her actions – 'I probe, I test ... slide through the crack ...'. In this way, the writer makes us believe she is getting through to Ash Girl and we begin to feel dread that sadness will win over hope. The idea that people in fairy stories live 'happily ever after' seems a distant dream to the audience at this point.

When Sadness really twists the knife by reminding Ash Girl that her father 'abandoned' her and 'no one's there for you ...' the scene really reaches its emotional height, or should that be 'depth' as surely Ash Girl has been brought to the brink of despair? Fortunately, the writer finally relents and lifts the mood. Owl appears – someone is there for her after all. In these ways, the writer has taken the audience on an emotional journey – mostly plunging downwards into darkness, but at the end finally beginning to see the light.

contextual comment linked clearly to dramatic effect

comment on overall dramatic structure of scene

final overview of scene's effect on audience

Comment:

This response shows sustained personal engagement with the task and extract. A wide range of skills displayed by the writer are analysed in depth, with very well-chosen references and links made across the extract. There is evidence of interpretation and deeper insights and context is handled sensitively and relevantly.

5 What advice might the writer of this response need to make even more progress? Use the table on page 240 to guide your ideas.

Check your progress:

What are the features of a *reasonably developed, relevant* personal response?

Knowledge	• You show how you know the text **well** by making reference to it and/or by quoting from it. • You make points that are **relevant** (close textual reference and/or quotation) to the task set.
Understanding	• You show a **sound** understanding of the text, reading beyond the surface to explore implicit meanings. • You **develop your ideas** on themes, characterisation or ideas.
Language and effects	• You write about **some** of the ways in which the writer uses **language, structure and form**. • You make **some exploration** of the **effects of the writer's choices** and how these effects are created.
Personal response	• You make your own honest and **considered** response to the text, appropriate to the task. • You show **some development of your own ideas** about the text and task.

What are the features of a response showing *sustained personal and evaluative engagement* with task and text?

Knowledge	• You show a **detailed** grasp of the text as a whole and a **deep** understanding of the task. • You support your **original** ideas with **carefully selected, well-integrated reference** to the text.
Understanding	• You show a **sophisticated understanding** of the implicit meaning of the ideas, characterisation and themes in the text. • You show your ability to **analyse, evaluate and interpret** the text in an **original** and **perceptive** way.
Language and effects	• You examine **in depth** the way the writer uses **language, structure and form** and you explore different **interpretations.** • You show the ability to make a **close analysis** of extracts from the text and (where appropriate to the question) respond to the writer's effects in the text as a whole.
Personal response	• You make a **convincing** response, showing deep interest, understanding and an involvement with both text and task. • You have your own individual **ideas and judgements** about the text and express them with **confidence and enthusiasm**.

Preparing for coursework

6

This chapter guides you through the process of developing your coursework. It will be relevant if you are taking the coursework route for your IGCSE™ Literature in English.

You will agree with your teacher which texts you would like to use for your coursework and what your coursework assignments should be.

There are two tasks that you must submit for your coursework:

- comparing poems – write an essay that compares two poems
- comparing texts – write an essay that compares two complete texts. One text must be drama, the second may be drama or prose.

The first half of this chapter helps you to prepare to write a coursework essay that compares two poems. You will work through the process of preparing, planning, writing and editing a coursework assignment using two poems. The framework outlined here can be applied to other poems and will support you as you write your own assignment on poetry.

The second half of this chapter helps you to prepare to write a coursework essay that compares two whole texts. In this case, one text is a drama text and one text is a prose text, but you can also compare two drama texts using the same approach. Again, you will work through a process of preparing, planning, writing and editing that you will apply to your chosen coursework texts.

The information in this section is based on the Cambridge International Education syllabus. You should always refer to the appropriate syllabus document for the year of examination to confirm the details and for more information. The syllabus document is available on the website: www.cambridgeinternational.org.

Preparing for a comparing poems coursework essay

How do I effectively explore the poems I select for comparison?

First, you need to find poems you can compare and contrast, ideally on a similar theme, or sharing other characteristics (for example, two sonnets). They will need to be rich in ideas and language so you can write a substantial response about them.

Start thinking

The following two poems will help demonstrate *how* to approach poems you have selected, providing you with a framework for comparison. If you are using poems you already know from the Anthology, you might have already done some of this work.

1 Read these two poems. It's important that on this first read-through, you do so without making notes. If you can, read the two poems aloud.

Try to think of the *feel* of the poems – their rhythm, pace (or lack of it) – and how certain words, phrases or lines make an impact.

Memory

Dawn hangs a crimson dusk
of all the Flame Trees in bloom
with all the **hibiscus**. Bare feet go
collecting animals in heavy dew.

Morning delivers new sun.
Smoke rises from little kitchens.
Every passing person calls out
'Good morning!'

Eyes go drowsy in blazing afternoon.
Golden wasps shimmer.
Clothes collect summer smells.

Swift brown bats litter dusk.
Anancy weaves in log cottages.
Grandma's knowing ripens.

Night ferments mango-walk.
The caring night pouches
busy sea and static hills
together with flatland palm trees.

James Berry

The Lighted Window

He said:
"In the winter dusk
When the pavements were gleaming with rain,
I walked thru a dingy street
Hurried, harassed,
Thinking of all my problems that never are solved.
Suddenly out of the mist, a flaring gas-jet
Shone from a huddled shop.
I saw thru the bleary window
A mass of playthings:
False-faces hung on strings,
Valentines, paper and tinsel,
Tops of scarlet and green,
Candy, marbles, **jacks**—
A confusion of color
Pathetically gaudy and cheap.
All of my boyhood
Rushed back.
Once more these things were treasures
Wildly desired.
With covetous eyes I looked again at the marbles,
The precious **agates**, the **pee-wees**, the **chinies**—
Then I passed on.

In the winter dusk,
The pavements were gleaming with rain;
There in the lighted window
I left my boyhood."

Sara Teasdale

Glossary

hibiscus: type of bright flowering plant

Anancy: spider hero of Caribbean folk-tales

tops: spinning tops

jacks: star-shaped small metal items used in a game called 'Jacks'

agate: form of quartz

pee-wees: small marbles, often made of clay

chinies: meaning not clear but possibly small Chinese dolls

Explore the skills

When you read poems for the first time, they can seem like a 'blur of words'. It helps to break down the poems by using familiarisation techniques.

2 On a copy of each poem, highlight, underline, and add questions that represent your first feelings and responses on reading the poem. For example:

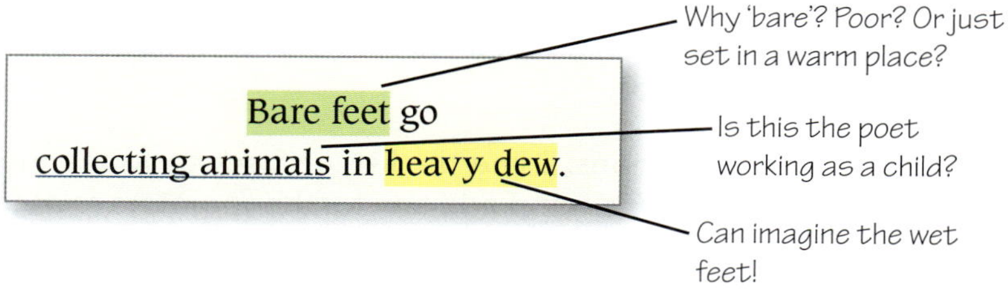

3. To help develop your understanding of imagery, make a drawing, a **collage** or a **mood-board** of what is being described in each of the poems. As you read through the verses or stanzas, add further images to your collection. Remember to include details about the imagery used. You could include labels too.

4. Now develop your familiarisation. Complete a table with notes about what happens, themes, tones and how you respond. Notice how this enables you to begin to compare and contrast the poems. You could do this with a partner.

Glossary

collage: collection or display of images and ideas linked to a theme

mood-board: similar to a collage, but with a deliberate goal of establishing a particular mood or emotion

	Memory	The Lighted Window
What happens in the poem? What story (if any) does it tell? (This might be as simple as 'a poet describes the sea'.)	*A series of images taken from one day are described.*	
What is the setting?		*A wintry city street*
Who, if anyone, is speaking? And from what **perspective?** (For example, a mother to her child?)		*Seems to be a* ***framed narrative*** *- poet introduces a man who gives his account.*
What seem to be the themes of the poem? (For example, 'growing old'?)		
What is the tone/mood? (For example, is it comical, bitter, thoughtful, angry, etc?)	*The tone feels light and affectionate in remembering happy past times.*	
What, if anything, changes or develops as the poem develops? (Does the speaker change their view or reveal something new?)		
What appeals to you about the poem?		
What, if anything, do you find puzzling or uncomfortable in the poem?		
Why do you think the poem has been written?		

5. Now that you have completed the table, can you see any obvious similarities or differences? List at least two of each.

Key term

framed narrative: a story within a story

Develop the skills

This next stage shows how you can develop a more detailed understanding of techniques the poets use in these or your chosen poems to convey their ideas.

6. Look at the terms listed below and their definitions. Using the list, go back to your annotated copies of each poem – or your own chosen poems – and add any further pointers related to these techniques.

Technique	Explanation
Form	What is the shape and structure of the poem on the page? For example, number and regularity of lines or verses; whether the poem is a particular form such as a sonnet, or is a 'freer' form.
Word choice	What particular words has the poet chosen? What do they mean? Are there links between the words. (For example, do they have a common semantic field, such as words related to the sea?)
Figurative language	Has the poet used similes, metaphors and other imagery? What do these literary techniques suggest or imply? For example, *'the caring night'* **personifies** the night as if it were a parent or other caring figure looking after the land and people.
Sound techniques	Has the poet used alliteration, assonance, sibilance, monosyllables, etc.? What is the effect created? Has the poet used rhyme? What rhythm, if any, does the poem have?
Tense and time	What verb tense does the poet use? (Do they use 'go' or 'went' or both, perhaps?) Does the poet write about the present, the past or the future – or a combination of these times?
Other devices or techniques	Listing, caesura, enjambment

You must do more than just list techniques. You need to explain what effect that technique or language choice has on the reader, and how it contributes to the meaning of the poem.

For example, a sample response might note how the poet lists items: *False-faces hung on strings / Valentines, paper and tinsel / Tops of scarlet and green / Candy, marbles, jacks*— and then comment: 'listing of items one after another creates sense that watcher is overwhelmed by what he has seen...'

7 Do you agree with this statement? Is there anything in the rest of the poem that would support this view?

8 Now, that you have looked at the ideas and the techniques, can you see any obvious points of similarity or difference? If so, jot down two or three quick ideas, for example:

Theme: both deal with childhood memories but in one the voice is very specific (a man passing a window) whereas we don't really know who is narrating the other.

Apply the skills

9 Write one paragraph on each poem, giving a personal response to them, explaining what you think the poets are trying to say, and how the language or ideas have an impact on you. Practise comparison by adding at least one of the points of comparison you noted down earlier.

Check your progress:

- I can read and make useful notes that help me understand the basic ideas in a poem.
- I can generate detailed notes that help me understand a wide range of ideas and techniques.

Structuring your poetry coursework

How do I plan and organise my ideas effectively?

Start thinking

You need to show that you can compare how the poets use language, form and structure to communicate ideas and to convey meanings and feelings.

1. With this in mind, decide which of the following are strong coursework essay titles?
   - **a)** Describe the memories being presented in these poems.
   - **b)** Compare how the poets convey their thoughts and feelings about memory and its impact.
   - **c)** What makes the poets' different portrayals of memories particularly striking to you?

Remember that you can change the focus of your title as you explore the poems, if you find that another approach will suit you better.

Explore the skills

Assume that the final title for your practice piece worth 20 marks is going to be:

> *Compare how the poets convey their thoughts and feelings about memory and its impact.*

You have already generated some ideas from your initial reading of the poems. Now it is time to relate those ideas to the essay task you have selected. The key words here are:

- **Compare** – what are the similarities and differences between the poems?
- **how** – what techniques do the poets use?
- **thoughts and feelings** – what emotions or ideas are suggested?
- **memory and its impact** – how is this particular theme explored?

There are different ways to plan your essay. For example: making a list, creating a flow chart, a storyboard, or a spider-diagram. Here, a student has started a spider-diagram for the first poem.

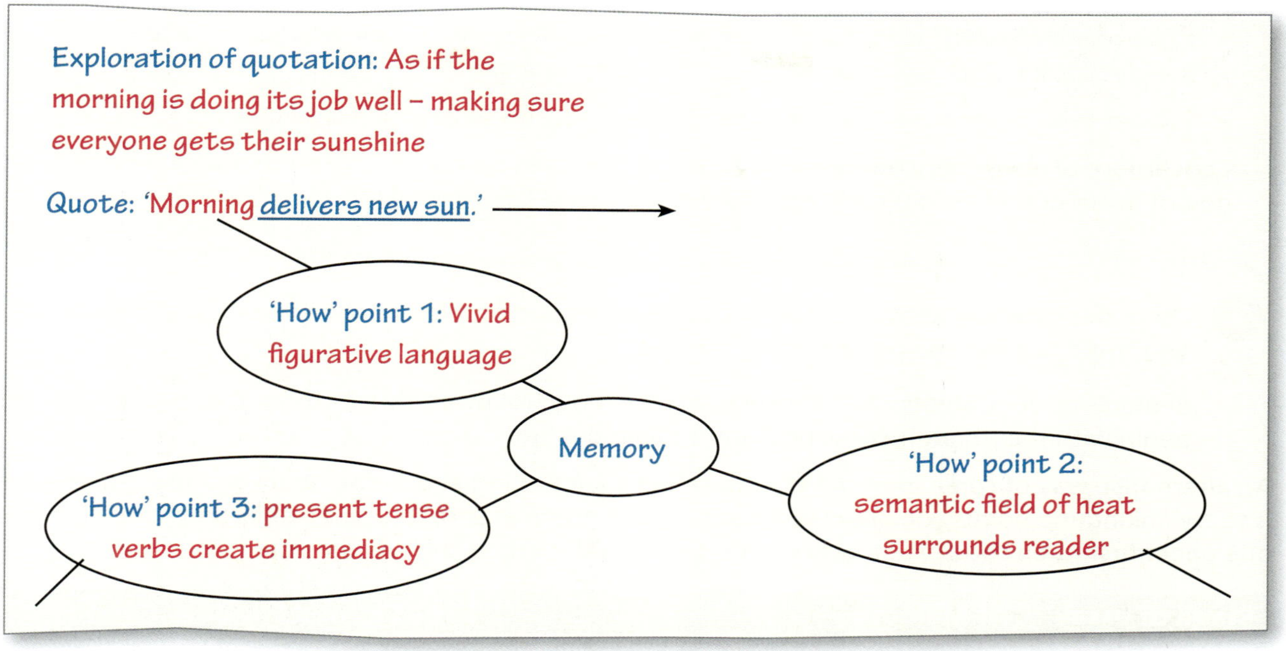

2 **a)** Copy and complete Points 2 and 3 on the diagram.

b) As in Point 1, find suitable quotations for Points 2 and 3 from other parts of the poem. Add an explanation or exploration as shown.

Through the different listing and generating ideas techniques you have learned about in Lessons 6.1 and 6.2, you will now have a good sense of how the poems are similar and different.

Develop the skills

You now need to reorganise your points into an essay plan that will sequence your ideas into a logical order. For example:

Introduction: You will need to introduce the poems and the focus of your essay ('thoughts and feelings about memory and its impact'). You will also need to compare the two poems in some way right from the start, for example setting out the basic similarity. *Both poems relate to childhood memories; the first, looking back to….*

First half of essay: body paragraphs exploring points about 'Memory'.

- Written in the present tense, Berry evokes a feeling of immediacy through the use of….
- Further imagery creates a sense of….

Second half of essay: body paragraphs exploring points about 'The Lighted Window'. Here, connections (these can be similarities, differences or both) should be made with the first poem.

- *Unlike 'Memory', 'The Lighted Window' is written in the past tense, suggesting a feeling of ancient time and things that have long gone, for example....*
- *The key imagery in the poem is not related to nature and fruitfulness but....*

Conclusion: Give an overview, drawing together the main points of contrast and similarity, but do not introduce any completely new points.

3 Using the structure above, complete your planning, adding ideas for each half of the essay. You could number the paragraphs if it helps.

Remember, your points can be focused on the 'how' followed by the 'thoughts/feelings' or begin with the 'thoughts/feelings' and explain the 'how' afterwards.

An alternative way of comparing the poems, rather than writing about one poem and then the next, is to try linking the points you are making about each poem *as you go along* rather than dealing with one poem first, then the next. In order to do this, a table such as this could help:

Stage of essay	Memory	The Lighted Window
Introduction	Link both poems together in a general introduction as you would for the original structure above.	
Body Paragraph 1: *Time/voice is very different*	*Written in present tense – creates immediacy ('Bare feet go')*	*Past tense – man telling story – creates sense of distance ('...when the pavements were gleaming with rain')*
Body Paragraph 2: *Setting: Nature versus the industrial*	*Semantic field of fruit, aspects of sun and dark, things growing ('mango' 'ripens', etc.)*	*Man-made objects, worthless in one way ('cheap', 'gaudy'), not real ('false-faces')*
Body Paragraph 3: *Rhythm and 'flow'*	*Short lines follow day as it progresses ...*	
Body Paragraph 4		
Further paragraphs		
Conclusion	Synthesise ideas and overview of the poems but do not repeat things in detail or introduce any major new ideas.	

Apply the skills

4 Complete the plan above adding additional paragraphs/ points, which you can compare as your essay progresses.

Check your progress:

- ▲ I can create a basic plan for my essay that addresses each poem in turn.
- ▲▲ I can create a detailed plan for my essay that includes paragraphs comparing aspects of each poem.

Developing writing skills for poetry coursework

How can I make sure I explain my ideas clearly and thoughtfully?

Start thinking

You will remember the key words and phrases in the practice essay title.

> Compare how the poets convey their thoughts and feelings about memory and its impact.

This introduction needs to include:

- reference to the poems you will be covering
- reference to the key terms in the question
- an indication of how you are going to approach the question
- (if possible) initial, broad links between your chosen poems.

> In both 'Memory' by James Berry and 'The Lighted Window' by Sara Teasdale, striking linguistic effects are used by the poets to highlight different memories of childhood. Using a variety of techniques, the poets at times employ similar – but also sometimes strikingly different – methods to present thoughts about the past and its impact.

1 Do you think this is an effective introduction? What could be added or made clearer?

Explore the skills

You have already begun to plan your essay structure, considering how many body paragraphs you will need and what to include. However, how you structure the paragraph itself is particularly important. To show that the points you are making are relevant to the essay title, you will need to refer to the title throughout your essay. (You can also use synonyms such as 'emotions' for 'feelings'.)

Read these two sample paragraphs. Paragraph **A** uses the simpler format of dealing with one poem only. Paragraph **B** tackles both poems at the same time.

A.

The tone of 'Memory' is one that suggests life and fruitfulness, unlike 'The Lighted Window'. This is particularly evident in the references to the trees 'in bloom' and the verb used to describe the way the night 'ferments'. Even 'Grandma … ripens', while the spider is at work, and the sea is 'busy'. Overall, these words and phrases suggest everything is fertile and growing, rich and comforting.

B.

The tone of both poems is clearly different. In 'Memory' many of the references relate to life and fruitfulness, for example in the way the trees are 'in bloom' and the verb used in the way the night 'ferments'. Even the memory of the spider is of it being at work, and the sea is 'busy'. In contrast, the things that hang in the shop in 'The Lighted Window' are still and lifeless – and even though they are colourful, the poet calls them 'pathetically gaudy and cheap'. The 'false-faces' – probably masks – hanging down are rather scary, too, adding to an overall feeling of foreboding.

2 **a)** What poetic aspect is the focus of *both* paragraphs – as introduced in their first, topic sentence?

b) What two initial quotations from 'Memory' in both paragraphs support the point being made?

c) What additional quotation does paragraph **A** include about 'Grandma'?

d) What phrase in paragraph **B** signals that the writer is going to explore differences when commenting on 'The Lighted Window'?

3 Both paragraphs deal with overall effects.

a) What adjectives does the writer of paragraph **A** use at the end to describe these effects?

b) What overall 'sense' does the writer of paragraph **B** say is created by the 'false-faces'?

4 How well has each sample response stuck to the focus of the essay task? Check the paragraphs for key words (include synonyms).

Develop the skills

You are going to write a paragraph following **one** of the two approaches above.

Look at the two paragraph structures and decide which to use:

A: Deals with one poem

Sentence 1 (topic sentence): Introduce the aspect of the poem you want to discuss. Briefly, refer to the other poem's similarity or difference but do not go into detail – you will be tackling the other poem in your other half.

Sentence 2: Explain how the poet addresses this aspect, and what they have to say. Include at least one relevant quotation, which you insert fluently into your sentence.

Sentence 3: Develop the point, adding further evidence from the first poem.

Sentence 4: Sum up the point and what it tells the reader, or say what its impact is.

B: Deals with both poems

Sentence 1 (topic sentence): Introduce the aspect of the two poems you want to discuss.

Sentence 2: Explain how James Berry in 'Memory' addresses this and what he has to say. Include at least one relevant quotation, which you insert fluently into your sentence.

Sentence 3: Develop or extend the point, if you can, with further evidence or references.

Sentence 4: Begin with a comparing or contrasting connective (see below) and explore the same aspect in 'The Lighted Window'. Include relevant quotations.

Sentence 5: Develop and extend the point – or you may wish to draw an overall conclusion between the two poems.

5 **a)** Now, choose an aspect from the poems to write about. (You will need to go back to your earlier notes.)

b) Write your paragraph.

Here are two possible starting points:

Approach **A**: *'The Lighted Window' demonstrates how seemingly small, unexpected moments can trigger very emotional responses, rather than the gentler reflections of 'Memory'. For example, when the man…*

Approach **B**: *Another key difference between the poems relates to the voice and perspective of the two speakers…*

Use comparison/contrast connectives such as 'Similarly', 'In the same way', 'On the other hand'.

The final paragraph of your coursework piece should be a conclusion. Include:

- reference to both the poems you have been discussing
- a summary of the main findings of your essay
- an interesting final idea to make an impression at the end of your essay.

It's a good idea to start this final paragraph with a formulation like: *In conclusion, ... In summary, ...* or *In reviewing the two poems, ...*

6 Identify the features listed above in this conclusion.

> In conclusion, both 'Memory' and 'The Lighted Window' address the way in which memories can rise to the surface in the present day. Although the spark in 'The Lighted Window' is a momentary, almost shocking image of what childhood was like for the narrator, the speaker in 'Memory' does not mention any one sudden remembrance nor do they specifically mention themselves, instead describing the past through a series of individual memories, rather like a montage, which might be true for many Caribbean children looking back. What both poems reveal is that memory's impact can be rich and rewarding or, in reminding us of pleasures long gone, that adult life can never be the same.

7 **a)** Read through the essay plan you developed in Lesson 6.2 and decide what you would like to say in your conclusion.

b) Write your final paragraph. You could try writing two different conclusions, then choose the one you think is more successful.

Remember you are writing a serious, academic essay for this coursework piece. Avoid the everyday *colloquial* (chatty) tone you might use if you were discussing these poems with your friends. Aim for a formal tone as shown in the examples you have read.

Apply the skills

Writing and drafting

8 Now it is time to plan, draft and write your own coursework using the poems you choose.

Step 1: Choose two poems with points of comparison. Make sure these are long and rich enough in language and ideas for you to write an extended essay.

Step 2: Generate ideas about the poems, using the techniques from Lessons 6.1 and 6.2.

Step 3: Plan your essay, using either the simpler 'Half and half' approach (dealing with one poem first, then the other) or the slightly more demanding 'As you go along' approach (comparing aspects of both poems in each paragraph).

Step 4: Write your essay, making sure each paragraph introduces key aspects, supports ideas with quotations, develops and extends the points made, and concludes effectively, sticking to the core focuses of the task.

Step 5: Review and proof-read, making sure your style is clear, and your spelling and grammar are secure.

Check your progress:

- ▲ I can write clear, focused paragraphs with well-chosen examples.
- ▲▲ I can write clear, but detailed paragraphs that fluently move between both poems.

Evaluating your comparing poems coursework

How do I know what needs improving?

Start thinking

Look again at the title of the coursework response you explored in the previous three lessons.

> **Compare how the poets convey their thoughts and feelings about memory and its impact. [20]**

1. Using the content you have developed, complete your practice coursework essay, worth 20 marks, if you haven't already done so. Next, check the table on page 284 *Coursework evaluation chart* and decide if your work falls broadly into the first or second category (or outside them).

Explore the skills

2. Go through your own essay, adding annotations (both positive and where there is room for improvement) based on the criteria on page 284 .

Develop the skills

3. Now read Response 1 along with the annotations. Think about what is done well and what advice you could give for improvement. Write your advice in bullet points.

Response 1: Extracts from a comparative poetry response

Both 'Memory' by James Berry, and 'The Lighted Window' by Sara Teasdale are about different memories. The first is quite subtle because we have to work out it is about memories, while the second states clearly that the speaker is looking back on his childhood.

'Memory' uses the stanza to present various times of day with vivid imagery of nature and other living beings. It begins with the dawn and half-rhymes of 'bloom' and 'dew' before progressing to show us morning, afternoon, dusk and night. This could be one day or represent any day in the poet's childhood.

The images are presented in single, clear descriptions, which use the senses. 'Bare feet ... in heavy dew' makes you almost feel the touch of water on you. The 'golden wasps' that 'shimmer' uses onomatopoeia to convey both the sound and look of hovering insects. Later, the poet personifies the 'caring night' suggesting comfort and protection. The use of the verb 'pouches' implies the night is gathering the world in like a mother to a child.

The slow pace of the poem is obvious because of the short lines with full stops. These make the reader pause and take each image in. This makes me imagine I am watching these moments as they slowly pass by.

The combination of these memories, which are described in the present tense, makes me think they are still alive in his mind. Berry is known for his work drawing on his Caribbean roots, so the references to 'hibiscus', 'Flame' and 'palm' trees, the mythic spider 'Anancy' and the rows of mango trees show a knowledge of those islands and the importance of nature to people there.

Different memories are presented in 'The Lighted Window' by Sara Teasdale. It is also presented in a very different form. It is a framed narrative in that it is told by a man, as if to the poet – 'He said'. The use of speech marks makes it sound like a story told on a winter's night.

[...the essay continues here]

Annotations:

- a clear start focused on overall theme
- a general comparison clearly stated
- reference to structure, if somewhat basic
- poetic techniques mentioned but not their impact
- good personal response to and analysis of language
- good background but is it relevant?
- contrasting phrase introduces second part of response
- language techniques identified with a basic explanation

The poem begins with the man setting the scene and time, in this case a 'winter dusk'. Unlike 'Memory', the poem sticks to this one time and place. There is drama in the use of the word 'Suddenly', which might make the reader think some horrible act in the 'dingy street' was about to take place. In fact, it is just a bright gas-jet that shows up a shop. Like 'Memory' there is the use of personification in the phrase, 'Huddled shop'.

good personal response to and analysis of language

poetic techniques mentioned but not their impact

In this shop, the speaker sees lots of childhood items and uses listing to create an overall effect of a mass of things hung up. It is a very visual account with references to colour – 'tops of scarlet and green', for example. But the adult speaker sees them as they are now – a 'confusion' and 'pathetically gaudy and cheap'. But his memory reminds him that they were once 'treasures' that were 'wildly desired'. For a moment, he becomes a child again. Many of these items are unfamiliar to the reader now – such as the 'pee-wees' and the 'chinies', plus masks called 'false-faces'. So, the poem seems old-fashioned and about a different world than ours. Other poems by Teasdale, such as 'Spring Night' and 'There will come soft rains', have a similar bittersweet tone and use natural observation to get across feelings of sadness or loss.

well-chosen quotations

links to other works by the poet, but not needed

There are lots of unanswered questions in the poem. For a start, we know the speaker is anxious and unhappy due to his 'problems that never are solved'. But we don't know what these are. Maybe we are supposed to think these are just the usual problems you face as you get older. Later, it says he looked with 'covetous eyes', which means eyes that wished to own these items. This could suggest he was never able to have them, or just that he wished that simple, cheap items were all he had to worry about having now.

attempt at interpretation, but perhaps too much guess-work

The final stanza is separated because it creates a neat ending, which repeats the two opening lines. It is like the speaker has come out of his dream, back to reality. The reality is less appealing than the memories, with the 'winter' and the 'pavements … gleaming with rain' giving a sombre feel.

relevant reference to how the structure serves the theme

[…the essay continues]

Comment:

This answer is reasonably developed, relevant and presents some personal response. There is some effective comparison and understanding of the deeper implications of both poems. Some response is made to both writers' use of language and this is backed up with some use of supporting evidence.

4 Now read a second response to the same question. Make notes about what is an improvement on the first response.

Response 2

Both 'Memory' by James Berry and 'The Lighted Window' by Sara Teasdale present contrasting reflections on childhood, separated not only by time, weather and location, but also in tone and mood. We are reminded that memory is personal, and selective, but also creates different impacts in the mind.

strong comparative approach established from the start

Whilst one implies a warmth and tenderness in the birth of the 'new sun' and the 'caring night' as the day ends, the other has an almost claustrophobic, dark quality in which the gloomy, rainy streets are only brightened by 'a flaring gas-jet'. The second emphasises hard industrial life; the first, the innocence of island living.

excellent, interpretative impact of the two poems

An exploration of tone is useful in understanding the two poems. In 'Memory', the slow-paced stanzas in which the poet sets out the passing day, seem to be in the present moment, due to the use of the present tense. The 'flame trees in bloom' and the 'blazing afternoon' suggest the way these moments still live tenderly in the poet's memory. The beauty of the dawn's colours, the way the clothes almost breathe like living things collecting 'summer smells' and the 'caring night', which personifies the passing of time, add to the comforting effect of Nature. In contrast, Teasdale, in 'The Lighted Window' presents the city as inhospitable and even dangerous. It's winter and the roads are 'dingy' and 'gleaming with rain', a pathetic fallacy that adds to how 'hurried, harassed" the man feels. The gas-jet is bright, but the poet introduces it with the adverb 'Suddenly', as if in shock.

topic sentence sets out overall way in which the analysis will be approached

language feature followed by examples and effect

variety of poetic techniques explored and explained

The tone develops as the poems progress. In 'Memory' a series of images is introduced by simple verbs of movement – 'rises', 'shimmer', 'litter', 'weaves' and so on. There is a semantic field of fruitfulness and growth – in the 'flame' and 'palm' trees, in the mention of 'golden wasps', 'brown bats' and 'Anancy' (the mythic name for spiders) – and in the idea of things growing and developing. The spider weaves his web; the night 'ferments mango-walk' and even Grandma becomes wiser as her 'knowing ripens'. All the world is connected, in a good way.

However, in 'The Lighted Window' the appearance of the window in the darkness is dream-like. But the objects the speaker lists don't bring much joy. They are presented as tacky and perhaps even frightening. The masks are called 'false-faces', which could be a metaphor for the world that gives the speaker his worries; the colourful toys are 'pathetically gaudy and cheap'. It seems as if things are out of his control as the memories 'rushed back'. The use of the adverb-adjective 'wildly desired' adds to this. The speaker is facing his past painfully, both regretting it, yet realising life has changed.

Teasdale in the final stanza repeats the earlier lines, as if the poet is coming to his senses after momentary madness. The poem echoes other works of hers such as the bitter-sweet 'Spring Night', and even though it is a man speaking, it is maybe a reflection of her own short, and in places, unhappy life.

variety of poetic techniques explored and explained

sophisticated and appropriate summary of key ideas

fluent, and sophisticated movement between the two poems

sophisticated and appropriate summary of key ideas

use of technical language leads to important, personal interpretation

contextual information is relevant to the identified tone

Comment:

This is a really perceptive comparison showing personal engagement with task and text. It is a sophisticated analysis. The writer of the response sustains personal engagement with the task – and with both the poems – throughout the essay. There are signs of individuality, insight and flair throughout this sensitive and skilful answer.

5 What other aspects (not highlighted) in the response impressed you? Make any notes about skills or content that added to the success of this response.

Apply the skills

6 Use your notes on what makes a successful response with the criteria on page 284 both to improve your practice essay and to help you redraft your own coursework essay.

Preparing for a comparing texts coursework essay

How do I generate ideas for my drama or drama and prose coursework essay?

The purpose of Lessons 6.5 to 6.8 is to provide you with a framework to support the process of preparing, planning, writing and editing your comparing texts coursework essay.

You will write your coursework essay on a play and another whole text, which could be another play or a prose text.

Start thinking

1 What do you think the challenges are of writing a much longer essay?

Though the skills are similar, writing an essay for coursework is quite different from writing an essay in an examination. You will have much more time to develop your ideas in detail and it is important that you use that time effectively. Consider these five stages of completing your coursework essay:

1. Choosing your title
2. Research, developing ideas and planning the essay
3. Writing a first draft
4. Revising and editing the first draft
5. Writing the final version of the essay

The final version, which will be assessed, depends on successful completion of the previous four stages.

Explore the skills

Your essay will compare the ways in which the two writers present a key common element between the texts, such as theme, characters, or setting. You will need to decide on your essay title and what you want to compare. A successful essay title will:

- explicitly ask for comparison
- focus on the writers' techniques – *how* the texts are written.

An effective essay title may use words and phrases to ask about the writers' *presentation*, or *how* they *present*, *explore*, or *convey* the feature you have chosen to compare.

2 Look at these sample essay titles. Think about how each focuses on the requirements of the task and rank them in order of effectiveness.

A. Discuss how Shakespeare and Williams present the characters of Juliet in *Romeo and Juliet* and Laura in *The Glass Menagerie*.

B. Compare how Odimba and Adichie explore the relationships between daughters and parents in *Princess & The Hustler* and *Purple Hibiscus*.

C. Compare migration in Gupta's *The Empress* and Desai's *Fasting, Feasting*.

D. 'Justice will always be done'. Compare justice in *An Inspector Calls* and *The Merchant of Venice* in the light of this comment.

Choosing and developing your area of comparison

To illustrate the process of preparing and writing coursework, these lessons will compare Stephen Hoo's play *Jamaica Boy* with Andrea Levy's novel *Small Island*.

Here is a brief introduction to each text:

Jamaica Boy focuses on the relationship between Ophelia and Chris. Ophelia is a Jamaican woman in her 60s, living in London. Chris is a teenager who has been in trouble with the law. He helps Ophelia in her garden as part of his community service. The play alternates scenes in London with scenes in Jamaica when Ophelia was 19 years old.

Small Island moves in time and place between Jamaica and London, before, during and after the Second World War, although there are also chapters set elsewhere in England and in India. Gilbert and Hortense migrate from Jamaica to England in the hope of better opportunities. They rent a room in Queenie's house in London but face difficulties and some hostility when seeking work.

3 **a)** Look at these preliminary notes comparing the two texts. What obvious connections have been identified?

	Jamaica Boy by Stephen Hoo	*Small Island* by Andrea Levy
Form	Drama: play	Prose: novel
Themes	Immigration, racial identity, overcoming challenges, developing relationships	Immigration, racial identity, overcoming challenges esp. racism, developing relationships
Setting	Jamaica and London	Jamaica, England esp. London, India

	Jamaica Boy by Stephen Hoo	*Small Island* by Andrea Levy
Time period	1960s and 2000s	Pre-, post- and during WW2
Structure	Alternating scenes between Jamaica and London	Frequent shifts of time, place and narrator
Key characters	Ophelia, Chris	Hortense, Gilbert, Queenie, Bernard
Outcome	Hope – renewed contact with roots	Hope – new life, house and adopted baby

b) Now complete a similar table for your own texts. This will help you identify areas that they have in common, which will allow comparison.

4 **a)** Look at your table. What areas of comparison might interest you? Some areas may have more interest to you than others; some may provide you with more fruitful areas for discussion.

A sample response studying *Jamaica Boy* and *Small Island* might choose to explore some of the possible areas for comparison further using mind-maps. This will reveal how interesting or fruitful the area of comparison might be.

b) The mind-maps below show a thinking process. How do you think similarities and differences noted on the 'migration' mind-map? How is colour used?

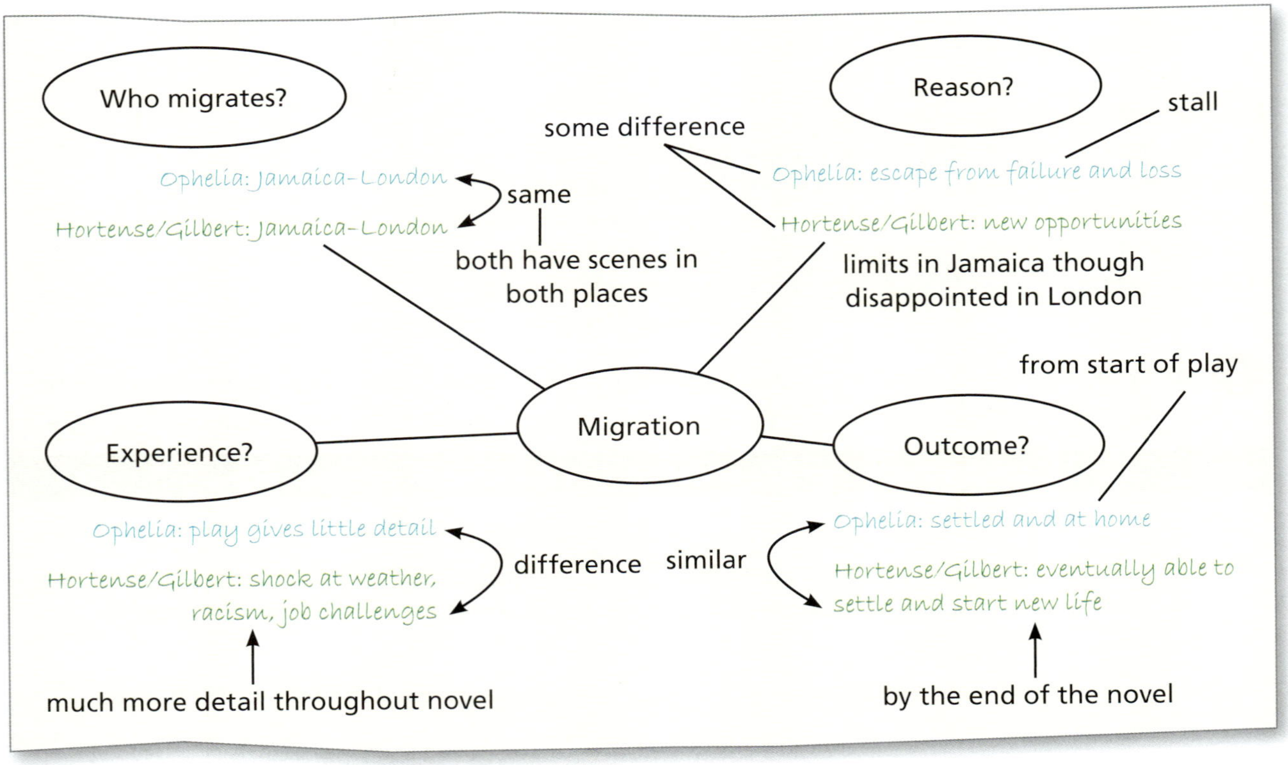

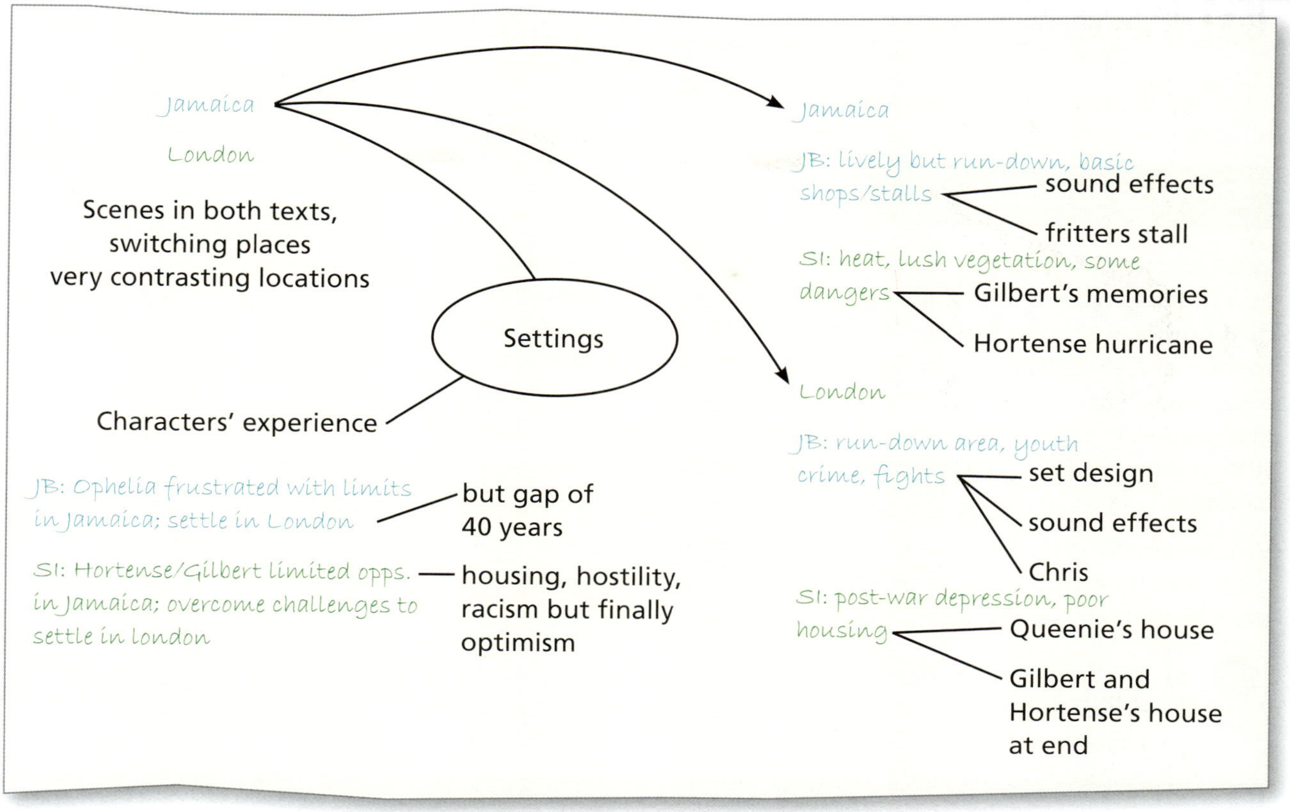

c) Working on your own texts, choose two or three areas of comparison that might interest you from the possibilities you have identified in your table.

d) Explore your possible areas of comparison by completing mind-maps. These will help you identify which will be most productive and interesting for your coursework essay.

5 From the notes and mind-maps in the example above, we are going to concentrate on the settings of *Jamaica Boy* and *Small Island*, and use this coursework title:

> Compare how Stephen Hoo and Andrea Levy present Jamaica and London in *Jamaica Boy* and *Small Island*.

Notice the key words in this question:

- 'Compare' – a clear instruction to discuss similarities and differences between the texts
- 'how' and 'present' – the comparison is looking at the writers' choice of techniques and their effects
- 'Jamaica' and 'London' – the two key settings in the texts.

Using your chart and mind-maps, you need to construct your own coursework title along similar lines.

6 **a)** Look back over your mind-maps and choose your focus for comparison to use in your coursework essay.

b) Write your own essay title.

Develop the skills

You can compare your texts in a number of ways. You might look at a theme, for example, and organise your paragraphs around different aspects of a theme. The sample question is asking you to look at how settings are presented, so the paragraphs of your essay could focus different aspects of the settings that you have explored in the two texts. So, one paragraph might explore how (the setting of) Jamaica is portrayed as 'lively and upbeat', for example.

Whatever your title and focus, you will need to explain and compare the various techniques that writers use to present or explore your chosen focus.

7 **a)** The table below shows techniques that writers use in drama and prose texts. Add to the techniques used in each form. Look back at Chapters 3 and 5 to help with this.

	Drama	Prose
Structure	Chronology; acts and scenes; entrances and exits	Chronology – flashbacks, …; juxtaposition; revealing or withholding information; chapters; paragraph and sentence lengths …
Characterisation	Costume, props, dialogue…	Description, appearance, dialogue, actions, language, views of other characters, contrast with other characters, character development…
Setting	Stage set, lighting, sound…	Description, language…
Voice	Individual characters' dialogue, monologue…	Narrative voice, perspective, character dialogue, interior dialogue/thoughts…
Language/imagery	Within characters' speech, visual imagery, patterns and repetitions, emphasis, pace, sounds such as alliteration, onomatopoeia…	In narrative, description, character dialogue, metaphor, patterning, semantic fields, emphasis, pace, sounds such as alliteration, onomatopoeia…

b) Identify which of these techniques the writers use in your texts. Give examples.

You need to think about how the writers of your texts use these techniques, exploring similarities and differences between them. This will help you compare *how* the writers present their ideas, rather than just *what* ideas they present. So, for example:

How the use of **structure** [technique] creates a **sense of place** [effect/your essay focus] or

How techniques of **characterisation** develop a **theme**.

c) Write some notes on how the techniques you have picked out develop your chosen essay focus.

In your essay, you should work closely with the texts to develop detailed examples. The sample response comparing the presentation of Jamaica and London in *Jamaica Boy* and *Small Island* has chosen some initial extracts to focus in on: Read the extracts.

Text 1: *Jamaica Boy*

Extract 1

1960s JAMAICA – Rocksteady music fades with radio broadcast interference.
RADIO BROADCASTER: Good morning, Kingston! This is Radio Jamaica and it is 6.30am!

Extract 2

PRESENT DAY LONDON/CROYDON – The back of a brick house. A back garden/allotment. A ton of mess. A shed.

Text 2: *Small Island*

Extract 1

A hurricane can make cows fly. It can tear trees from the ground, toss them in the air and snap them like twigs. A house can be picked up, its four walls parted, its roof twisted, and everything scattered in a divine game of hide-and-seek.

Extract 2

I never dreamed England would be like this. So cheerless. Determined, I held my breath but still I could hear no birdsong. The room was so pitiful on the grey morning light. I thought it tumbledown last night but daylight was happy to show me more of its filthy secrets. Plaster missing from a bit of a wall. Jagged black lines of cracking everywhere. A missing handle of the chest of drawers. No basin in the sink. And there were lacy white patterns on the windowpane. Frost.

8 The writer has made a chart. Using the extracts, work closely with the text to complete it.

	Jamaica Boy	Small Island
	Extract 1	**Extract 1**
What is the setting?	Jamaica 1960s, morning	Jamaica, approx 1947 Destruction of a hurricane
• **What does the extract suggest about the setting?** • **What impressions or mood are created?**	Energetic, lively, positive, friendly...	Wild in nature, potentially dangerously destructive
• **How does it create this impression? What techniques are used?** • **What effects are created?**	Use of sound: Rocksteady music – creates a sense of joy Voice of radio presenter bursts in with early morning greeting. Combined with use of exclamation creates sense of ...	
	Jamaica Boy	**Small Island**
	Extract 2	**Extract 2**
• **What is the setting?**		
• **What does the extract suggest about the setting?** • **What impressions or mood are created?**		
• **How does it create this impression? What techniques are used?** • **What effects are created?**		

By working closely on extracts like this, you can gain the detailed understanding of the two texts that you will need in this extended essay. You will need to consider extracts from across the whole text to get a sense of how ideas change and develop.

9 **a)** Go back to the focus of your essay question.

- Choose three extracts from across each of your texts.
- Read and annotate them, picking up on writers' techniques and how they develop the ideas in your essay.

b) Create a table like the one above to compare the focus of your essay across the two texts.

- What is the writer communicating about your chosen focus in each extract?
- *How* does the writer do this and what techniques do they use?
- Include aspects of form and structure as well as other writers' techniques in your comparison.

Check your progress:

- I can read and make useful notes about the key ideas in my texts.
- I can produce detailed notes that develop my understanding about my texts and the techniques used by the writers.

Planning your comparing texts coursework essay

How do I organise my ideas for the essay into a clear plan?

Start thinking

Look at the mind-map below. It identifies key ideas about Jamaica and London to compare in each paragraph, and it begins to draw links between them.

Create a mind-map for your texts that identifies key ideas to compare around the focus of your essay title.

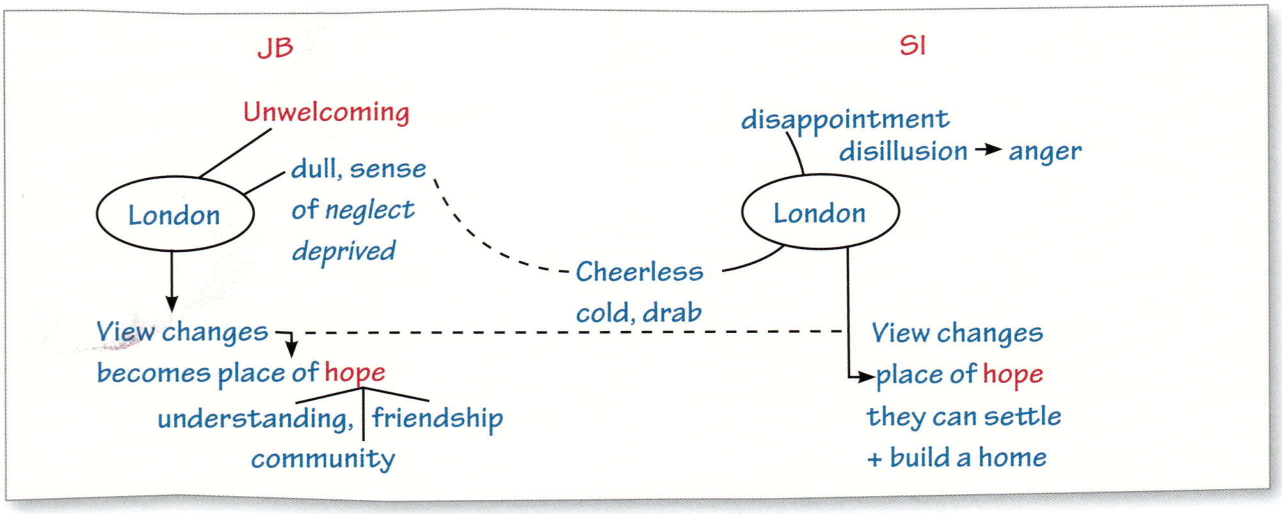

Explore the skills

Look back at your notes, making sure you now have full notes on:

- key scenes/episodes from across each text that are relevant to your title
- what ideas the writers explore about your chosen focus or theme
- the writers' techniques used in the key scenes/episodes and their effects on the audience/reader
- similarities and differences between the texts.

You will need to show how the ideas in your texts are developed using evidence of writers' techniques. The notes below show a writer gathering evidence and exploring how a key idea is explored using writers' techniques.

Here is an example:

Key idea	Quotation	Explanation/Interpretation
London JB *London is run down and ugly*	'The back of a brick house. A back garden/allotment. A ton of mess. A shed.'	Listing for designer: creates visual impression of neglect for audience.
London SI *Hortense sees poverty, neglect ugliness and cold in London*	'Jagged black lines of cracking everywhere. A missing handle of the chest of drawers. No basin in the sink. And there were lacy white patterns on the windowpane. Frost.'	Hortense's perspective: list emphasises number of faults she sees. Sentence fragments suggest her shock.

Using the notes on this chart, the writer has developed a point on *Jamaica Boy*:

In 'Jamaica Boy', London is presented as neglected, urban and ugly as shown by the stage directions that describe the scene as the 'back of a brick house' with 'A ton of mess'. This would look unappealing to the audience, especially with the piles of rubbish the designer could include.

3 **a)** Use the information on the chart to support and explain the key idea about *Small Island*.

b) Write about a key idea from each of your texts, using this model.

Develop the skills

It is now time to organise your points into a structure that leads the reader through your ideas in a logical way. Look at this first approach to structuring your essay.

Introduction: This needs to give an initial focus on the key terms of the essay and introduce the texts. It needs to show why the two texts are being considered together.

> Both 'Jamaica Boy' and 'Small Island' present characters who move from Jamaica to London and the action of the texts shifts between the two settings.

Key term

sentence fragment: a phrase, lacking a subject or main verb, that is punctuated like a full sentence

First section of the essay: Paragraphs exploring points about the *first text*.

- The settings in the 'Jamaica Boy' are created for the stage, with the vibrancy of Jamaica first presented to the audience using sound effects.........
- London in the play is presented as ....by.........
- ....

Second section of the essay: Paragraphs exploring points about the *second text*, making connections with the first text.

- As with 'Jamaica Boy', Hortense and Gilbert also describe Jamaica as a place of limited opportunities...
- There are similarities in the way the novel and the play present London. Both Hortense and Gilbert find London to be run-down and are at first disillusioned...
- ....

Conclusion: Draw together your main points of comparison to form a final judgement, but do not summarise what you have already written.

4 Using this kind of structure, complete a plan for your own essay, including your key ideas for each section.

Apply the skills

A second way of structuring the essay is to blend your discussion of the two texts within your paragraphs. This method makes comparison a more consistent feature and can lead to a more sophisticated essay.

Here is an alternative plan for the *Jamaica Boy/Small Island* essay:

- **Introduction**: Same introduction as the previous plan.
- **Paragraph 1**: Explore the *vibrancy* of Jamaica, contrasting its presentation in *JB* with the use of sound effects, with its presentation in *SI* with its descriptions of natural life and storms.
- **Paragraph 2**: Explore the *challenges* of Jamaica in both texts, comparing the movement of Ophelia's stall in *JB* with Gilbert's failed business ventures in *SI*.
- **Paragraph 3**: Explore the sense of *London's dilapidation* in both texts, comparing Hortense's first impressions in *SI* and the set design details in *JB*.
- **Paragraph 4**: Explore the *hope* given by London, comparing Ophelia and Chris's phone calls with description of Hortense and Gilbert's new house.
- **Conclusion**: Same conclusion as the previous plan.

5 Complete your own alternative plan, adding points and paragraphs where necessary.

Check your progress:

- I can make a plan for my comparative essay that looks at each text in turn.
- I can make a detailed plan for my comparative essay that blends discussion of both texts together.

Writing a comparing texts coursework essay

How do I explain my ideas in a clear, supported way?

Start thinking

1 Look back at your notes so far. Check to see if there are any gaps, or points where you do not have supporting quotations. Make any additions you think are necessary.

Explore the skills

In this lesson, you are going to focus on structuring and writing paragraphs for your comparative essay, worth 30 marks, starting with the introduction. Look again at the key terms of our working essay title:

> Compare how Stephen Hoo and Andrea Levy present Jamaica and London in *Jamaica Boy* and *Small Island.*

It is important to acknowledge the terms of the title in the opening to your essay.

Check that your introduction:

- identifies the two texts you will be discussing
- links those texts in a way that is relevant to the title
- makes clear reference to the terms of the title.

2 a) Look at the following introduction. Do you think it follows this guidance clearly?

> Stephen Hoo's play 'Jamaica Boy' and Andrea Levy's novel 'Small Island' both focus on characters who migrate from Jamaica to London. Both texts present both locations. While there are similar views of Jamaica and London, as a dramatist and a novelist, the writers use quite different methods to present these settings to the audience and reader.

b) Would you make any changes to this paragraph? Can you think of ways to improve it? Think about the degree to which each sentence is relevant to the task.

Referring back to the essay title: You can use similar terms to those used in the task wording to avoid repetition in your essay. So, you could use 'portrays' or 'depicts' as well as 'presents', for example.

In lesson 6.6, you prepared a plan for your essay, with key ideas for your paragraphs. You will need to structure each of your paragraphs carefully, using your supporting quotations and explanations.

3 Read excerpts **A** and **B** from essays using the two different approaches from Lesson 6.6. Answer questions **a)** and **b)** in the annotations.

A. Discussing the texts separately

The play 'Jamaica Boy' presents Jamaica on stage for the audience firstly through sound effects to create a sense of Jamaica's energy and vibrancy. The stage directions indicate '1960s JAMAICA – Rocksteady music fades with radio broadcast interference.' Rocksteady was a typical music genre of Jamaica and the sounds the audience hears transport them to the Jamaica of this time. The Radio Announcer also sounds excited through the use of exclamation marks after his sentences: 'This is Radio Jamaica and it is 6.30am!'

Jamaica in 'Small Island' is also presented...

a) Look at the topic sentence in **A**. At the beginning of the paragraph, it indicates what the focus will be. How effective is the topic sentence in **B**?

a context reference develops the point about sound

the structure in **A** makes comparative points in separate paragraphs

B. Discussing the texts together

The two texts present Jamaica in different ways, with the play initially using sound effects and the novel using the details of description. Hoo begins the first Jamaica scene with sound effects, using typical '1960s... Rocksteady music' to create the impression of a lively island. Levy, however, gives the reader of 'Small Island' an impression of the produce and wildlife of the island, with references to 'star apples, raspberries and mangoes' in Hortense's narration making it sound lush and productive, while it seems to teem with wildlife with references to 'tiddlers', 'woodpeckers' and 'scorpions'.

b) The sample response uses the same quotation as in **A**. What is the difference in the way the two sample responses use it?

a useful contrasting word, which shows the student is using a different approach in this version

quotations are incorporated into the sentences

4 How successfully does each paragraph respond to the essay title? Use this checklist:

- Does the paragraph have a clear topic sentence?
- Does it use quotations and/or references to support its points?
- Does it include comments on how the techniques work?
- Does it fit within a comparative structure?

Develop the skills

Using what you have learned, you are going to write a paragraph of your own about your two texts. Follow either of the two approaches.

A Discussing the texts separately

Topic sentence to introduce the focus of the paragraph.

↓

Explain the key point, including a supporting quotation, blended into your sentence.

↓

Develop the point, using further evidence from the text.

↓

Explain the effect on the audience or reader.

B Discussing the texts together

Topic sentence to introduce the focus of the paragraph with reference to both texts.

↓

Explain the key point about Text 1, including a supporting quotation, ideally blended into your sentence.

↓

Develop the point, using further evidence from the text.

↓

Use a comparative word or phrase to explain a connected key point in Text 2. Ideally, blend your quotation into your sentence.

↓

Develop the point with further evidence from Text 2.

↓

You may be able to comment on the differing effects on the audience or readers.

5 Go back to the plan you made earlier and choose a topic sentence to write about in a paragraph. Using the planning structure you prefer, write your paragraph.

Use connectives from the box when moving from text to text:

Similarities	Differences
Similarly…	On the other hand…
While…	However…
Text 1 also…	In contrast…
In comparison…	Unlike Text 2…
In addition…	Conversely…
Likewise…	Text 1 differs…

Finish your essay with a conclusion. A successful conclusion will:

- pull together the main points of comparison from the essay
- make reference to the terms of the title
- present a final view or judgement but doesn't summarise.

Read this conclusion to the essay on *Jamaica Boy* and *Small Island*.

> While the texts give slightly different impressions of Jamaica, their presentation of London is remarkably similar. As a play, 'Jamaica Boy' seeks to immerse the audience in the worlds of the two settings through sound effects and the visual details of Stephen Hoo's set design. Andrea Levy, on the other hand, relies on prompting the reader's imagination through details in the narrative, and particularly Hortense's perception of the two locations. In their different ways, however, both the play and the novel create a nostalgic view of Jamaica, and present London as initially forbidding, but a place where immigrants can eventually thrive.

6 **a)** How successfully does this paragraph fulfil the requirements of a conclusion?

b) Using your notes and plan, write a conclusion to your own essay.

Apply the skills

Now you have worked through the process of comparing, planning and structuring your coursework, it is time to start writing your own essay.

7 Write your essay. This will be your full first draft.

Checklist for success

- ✔ Choose the essay plan that you are most confident with. Identify the topic sentences for each paragraph. Make sure you have clear points of comparison, that you have enough to say, and that it is organised in a logical order.
- ✔ Show how the techniques the writers use affect the audience or reader and develop the ideas presented.
- ✔ As you write your essay, ensure each paragraph has a clear topic sentence, focuses on the task and uses evidence from the texts to support its points.
- ✔ Review, edit and proof-read your first draft essay once completed. Use the grid on page 284 to understand the features of a better answer.

Check your progress:

- ▲ I can structure an essay with relevant paragraphs about two texts, including support from those texts.
- ▲▲ I can structure an essay with detailed, analytical paragraphs that compare and contrast the writing of two texts.

Evaluating your comparing texts coursework

How can I improve my coursework essay?

Start thinking

When you have completed a draft of your essay, you will need to read through it critically to identify strengths and areas for improvement.

1. Start by checking that you have included the following points:

- Have you clearly addressed the question in the opening paragraph?
- Do your paragraphs begin with directed topic sentences?
- Do you support your points with references and quotations?
- Do you comment on the effects of the writers' choices of language and other techniques?
- Do you include words and phrases that indicate your comparison?

Explore the skills

Read the following response to the practice question below. Use the annotations and the list above to note what the essay does well, and where you would offer advice for improvement.

Compare how Stephen Hoo and Andrea Levy present Jamaica and London in *Jamaica Boy* and *Small Island*. [30]

Response 1: extracts from a comparing texts coursework essay

Parts of both 'Jamaica Boy' and 'Small Island' are set in Jamaica and London. This is because central characters, Ophelia in the play and Hortense and Gilbert in the novel, move from the Caribbean to England. Each text presents these places in different ways.

opening paragraph clearly focuses on the texts and the task

Jamaica in 'Jamaica Boy' is first presented as lively and upbeat because Stephen Hoo uses the sounds of music and a radio broadcaster to create the idea of the island. The radio plays 'Rocksteady music' that is 'Jolly and cheerful'. This music is typical of Jamaica. The radio announcement uses exclamation marks, saying 'Good morning, Kingston!', which shows he is enthusiastic. On the other hand, Jamaica is also seen as a place where opportunities for work are limited. Ophelia and her brother Clinton run a small stall selling banana fritters, which they have to keep moving as they look for better business. It is a 'makeshift' stall, with a 'blue tarpaulin' with 'gas canisters, frying baskets', which shows the audience that it is a small business. Even when they can make their stall better when Chong lets them use the space outside Lim's shop, it does not last long. The new 'garish sign' saying 'The Original. Chinese. Jamaican. Banana Fritters' shows they are confident and they do good business. Ophelia says 'We almost sold out. Word go round. Phone burning up', but Mr Lim does not let them stay because he wants more of the profit. This shows how difficult it is to make a successful living in Jamaica.

recognition of the use of sound effects in drama

focus on detail of the writing

acknowledges the audience to show awareness of drama

quotations are integrated, but could have more analytical comment

[...essay continues]

Andrea Levy also presents Jamaica as a typical Caribbean island. Gilbert remembers:

> 'In the evening light I sat to eat mango alone under the refuge of the guango tree ... I could hear Aubrey in the neighbouring farm whistling to call his cows to take them to their night meadow. A black dash of crows flew home against the sky. A tree lizard scuttled up the bark licking grubs with its lightning tongue. Cicadas hissed rhythmic as cymbals.'

The fruits like 'mango' and 'guango' and the animal 'tree lizard' sound tropical and Levy uses many sounds to convey Jamaica. The use of 'hissed' is onomatopoeia and describing the 'cicadas' as 'cymbals' is Levy using a simile. Hortense also refers to 'star apples, raspberries and mangoes', 'tiddlers', 'woodpeckers' and 'scorpions', making Jamaica sound exotic. Levy also presents Jamaica as a place that can be dangerous, where a hurricane can pick up a house and make 'its four walls parted, its roof twisted, and everything scattered'.

comparative links made between the texts

very long quotation – is it all needed or would selections be better?

identifies but does not develop comments on the effects of the techniques

Like Ophelia in 'Jamaica Boy', Gilbert and Hortense also think there are better opportunities away from Jamaica in London. — *comparative links made between the texts*

London is a big city and is very different from Jamaica. Stephen Hoo used 'Rocksteady music' to represent Jamaica but he uses a 'dirty London grime track' to present London using sound. He also uses a set that looks ugly: 'The back of a brick house. A back garden/allotment. A ton of mess. A shed.' This makes London seem very unappealing and a place I would not like to visit. However, this is Ophelia's house in London and she seems settled and happy with Chris helping her tidy her garden.

recognition of the use of sound effects in drama

shows basic personal response

[...essay continues]

It is different in 'Small Island' because Hortense and Gilbert eventually see London as a place of hope. At the beginning, Gilbert describes the 'Mother Country' using a metaphor: 'Mother has a blackened eye, bad breath and one lone tooth that waves in her head when she speaks.' This shows he is disappointed. Hortense also finds London 'cheerless' and some people are hostile. A neighbour, Mr Todd is depicted as racist when he says that foreign people are 'all right in their own country' but he thinks that 'they would turn the area into a jungle' if they lived near him. However, at the end of the novel when Hortense and Gilbert get their own house, they are more hopeful for their future in London. Even though the house is run-down, Hortense says: 'We can fix it up.' This shows she is now optimistic about living in London.

comparative links made between the texts

identifies but does not develop comments on the effects of the techniques

[...essay continues]

Because 'Jamaica Boy' is a play and 'Small Island' is a novel, Stephen Hoo and Andrea Levy use different methods to present Jamaica and London. Stephen Hoo uses a lot of sounds and the set but Andrea Levy uses a description of what the characters see. They both present Jamaica as a lively but difficult place to live and they both show London as run-down. In both texts, though, the characters come to like London.

draws together points for the conclusion

Comment:

There is some relevant comparison in the essay, which shows knowledge of both the play and the novel, with relevant quotations. The sample response shows understanding of the writers' techniques, but could develop their comments on how they achieve their effects.

2 There are some clear strengths to this essay, as well as some aspects that could be improved. What advice would you give to improve this essay? Pick out two or three key points.

3 Now read extracts from another response to the same title, thinking about what makes this a superior essay to the one you have just read.

Response 2: extracts from a comparing texts coursework essay

Compare how Stephen Hoo and Andrea Levy present Jamaica and London in *Jamaica Boy* and *Small Island*. [30]

Jamaica and London are the two locations that are central to both Stephen Hoo's play 'Jamaica Boy' and Andrea Levy's novel 'Small Island'. In both texts, the central characters – Ophelia in the play and Hortense and Gilbert in the novel – migrate from Jamaica to London in search of greater opportunities, and the action moves between the two places.

Both writers present Jamaica as a lively, fertile and colourful place, though the methods they use are different. Hoo immediately immerses the audience in the sounds of the island, with 'Rocksteady music', a traditional Jamaican style, and the Radio Broadcaster excitedly announcing, 'This is Radio Jamaica and it is 6.30am!' The first action the audience sees is also lively. Ophelia 'bursts out' of the shop, 'chased' by Chong, before they 'embrace'. The energetic movements also create the idea of vitality and youthfulness in Jamaica. Levy also gives the reader a youthful view of Jamaica, though in the novel it is presented through Gilbert's and Hortense's first person narrative perspectives as young people. Gilbert's description of Jamaica includes references to nature, including 'mango', 'guango tree', 'crows', 'tree lizard' and 'cicadas', which give the idea of abundant life.

clear opening, relevant to the question, highlighting the difference in forms

clear points of comparison and contrast between the two texts

personal interpretation and response

thoughtfully explored understanding of the techniques and effects of drama

quotations are carefully integrated into the sentences

clear points of comparison and contrast between the two texts

thoughtfully explored understanding of the techniques and effects of prose

The sense of liveliness is emphasised by the use of metaphor in the reference to the lizard's 'lightning tongue' and the onomatopoeia of the insects, which 'hissed rhythmic as cymbals'.

[...essay continues]

Though Jamaica is presented as an attractive location in many ways in both 'Jamaica Boy' and 'Small Island', Hoo and Levy show their characters are dissatisfied by the limitations of their ambitions in the Caribbean. The difficulties faced by Ophelia and Clinton are made very clear to the audience. At first their stall is presented as 'makeshift', with the stage directions referring to 'blue tarpaulin', which the audience would recognise as a flimsy covering. When it is moved to Lim's shop at Chong's suggestion, their momentary success is represented visually with the new sign, comically reading 'The Original. Chinese. Jamaican. Banana Fritters'. Although the stage directions describe this as 'garish', the audience would recognise the bold colours as a sign of confidence. The success is also clear in Ophelia's excited speech of short phrases: 'We almost sold out. Word go round. Phone burning up.' The audience would therefore share her frustration when they see her physically have to move the stall back across the stage when Lim refuses to let it stay outside his shop. This is similar to Gilbert's various failed business opportunities in 'Small Island', like the loss of his and Elwood's bee hives. Though Elwood refers to the loss as 'a little setback', Gilbert knows the truth and sees Jamaica as an island of 'Angry young men ... fighting with each other over this tiny scrap of land.' Hortense also sees limited opportunities for using her teaching certificate...

[...essay continues]

Gilbert's and Hortense's narratives in 'Small Island' show their disappointment with London, whereas 'Jamaica Boy' does not show Ophelia's arrival, only showing her as a woman in her 60s, about 40 years after her immigration. However, there are still similarities between the novel and the play. Gilbert's narrative voice shows his disillusion with the idea of the 'Mother Country', developing the metaphor to describe England as a 'filthy

thoughtfully explored understanding of the techniques and effects of prose

personal interpretation and response

clear points of comparison and contrast between the two texts

thoughtfully explored understanding of the techniques and effects of drama

personal interpretation and response

thoughtfully explored understanding of the techniques and effects of drama

personal interpretation and response

clear points of comparison and contrast between the two texts

thoughtfully explored understanding of the techniques and effects of prose

clear points of comparison and contrast between the two texts

thoughtfully explored understanding of the techniques and effects of prose

tramp' and 'This twisted-crooked weary woman. This stinking cantankerous old hag'.

The powerfully insulting language of this personification shows Gilbert's feelings clearly. Hortense too comments that London is 'So cheerless', the short sentence fragment emphasising her dismissive view. These impressions of London are similar in 'Jamaica Boy'. In contrast to the 'Rocksteady music' for Jamaica, Hoo uses a 'dirty London grime track', music often associated with deprived urban areas, to indicate the change of location. London is also presented visually to the audience in the set design. The stage directions detail 'The back of a brick house. A back garden/allotment. A ton of mess. A shed.' The audience can see nothing attractive on stage and the designer can use all kinds of rubbish to make the 'mess'. The background of Chris, the young offender sent to help Ophelia tidy the garden, also indicates that London is a place where young people can easily become involved in crime. Hoo often uses the sounds of 'police sirens' in the background to emphasise this.

[...essay continues]

However, while London may seem unattractive in these two texts, it is also ultimately a place of hope. In 'Jamaica Boy', Chris succeeds in restoring Ophelia's garden, even growing vegetables, and progresses to helping her inside the house too. The change from the earlier 'mess' is a visual indication of the developing understanding and relationship between Ophelia and Chris, who are friends by the end of the play, replacing Ophelia's early suspicion and Chris's hostility. Levy includes something similar at the end of 'Small Island' when Gilbert and Hortense visit their first house. In a passage of dialogue, Gilbert admits that 'It is very run-down', but Hortense shows a new optimism in her reply: 'We can fix it up.' Family relationships are important in this optimism too. As well as the understanding between Ophelia and Chris, Hoo ends the play with Chris showing Ophelia how to use a mobile phone to contact her brother in Jamaica for the first time in decades, while Gilbert and Hortense are keen to repair the house to provide a home for the their newly-adopted son.

thoughtfully explored understanding of the techniques and effects of prose

clear points of comparison and contrast between the two texts

thoughtfully explored understanding of the techniques and effects of drama

thoughtfully explored understanding of the techniques and effects of drama

personal interpretation and response

clear points of comparison and contrast between the two texts

thoughtfully explored understanding of the techniques and effects of drama

clear points of comparison and contrast between the two texts

thoughtfully explored understanding of the techniques and effects of prose

Jamaica and London are very different settings and there are similarities in how they are viewed by Hoo and Levy in the two texts. As 'Jamaica Boy' is drama, however, and 'Small Island' is prose, the methods used by the writers to portray the locations need to be different. In these different ways, both texts give their audience and readers the idea that, with resilience and courage, characters can make a success of migration from one place to another and create a life for themselves in London, even if it is initially forbidding.

clear points of comparison and contrast between the two texts

clearly formed conclusion with an overview of the texts and the essay.

Comment:

This essay sustains a perceptive comparison, based on detailed knowledge of the play and the novel. Quotations and references are well integrated, with thoughtfully developed appreciation on the methods and effects of dramatic and prose writing.

4. Refer to the level descriptors on page 284. What evidence do you find for a *detailed* and *convincing* essay fitting the higher level? Pick out features that you can incorporate into your own essay.

Apply the skills

5. Annotate your own first draft essay with improvements you want to make. Use the table on page 284 along with the bullet points and annotations from this lesson.

6. Write an improved draft of your comparing texts coursework essay.

Coursework evaluation

Coursework evaluation chart: comparing poems and comparing whole texts

What are the features of a *reasonably developed, relevant* comparison?

Knowledge	• You show how you know the texts well by making reference to it and/or by quoting from them. • You make points that are **relevant** to the task set.
Understanding	• You show a **sound** understanding of the texts, reading beyond the surface to explore implicit meanings. • You **develop your ideas** on themes, characterisation or ideas.
Language and effects	• You write about **some** of the ways in which the writers use language, structure and form. • You make **some exploration** of the effects of the writers' choices and how these effects are created.
Personal response	• You make your own honest and **considered** response to the texts. • You show **some development of your own ideas** about the texts and task.

What are the features of a response showing *sustained personal and evaluative engagement* with task and texts?

Knowledge	• You show a **detailed** grasp of the texts as a whole and a **deep** understanding of the task. • You support your **original** ideas with **carefully selected,** well-integrated reference to the texts.
Understanding	• You show a sophisticated understanding of the implicit meaning of the ideas, characterisation and themes in the texts. • You show your ability to **analyse, evaluate and interpret** the texts showing **individuality and insight**.
Language and effects	• You examine **in depth** the way the writers uses **language, structure and form** and you explore different **interpretations**. • You show the ability to make a **close analysis** of extracts from the texts and (where appropriate to the question) respond to the writers' effects in the texts as a whole.
Personal response	• You make a **convincing** response, showing deep interest, understanding and an involvement with both texts and task. • You have your own individual **ideas and judgements** about the text and express them with **confidence and enthusiasm**.

Glossary of key terms

abstract: the opposite of concrete; something that cannot be seen, like an emotion

achronological: events are told in a different order from the order they occur in time

adjectives: words that describe a noun

adversary: enemy or rival

alliteration: repeated consonant sounds at the start of a sequence of words

ambiguous: open to more than one interpretation

analepsis or flashback: the story cuts backwards in time to an event that happened earlier

anaphora: the deliberate repetition of the first part of a sentence for effect

antagonist: a character who opposes the hero or heroine

archaic language: words no longer in everyday use, and which give the impression of coming from a historical time period

assonance: the repetition of vowel sounds in a sequence of words with different consonant beginnings

atmosphere: the mood of a text

auditory: relating to hearing

autobiography: someone's life story told from their own point of view

biased: taking a particular side

Bildungsroman: German term meaning 'education or growth novel'

caesura: a break within a line of verse created by punctuation, especially the end of a sentence

central theme: key idea or theme that occurs throughout a text

chorus: from Greek theatre, a person or group that provides a critical commentary or explanation of the action

chronological: events are told in the order they occur in time

clause: a supplementary part of a sentence

cliffhanger: an ending that leaves the reader in suspense

colloquial: informal, chatty language

connotations: the associations brought to mind by a word or phrase

context: background to a text that aids in understanding the text

conventions: the usual rules or expectations of a text type

diction: the speaker's style of expression and the wording or phrasing they use

empathises: able to put yourself in the shoes of someone else and understand their situation

enjambment: a continuation of a phrase beyond the end of a line of poetry

epigraph: a short phrase at the beginning of a text that summarises the content or themes

exclamations: phrases or sentences that indicate surprise, shock or anger

extended metaphor: an image that is extended across a piece of writing

fiction: text dealing with imagined scenarios, imagined characters and events

first person: the narrator is within the story, giving their own point of view

first person plural: voicing the collective thoughts of several narrators

flashback: the story cuts backwards in time to an event that happened earlier

flaw: a character weakness, such as pride

foreshadow: hint at events that will come later in the plot

form (poetry): the type of poem, which may follow rules about a set number of lines, a set rhyme scheme and a set metre or rhythm for each line

form (prose): a set of agreed conventions or rules, which give an identifiable shape to a piece of literary writing

framed narrative: a story within a story

free indirect style: a third person narrative where the narrator adopts the voice of a character, seeming to merge first person subjectivity with third person narration

genre: category or type of story

Gothic literature: a popular form of storytelling that came to prominence in the 18th century. It is a very broad genre but often includes supernatural or dream-like happenings; a villain who seeks to destroy or corrupt an innocent, younger person; gloomy, remote settings such as castles or ruins in mountainous areas or forests

hybrid: a text combining conventions of two or more genres

hyperbole: exaggeration for effect

imagery: vivid pictures created by words and phrases

infer: work out from clues

instigate: to bring about or set something in motion

interact: how people behave towards each other

internal rhyme: rhyme within the lines of a poem

ironic: when words and their apparent meanings are deliberately the opposite of the situation or intended meaning

literal: the usual, basic meaning of a word or image

metaphor: a stronger form of comparison that states that something *is* something else

metaphorical: symbolic or figurative meaning of a word or image

minor character: a character who may influence a story but is not the main focus

minor sentences: phrases that stand for a whole sentence but omit an element, such as the subject

modal verbs: an auxiliary (or additional) verb that helps express levels of necessity or possibility

monologue: any long speech made by a character

mood: the feeling or atmosphere of a piece of writing

motif: recurring image or idea

motivations: reasons for a character's behaviour

multi-dimensional characters: characters who have a range of aspects to them – perhaps surprising ones (for example, an apparent villain who we learn is a carer for his old mother)

multiple narrators: many narrators providing a range of perspectives on the same event

narration: the telling, or manner of telling, of a story

narrators: people telling stories

neologism: a newly invented word

non-fiction: text dealing with the real world, concerning real people and events

non-metrical: without a regular rhythm

omniscient narrator: all-seeing – the narrator knows everything about the character and the story

onomatopoeia: the sound of the word matches its meaning

oxymoron: combination of opposing ideas, for example 'white blackness'

passive voice: a form where the subject of the sentence is acted on by the verb

pastoral: of the countryside

pathetic fallacy: when human emotion is attributed to a natural scene, often the weather

person: point of view from which communication is delivered

personification: the attribution of human characteristics to things, abstract ideas

plosive: repetition or grouping of /b/ /p/ /t/ /d/ sounds

prolepsis or flash-forward: the story cuts forward in time to an event that will happen later

prop: objects that are used by actors (for example, a cup or a letter)

protagonist: the leading character in a drama

pun: usually playing on two meanings of the same word or two words with the same sound to create humour. For example: 'I know the best *plaice* to buy fish'

qualifier: a word or phrase used to modify an adjective, adverb or verb in order to specify its meaning

quest: a journey in search of something or someone

reading: a way of interpreting a text

repetition: repeated words or phrases for impact or rhythmic effect

secondary theme: a less important theme or idea that is either explored in less depth or is only relevant to certain parts of the text

second person: often found in advertising and poetry, this directly addresses the reader

semantic field: a set of words or phrases that can be grouped by their meaning, linked to a particular subject, for example: 'battle', 'helmet', 'gun', 'enemy' are from the semantic field of war

sentence fragment: a clause punctuated like a full sentence, but might not contain a subject or main verb (see also minor sentence)

set: the objects – such as walls or furniture – that create the background for a play

sibilance: when words near each other begin with the same letter

simile: comparison made between two different objects, people, and so on, using the word 'like' or 'as'

soliloquy: longer speech made by a character when they are on their own, which reveals their thoughts

speaker: the person in a poem who 'speaks' or describes the events

staging: the set, props, lighting and design that create the space in which a play takes place

stanza: a group of lines forming a section of a poem

statement: sentence in which a main idea or event is declared

status: level of power

stock characters: characters with very recognisable features or roles in stories (in fairy tales, these might be the evil stepmother or the handsome prince)

stresses: syllables on which the emphasis falls, creating rhythm

subjective: a personal view

sub-plot: a secondary plot, running alongside the main plot

superlative: adjective expressing the highest degree, for example best, most

suspense: anxious or fearful expectation

symbol: something used to represent something else, for example a heart could *symbolise* love

syntax: word order

theme: a key idea running through a text

third person limited: the narrator is outside the story. However, their scope is more limited, following just one character

third person omniscient: the narrator is outside the story. They seem omniscient (all-knowing), observing multiple characters and events

tone: the voice, attitude or feeling created by the writer's language choices

viewpoints: the positions from which stories are told

volta: a shift or change of direction in a poem

Acknowledgements

The publishers gratefully acknowledge the permission granted to reproduce copyright material in this book. Every effort has been made to trace copyright holders and to obtain their permission for the use of copyright material. The publishers will gladly receive any information enabling them to rectify any error or omission at the first opportunity. The publishers would like to thank the following for permission to reproduce copyright material:

An extract on p.11 from *The Piano Teacher* by Janice Y. K. Lee, copyright © Janice Y. K. Lee, 2009. Reprinted by permission of HarperCollins Publishers Ltd and Viking Books, an imprint of Penguin Publishing Group, a division of Penguin Random House LLC. All rights reserved; Extracts on pp.14, 15 from *The Island of Missing Trees* by Elif Shafak, Viking, copyright © Elif Shafak, 2021. Reprinted by permission of Penguin Books Limited; and Curtis Brown Limited; Poetry on p.17 "Yusman Ali, Charcoal Seller" by Ian Macdonald published in *Jaffo the Calypsonian*, Peepal Tree Press, 1994. Reproduced by permission of Peepal Tree Press; Extracts on pp.19, 21 from *Hope and Other Dangerous Pursuits* by Laila Lalami, copyright © Laila Lalami, 2005. Reprinted by permission of Algonquin Books, an imprint of Hachette Book Group, Inc.; An extract on p.20 from 'The Werewolf' from *The Bloody Chamber* by Angela Carter, Gollancz, 1979, copyright © Angela Carter. Reproduced by permission of the author's estate c/o Rogers, Coleridge & White Ltd., 20 Powis Mews, London W11 1JN; An extract on p.29 from *The Narrow Road to the Deep North* by Richard Flanagan, Chatto & Windus, copyright © Richard Flanagan, 2013. First published by Vintage in 2013, 2014. Reproduced by permission of The Random House Group Limited; Penguin Random House Australia Pty Ltd; and Alfred A. Knopf, an imprint of the Knopf Doubleday Publishing Group, a division of Penguin Random House LLC. All rights reserved; An extract on p.30 from 'The Bed Sitting Room' by Maureen Ismay, published in *Watchers and Seekers*', ed. Rhonda Cobham and Merle Collins, Cambridge University Press, 1990. Collection copyright © Rhonda Cobham and Merle Collins, 1987. Reproduced by permission of Cambridge University Press via PLSClear; An extract on p.31 from 'The Coalminer's Scarf' by Russell Celyn Jones, published in *Time Out Book of New York Short Stories*, ed. Nicholas Royle, p.5, Penguin. Reproduced by kind permission of the author; An extract on pp.40-41 from 'Madam's Sister' by Mbozi Haimbe, copyright © Mbozi Haimbe, 2019. Reproduced by kind permission of the author; Poetry on p.42 "Nettles" by Vernon Scannell, published in *New and Collected Poems 1950-1993*, Robson Books Ltd. Reproduced by permission of the Estate of Vernon Scannell; Poetry on pp.44, 45 "Marrysong" by Dennis Scott, 1989. Reproduced by permission of Peepal Tree Press; Poetry on p.52 "Between Walls" by William Carlos Williams, published in *The Collected Poems: Volume I, 1909-1939*, copyright © New Directions Publishing Corp, 1938. Reprinted by permission of The Permissions Company, LLC on behalf of New Directions Publishing Corp, ndbooks.com; and Carcanet Press Limited; An extract on p.62 from *Brighton Rock* by Graham Greene, Vintage Classics, copyright Graham Greene, 1938. Reproduced by permission of David Higham Associates Ltd; An extract on p.64 from 'The Wedge-Tailed Eagle' by Geoffrey Dutton, Macmillan, 1980. Reproduced by permission of the Licensor, The Estate of Geoffrey Dutton, c/o Curtis Brown (Aust) Pty Ltd; An extract on p.65 from *Keep the Aspidistra Flying* by George Orwell, Secker and Penguin Books, 2000, copyright © Eric Blair, 1936; the Estate of the late Sonia Brownwell Orwell, 1956; © renewed 1984; This edition © 1987, 1999. Reproduced by permission of A M Heath Literary Agency; Houghton Mifflin Harcourt Publishing Company and Bill Hamilton as the Literary Executor of the Estate of the Late Sonia Brownell Orwell. All rights reserved; Extracts on pp.72, 73 from *As I Lay Dying* by William Faulkner, published by Vintage 2004, copyright © William Faulkner, 1930, © renewed 1957/1958. Reproduced by permission of Random House, an imprint and division of Penguin Random House LLC; and W. W. Norton & Company, Inc. All rights reserved; An extract on p.79 from *The Thing Around Your Neck* by Chimamanda Ngozi Adichie, HarperCollins, 2009, copyright © Chimamanda Ngozi Adichie, 2009. Reprinted by permission of HarperCollins Publishers Ltd; and The Wylie Agency (UK) Limited; An extract on p.79 from *Paddy Clarke Ha Ha Ha* by Roddy Doyle, Vintage, copyright © Roddy Doyle, 1993. Reproduced by permission of The Random House Group Limited; and Viking Books, an imprint of Penguin Publishing Group, a division of Penguin Random House LLC. All rights reserved; Extract on p.80 from, *Changes* by Ama Ata Aidoo, 1991. Reprinted by kind permission of the Estate of the author; Extracts on pp.80-81 from *Anthills of the Savannah* by Chinua Achebe, Penguin Classics, copyright © Chinua Achebe, 1987. Reprinted by permission of Penguin Books Limited; and The Wylie Agency (UK) Limited; An extract on p.89 from *The Siege of Krishnapur* by J.G. Farrell, Wiedenfeld & Nicolson, 1973, copyright © J. G. Farrell, 1973. Reproduced by permission of the author's estate c/o Rogers, Coleridge & White Ltd., 20 Powis Mews, London, W11 1JN; and Orion Publishing via PLSClear; An extract on p.94 from *Kanthapura* by Raja Rao, 1938. Reprinted by kind permission of the Estate of the author; Poetry on p.119 "Lyric" by Hone Tuwhare. Reproduced by kind permission of the Tuwhare Literary Estate; Poetry on p.126 "The Fist" by Derek Walcott published in *Collected Poems: 1948-1984*, Farrar, Straus & Giroux, copyright © Derek Walcott, 1986. Reproduced by permission of Faber & Faber Limited; and Farrar, Straus and Giroux. All Rights Reserved; Poetry on p.129 "Sleep Training" by Siân Hughes, published in *The Missing*, Salt Publishing, 2009. Reproduced by permission of the author Siân Hughes; Poetry on p.132 "l(a" by E. E. Cummings, published in *Complete Poems: 1904-1962*, ed. George J. Firmage, copyright © the Trustees for the E. E. Cummings Trust, 1958, 1986, 1991. Used by permission of Liveright Publishing Corporation; Poetry on p.133 "Quick Draw" by Carol Ann Duffy, published in *Rapture*, first published in 2005 by Picador, an imprint of Pan Macmillan, copyright © Carol Ann Duffy 2005. Reproduced by permission of Macmillan Publishers; and c/o Rogers, Coleridge & White Ltd., 20 Powis Mews, London, W11 1JN; Poetry on p.136 "The Sleepout" by Les Murray, published in *New Selected Poems* by Les Murray, Carcanet, 2012, copyright © Les Murrya, 2007, 2012, 2014. Reproduced by permission of Carcanet Press Limited; and Farrar, Straus and Giroux. All Rights Reserved; An extract on p.140 from 'Why the Old Woman Limps' by Lupenga Mphande, published in *Heinemann African Poetry in English*. Reproduced by kind permission of the author; Poetry on p.142 "I'm nobody" by Emily Dickinson, published in *The Poems of Emily Dickinson: Variorum Edition*, edited by Ralph W. Franklin, Cambridge, Mass.: The Belknap Press of Harvard University Press, Copyright © 1998 by the President and Fellows of Harvard College. Copyright © 1951, 1955 by the President and Fellows of Harvard College. Copyright © renewed 1979, 1983 by the President and Fellows of Harvard College. Copyright © 1914, 1918, 1919, 1924, 1929, 1930, 1932,1935, 1937, 1942 by Martha Dickinson Bianchi. Copyright © 1952, 1957, 1958, 1963,1965 by Mary L. Hampson. Used by permission. All rights reserved; Poetry on pp.143-144 "Mrs Faust" by Carol Ann Duffy, published in *The World's Wife*, Picador, 1999, copyright © Carol Ann Duffy. Reproduced by permission of the author c/o Rogers, Coleridge & White Ltd., 20 Powis Mews, London, W11 1JN; Poetry on p.147 "English Girl East Her First Mango" published in *Mangoes and Bullets* by John Agard, Serpent's Tail, 1990, copyright © John Agard. Reproduced by permission of the author c/o Rogers, Coleridge & White Ltd., 20 Powis Mews, London W11 1JN; Poetry on pp.155-156 "Swami Anand" by Sujata Bhatt, published in *Sujata Bhatt: Collected Poems*, Carcanet, 2013. Reproduced by permission of Carcanet Press Limited; Poetry on p.172 "Harmonium" by Simon Armitage, published in *Book of Matches*, Faber & Faber, 2001 and *The Unaccompanied Poems*, Knopf, 2017 copyright © Simon Armitage. Reproduced by permission of Faber & Faber Limited and Alfred A. Knopf, an imprint of the Knopf Doubleday Publishing Group, a division of Penguin Random House LLC. All rights reserved; Extracts on pp.192, 193, 232-233 from *The Ash Girl* by Timberlake Wertenbaker, Faber & Faber, 2000, copyright © Timberlake Wertenbaker, 2000. Reproduced by permission of Faber & Faber Limited; Extracts on pp.194, 196 from 'Anowa' by Ama Ata Aidoo, published in *Contemporary African Plays*, Methuen, 1999. Reprinted by kind permission of the Estate of the author; An extract on p.195 from *Collins Drama – Treasure Island* by Ken Ludwig adapted from the novel by Robert Louis Stevenson, copyright © Ken Ludwig, 2007. Reprinted by permission of HarperCollins Publishers Ltd; An extract on p.201 from *Beauty and the Beast* by Laurence Boswell, Nick Hern Books. Reproduced by permission of Nick Hern Books; An extract on p.203 from *Humble Boy* by Charlotte Jones, Faber & Faber, 2000. Reproduced by permission of Faber & Faber Limited; Extracts on pp.204-205 from 'Scene One' from 'Ti-jean and His Brothers' from *Dream on Monkey Mountain* by Derek Walcott, copyright © Derek Walcott, 1970. Reproduced by permission of Farrar, Straus and Giroux. All Rights Reserved; Extracts on pp.206, 207-208 from *Private Peaceful* by Michael Morpurgo, adapted by Simon Reade, copyright © Michael Morpurgo, 2003. Stage adaptation, copyright © Simon Reade, 2004, 2012. Reproduced by permission of Berlin Associates Ltd; Extracts on pp.211, 212, 263 from "Jamaica Boy" by Stephen Hoo, published in *British East Asian Plays*, Aurora Metro Book, 2018. Reproduced by kind permission of the author; Extracts on pp.212-213 from *Waiting for Godot* by Samuel Beckett, copyright © Grove Press, Inc., 1954, © renewed 1982 by Samuel Beckett. Reproduced by permission of Faber & Faber Ltd and Grove/Atlantic, Inc. Any third party use of this material, outside of this publication, is prohibited; An extract on p.215 from 'A slight ache' published in *Complete Works, Vol 1* by Harold Pinter, Methuen, 1976, copyright © H. Pinter Ltd, 1962, 1964. Reproduced by permission of Faber & Faber Ltd and Grove/Atlantic, Inc. Any third party use of this material, outside of this publication, is prohibited; Poetry on p.242 "Memory" by James Berry, published in *A Story I Am In: Selected Poems*, Bloodaxe Books, 2011. Reproduced by permission of Bloodaxe Books, www.bloodaxebooks.com; and an extract on p.263 from *Small Island* by Andrea Levy, St Martin's press, 2014, copyright © Andrea Levy, 2004. Reproduced with permission of David Grossman Literary Agency; and Picador. All Rights Reserved.

The publishers would like to thank the following for permission to use reproduce pictures in these pages:

Key: t = top, b = bottom, l = left, r = right, c = centre

p7 PUSCAU DANIEL/Shutterstock; p9 Cebas/Shutterstock; p11 jannoon028/Shutterstock; p12 Masheter Movie Archive/Alamy; p13 Bruno Passigatti/Shutterstock; p14 Wirestock Creators/Shutterstock; p16l Kozlik/Shutterstock; p16r Kathy Hutchins/Shutterstock; p19 Best_photo_studio/Shutterstock; p21 Morocko/Shutterstock; p22 Jaydon Hartman/Shutterstock; p24cl sjbooks/Alamy; p24cr CBW/Alamy; p24l Ben Molyneux/Alamy; p24r sjtheatre/Alamy; p26 Carlos Amarillo/Shutterstock; p27 Lebrecht Music and Arts Photo Library/Alamy; p28 Michael Warwick/Shutterstock; p29 Bogdan Sonjachnyj/Shutterstock; p30 Tanya Dvoretskaya/Shutterstock; p33 Rosliak Nataliia/Shutterstock; p35 ART Collection/Alamy; p36 RosnaniMusa/Shutterstock; p39 amenic181/Shutterstock; p41 Tatsiana Hendzel/Shutterstock; p42 Foxtography/Shutterstock; p44 L7lb/Shutterstock; p46 Rosliak Nataliia/Shutterstock; p48 Rohane Hamilton/Shutterstock; p50 Triff/Shutterstock; p52t Peter Hermes; Furian/Shutterstock; p52b NaomiTurtle/Shutterstock; p55 connel/Shutterstock; p56 GIOVANE RIBEIRO MARTINS/Shutterstock; p57 The Print Collector/Alamy; p58cl JulioRV/Shutterstock; p58cr Robert Hoetink/Shutterstock; p58l alberto clemares exposito/Shutterstock; p58r Lucky Business/Shutterstock; p60t Korionov/Shutterstock; p60-61 Iakov Kalinin/Shutterstock; p62-63 Trinity Mirror/Mirrorpix/Alamy; p64 Liz Miller/Shutterstock; p65 Martin Charles Hatch/Shutterstock; p66 MorganStudio/Shutterstock; p68l Algol/Shutterstock; p68r Creaturart Images/Shutterstock; p69 Kichigin/Shutterstock; p72t kurhan/Shutterstock; p73b Lindasj22/Shutterstock; p76 Stephen Dorey - Bygone Images/Alamy; p79 Richard Awana/Shutterstock; p80 I and S Walker/Shutterstock; p81 Bossa Art/Shutterstock; p82 Album/Alamy; p85 David Bagnall/Alamy; p86 thislife pictures/Alamy; p88t Mitar Vidakovic/Shutterstock; p88c Martin Spurny/Shutterstock; p88b Supriyo Chatterji/Shutterstock; p90-91 AlokVerma/Shutterstock; p93 Everett Collection Inc/Alamy; p94 Jake Lyell/Alamy; p95 FotograFFF/Shutterstock; p96 Historic Images/Alamy; p98 chronicler/Shutterstock; p101 Danussa/Shutterstock; p105 Zamurovic Brothers/Shutterstock; p111 Aaltair/Shutterstock; p113 Collection Christophel/Alamy; p117 Art Library/Alamy; p118 Antonio Gravante/Shutterstock; p120 Hoika Mikhail/Shutterstock; p121 nienora/Shutterstock; p 122 Laborant/Shutterstock; p124 Richard090381/Shutterstock; p126 Improvisor/Shutterstock; p128 spatuletail/Shutterstock; p129 KieferPix/Shutterstock; p131 Fokin Oleg/Shutterstock; p132 Inna Reznik/Shutterstock; p134l Nando Machado/Shutterstock; p134c Platslee/Shutterstock; p134r Mistervlad/Shutterstock; p135 Songquan Deng/Shutterstock; p136 Jackson Stock Photography/Shutterstock; p138 Chronicle/Alamy; p140 marako85/Shutterstock; p142 Tadija Savic/Shutterstock; p145 New Africa/Shutterstock; p146 Art Library/Alamy; p147 cameilia/Shutterstock; p149 Marylin Vergel Rodriguez/Shutterstock; p150 Robsonphoto/Shutterstock; p151 Cristian_2nd/Shutterstock; p153 Victorian Traditions/Shutterstock; p155 Vasily Gureev/Shutterstock; p165 pixelparticle/Shutterstock; p172 Shyripa Alexandr/Shutterstock; p180 Volodymyr TVERDOKHLIB/Shutterstock; p183 jeremy sutton-hibbert/Alamy; p186 Heritage Image Partnership Ltd/Alamy; p187 Heritage Image Partnership Ltd/Alamy; p188 Geraint Lewis/Alamy; p189 Corina Daniela Obertas/Shutterstock; p191 Donald Cooper/Alamy; p194 Dean Drobot/Shutterstock; p195 Sueddeutsche Zeitung Photo/Alamy; p196 Hintau Aliaksei/Shutterstock; p197 James Dalrymple/Shutterstock; p198 Cinematic/Alamy; p199 United Archives GmbH/Alamy; p201 buteo/Shutterstock; p204 Nenad Basic/Shutterstock; p207 Moviestore collection Ltd/Alamy; p209 Geraint Lewis/Alamy; p210 Multishooter/Shutterstock; p211 Aoy_Charin/Shutterstock; p212 margaryta/Shutterstock; p213 Vibrant Pictures/Alamy; p214 dwphotos/Shutterstock; p216 Donald Cooper/Alamy; p217 Dark Moon Pictures/Shutterstock; p220 Geraint Lewis/Alamy; p221 Geraint Lewis/Alamy; p222 Prayoga Nugroho/Shutterstock; p223 Sergey Petrov/Shutterstock; p224 Sergey Petrov/Shutterstock; p225 Lebrecht Music & Arts/Alamy; p228 LapailrKrapai/Shutterstock; p232 Stacyann 105/Shutterstock; p237 Alex Cherepanov/Shutterstock; p239 welburnstuart/Shutterstock; p241 stavklem/Shutterstock; p242 SUPAKIT_N/Shutterstock; p243 CapturePB/Shutterstock; p247 icemanphotos/Shutterstock; p249 Anna Jedynak/Shutterstock; p252 Ground Picture/Shutterstock; p253 Emvat Mosakovskis/Shutterstock; p258 Wirestock Creators/Shutterstock; p259 Sevenstock Studio/Shutterstock; p261 Associated Press/Alamy Stock Photo; p267 stavklem/Shutterstock; p269 GOLFX/Shutterstock; p271 Chronicle/Alamy.